Visibility Interrupted

Visibility Interrupted

Rural Queer Life and the Politics of Unbecoming

Carly Thomsen

University of Minnesota Press
Minneapolis
London

The University of Minnesota Press gratefully acknowledges financial assistance for the publication of this book from Middlebury College.

Portions of this book have been previously published as "In Plain(s) Sight: Rural LGBTQ Women and the Politics of Visibility," in *Queering the Countryside: New Frontiers in Rural Queer Studies,* ed. Mary Gray, Colin Johnson, Brian Gilley, 244–65 (New York: New York University Press, 2016). A version of chapter 1 was published as "Matthew Shepard, Hate Crimes Legislation, and Queer Rurality," in *The Legacies of Matthew Shepard: Twenty Years Later,* ed. Helis Sikk and Leisa Meyer, 57–78 (London: Routledge, 2019). A version of chapter 3 was published as "The Post-Raciality and Post-Spatiality of Calls for LGBTQ and Disability Visibility," in "New Conversations in Feminist Disability Studies," edited by Kim Q. Hall, special issue, *Hypatia: A Journal of Feminist Philosophy* 30, no. 1 (2015): 149–66.

Published by the University of Minnesota Press
111 Third Avenue South, Suite 290
Minneapolis, MN 55401-2520
http://www.upress.umn.edu

ISBN 978-1-5179-1063-1 (hc)
ISBN 978-1-5179-1064-8 (pb)

Library of Congress record available at https://lccn.loc.gov/2021022936

The University of Minnesota is an equal-opportunity educator and

employer.

Contents

Introduction

Theorizing Queer Rurality and Calls for LGBTQ Visibility

Coming out—whether it is as lesbian, gay, bisexual, transgender, queer or allied—STILL MATTERS. When people know someone who is LGBTQ, they are far more likely to support equality under the law. Beyond that, our stories can be powerful to each other. In honor of National Coming Out Day, HRC honors all who have come out.

Human Rights Campaign

The #RuralPride campaign is a partnership between NCLR and the U.S. Department of Agriculture (USDA) *aimed at increasing visibility* of the LGBT community in rural America and identifying ways we can use federal advocacy to increase access to crucial services and resources for LGBT rural people and families. (emphasis added)

National Center for Lesbian Rights

I'm not real loud, and I never have been, but I am out, and I'm proud of everything about me. . . . But I don't go to parades, and do that stuff.

Nancy, white, forties, Minnesota

I don't feel you know like "Oh I'm gay, I'm an outsider and I need to" . . . I just feel like me. I don't feel any different than I was before I came out, so I just live my life normal. . . . I don't live it any different.

Nissa, Native, twenties, Minnesota

MORE THAN THIRTY YEARS after the first National Coming Out Day, gay rights supporters continue to hang their proverbial hats on the benefits of visibility and outness. In addition to celebrating National

Coming Out Day in October and partying at Pride events sprinkled throughout the month of June, one can also observe Lesbian Visibility Day, Asexual Awareness Week, International Transgender Day of Visibility, Intersex Awareness Day, Pan Visibility Day, and Bisexuality Awareness Week (which culminates in Bi Visibility Day). If the increasing number of LGBTQ visibility-promoting holidays is any indication, the collective affective attachment to coming out has only intensified over the course of the last three decades. As the Human Rights Campaign, the self-proclaimed largest LGBTQ civil rights group in the United States, tells us in the epigraph, "coming out . . . still matters" because leaving the shadowy closet and moving into the realm of visibility enables social progress and LGBTQ community building. Today, calls for LGBTQ visibility comprise the backbone of gay rights activism—a strategy emboldened by positing visibility as an uncontestable social good, as that which everyone *everywhere* desires. Indeed, the #RuralPride campaign quoted in the epigraph has as its goal "increasing visibility of the LGBT community in rural America." Good LGBTQ (loving) people, I'm talking to you. We have a problem. A visibility problem. And a rurality problem. But these problems, as I suggest here, are not those that gay rights supporters have sold with remarkable success: they are not problems of LGBTQ invisibility and the homophobic nature of rural places. The problems lie in how good LGBTQ (loving) people imagine and deploy gay visibility (Possibility! Freedom! Change!) and rurality (Homophobic. Backwards. Dangerous.). It is the contention of this book that these two problems are intertwined and, further, that rethinking the celebratory affects attached to visibility politics creates possibilities for rethinking the negative affects tethered to the rural, and vice versa.

This book examines various moments in which rurality and LGBTQ sexuality come into contact—in the work of gay rights groups, in cultural texts, and in the lives of LGBTQ-identified women in rural South Dakota and Minnesota. My goal is less to recuperate the rural than it is to understand how the rural has been produced as flat, homogenous, and the type of conservative, anachronistic place where LGBTQ people necessarily suffer. Doing so is, I suggest, epistemologically and politically useful, particularly in this moment in which liberals, progressives, and leftists have blamed the state of U.S. politics (i.e., Donald Trump's presidency) on rural places and people. What lessons might we learn from LGBTQ women in rural South Dakota and Minnesota about the rural more broadly? About LGBTQ politics? And about the relations between the two? What can we learn from those who are imagined as out of place in rural America but who choose to live there, and even claim that they feel happy, content, welcome, and supported by their neighbors?

Visibility Interrupted: Rural Queer Life and the Politics of Unbecoming examines the experiences, desires, and politics of LGBTQ women in the rural upper Midwestern United States in relation to broader ideas about rural place and LGBTQ sexuality. In so doing, this book—the first on LGBTQ women in the rural Midwest—grapples with what is, arguably, the most taken-for-granted idea among LGBTQ rights supporters: the inherent (personal and social) value of being "out, loud, and proud," an assumption that informs advocates' reliance on what I refer to as visibility politics and discourses. *Visibility Interrupted* is, then, as much a meditation on calls for LGBTQ visibility as it is an introduction to the lives and epistemologies of LGBTQ women in rural South Dakota and Minnesota.

More pointedly, *Visibility Interrupted* asks: How do LGBTQ movements produce space and place and how do these constructions influence cultural understandings of LGBTQ women in rural places? How do LGBTQ women in rural South Dakota and Minnesota negotiate, reproduce, and challenge these constructions, particularly in relation to ideas about LGBTQ community, identity, and visibility? How and what does the LGBTQ subject, in rural locales and beyond, *become* through visibility discourses? Harkening back to that classic feminist mantra—The personal is political!—how do we understand the relations between personal (in)visibility and political (in)visibility? What, after all, does it mean to be (in)visible? What are the intellectual and political stakes of calls for visibility, indeed, of making forms of marginalization that are not apparent "visible," particularly through identifying with one's ostensible oppression?

The literal and figurative distance between LGBTQ women in the rural Midwest and national gay rights organizations provides an intellectually and politically productive space from which we can begin to answer these questions by examining the unexplored problematics of visibility politics. My concern is less that the visibility strategies and discourses in question do not work for LGBTQ women in the rural

Midwest (or any other particular demographic) and more with what this estrangement reveals about the discourses and ideologies themselves. To reference briefly some of the arguments upon which I elaborate in the chapters that follow, calls for visibility create "authentic" gay subjects as those who are "out, loud, and proud" in a prescribed manner; position those who are not visible in such a prescribed way, as well as the places that ostensibly prevent such ways of being, as anachronistic; conflate coming out, being out, and being visible; and frame the elimination of homo- and transphobia—social problems everyone, rather than only those marginalized by its impacts, ought to work toward extinguishing—as contingent upon LGBTQ people being the right kind of subject or participating in social struggle in a prescribed ("out, loud, and proud") manner. *Visibility Interrupted* takes on these ways of thinking, which are the very ideas that render rural LGBTQ women unintelligible, in order to challenge the too-simple linking of visibility to rights, liberation, and social progress that happens in contemporary LGBTQ activism. In doing so, *Visibility Interrupted* examines the ways in which calls for visibility work in the service of metronormativity, post-raciality, and capitalism.

The sexual illegibility of rural queers that I discuss here provides critical accompaniment to visibility discourses and gestures toward the unbecoming characteristics of visibility politics. It is my position that rural LGBTQ women are illegible *not to rural people* but to urban people; self-identified liberals, progressives, and leftists; and gay rights groups, and, further, that rural LGBTQ women become illegible through visibility discourses. This argument creates new opportunities to revise assumptions about the ostensible relations among gay community, identity, and visibility, to challenge dominant conceptions of the nature of rural place, and to question the notion that LGBTQ visibility necessarily leads to rights, justice, or freedom.

Addressing the latter point is especially crucial in a moment in which visibility has become the political project—that which is desired, the method, and that which is celebrated—and when there are few discussions of the limits of visibility as a political goal. This point is deeply informed by Andrea Smith's critique of the common activist practice of articulating the forms of privilege one possesses prior to speaking. ("As a white person, I recognize my white privilege.") Smith suggests that such confessions rarely translate into political projects that work to undo the systems that create these very privileges, and instead, the act of confessing one's privileges—a practice that connotes one's "woke-ness"—becomes the political project itself (2013, 263). In much the same way, we ought to ask how, if at all, becoming visible dismantles those systems that create and perpetuate homophobia in the first place. It is my contention that visibility politics have precisely the opposite effect: the ubiquity of celebrations of LGBTQ visibility, through which becoming visible has become the political project, precludes collective social action. *Visibility Interrupted* offers new ways to interrogate and dismantle visibility politics.

Where Are the Women? On the Feminist Stakes of Thinking Sexuality Spatially

The arguments I advance here are indebted to the insights of scholars writing about sexuality and place, and particularly queer sexualities and rural place.[1] Over the last two decades, rural queer studies has become an increasingly vibrant subfield within LGBTQ studies, evidenced by rural queer studies anthologies, conferences, and networks. Still, very little rural queer studies scholarship focuses on LGBTQ sexualities in the Midwest, a strange oversight considering that the Midwest is the largest geographic region in the United States.[2] In addition, rural queer studies, like LGBTQ studies more broadly, continues to center men, despite the fact that women and people of other genders make up more than half of the population.[3] In fact, there is not a single book that focuses on LGBTQ women in rural places. It is not just in academic scholarship where one might notice a dearth of rural LGBTQ women (Midwestern or not); very few cultural representations of rural LGBTQ women exist, a point upon which I expand in chapter 5. Such omissions are especially worth exploring in a moment in which LGBTQ people are consistently interpellated into authentic subjectivity via visibility discourses. Put otherwise, when visibility is at a premium, these types of ostensible "invisibilities" are particularly worth interrogating.

Rural queer studies scholars, who have challenged the assumption that the lives of LGBTQ people in rural places are defined by homophobia, violence, and fear, provide tools for doing so. In fact, scholars have argued that there are no more hate crimes per capita in rural areas than there are in urban places and, further, that such crimes are enabled by the types of anonymity that do not typically exist in rural places (Gray 2009, 90). A reduced number of hate crimes does not, of course, necessarily mean that LGBTQ people in rural places feel less discriminated against or feel supported, welcome, or safe—but this is, in fact, what scholars have found. John Howard suggests that life for rural queers is characterized by negotiations, including "fewer public displays of affection, a greater feeling of rootedness, less pride in outness, *more of a sense of safety*" (2006, 101, emphasis added). More recently, scholars surveyed 632 "sexually active" gay men and lesbians who live in towns with populations of 10,000 or less. They found that "rural gay persons fare no worse than their urban counterparts when it comes to their sense of wellbeing—a pattern of findings that holds for both men and women. . . . If anything, the results from this study suggest that living in the largest cities may be detrimental to gay people's wellbeing, although more so for lesbians than for gay men" (Wienke and Hill 2013, 1271). The following reasons, according to these sociologists, may account for this gendered difference: lesbians' income is less than that of gay men (because women earn less than men), lesbians are more likely to be raising children than are gay men, and LGBTQ subcultural scenes are largely dominated by gay men. Emily Kazyak provides an alternative explanation. She suggests that, while "both lesbian women and gay men gain acceptance by doing masculinity" in rural places, the positive value masculinity confers in many rural places may translate into greater acceptance of lesbians than effeminate gay men (2012, 826). The gendered make-up of rural LGBTQ life, then, ought to make us consider for whom these spaces are unbecoming and for whom they are, actually, liberating.

As it turns out, analyzing the gendered make-up of *urban* LGBTQ life might lead to similar revelations. As Amin Ghaziani notes in his discussion of "lesbian geographies," "When we think about gay neighborhoods, many of us are not immediately imagining lesbians" (2015, 62). That gay men often stand in for an imagined LGBTQ community makes it difficult to see that, as Ghaziani says, "lesbian geographies are quite distinct." To make the point that "coupled women tend to live in less urban areas, while men opt for bigger cities," Ghaziani examines 2010 census data on "same-sex male couple" and "same-sex female couple" households (62). (Unfortunately, census data does not lend itself to analyzing LGBTQ single people, as it only asks questions about "same-sex partner households" [63].) Of the ten zip codes with the highest percentage of households headed by same-sex men and women couples, only three of them overlap. Perhaps most striking, Ghaziani shows that in the Castro district of San Francisco, which remains the imagined pinnacle of gay life, 14.2 percent of households are headed by gay men couples, but only 1.9 percent by women couples. In Provincetown, Massachusetts, which has the highest percentage of women couple households in the country and has long been known as a lesbian haven, men couples actually constitute more than twice as many households as those of women (11.5 percent to 5.1 percent) (62). This data ought to encourage us to consider who is sacrificed in the name of some imagined LGBTQ community, and the deeply sexist, classist, and racist nature of these unbecoming sacrifices.

Building upon the work of other rural queer studies scholars, it is my contention here that we can learn a great deal about gender, sexuality, and place from those who will never make such a "Top 10" list in the first place. Furthermore, I suggest that rural queers are unbecoming, not for rural folks, but because the metronormativity of hegemonic and LGBTQ subcultural narratives renders them untenable and illegible. What I add to this illuminating body of work is not only a focus on LGBTQ women and the rural Midwest, but a deep and sustained analysis of the ideologies undergirding and ramifications of visibility politics. At the same time, it is this focus on the lives of LGBTQ women in the rural Midwest—an understudied demographic that prioritizes their rurality and possesses understandings of LGBTQ community, identity, and visibility that differ sharply from those of national lesbian and gay rights groups—that calls visibility politics into question in new ways.

This point speaks to the feminist stakes of my argument: I unapologetically theorize about, from, and in terms of women. When I started this project a decade ago, I decided to focus on women simply because little rural queer studies work had. Today, I do so less with a belief in the power of equitable representation and more out of the realization that women can teach us something particular about the metronormative logics that subtend the project of LGBTQ visibility. How can we make sense of the tension between the persistent idea that cities are best for LGBTQ people and the facts that LGBTQ women are less likely to live in urban spaces and are more likely to report higher levels of happiness outside of cities than are people of other genders? I fear that the answer to this question is deceptively transparent: sexism. Perhaps the city-centric nature of LGBTQ studies and activism reflects not just disdain for rural life—as other rural queer studies scholars have argued convincingly—but also disdain for women. One of the most important feminist contributions of this book is the simple, but heretofore unmade, point that metronormativity not only disproportionately impacts women but is itself sexist.

To say that sexism is real, that women continue to constitute a group that experiences the world in ways that are distinct from people of other genders, seems a banal point. Equally banal is the point that different women experience the world differently from one another in ways that are mediated by all kinds of factors, including race, gender presentation, class, ability, sexuality, geography, age, and education. But in a world in which support for LGBTQ people and gay rights have advanced in ways that are not true for women and issues that disproportionately impact women, queer theory could do better at considering why.[4]

Deconstructing the Title, Constructing the Argument

Throughout this book, I work to interrupt commonly accepted ideas about visibility and its social and political value, and I do so, in part, through developing the theoretical concept of "unbecoming." Unbecoming, a term I use as a double entendre, is precisely how the LGBTQ women in rural South Dakota and Minnesota with whom I spoke found many of the approaches of mainstream gay rights groups: unattractive, unseemly, improper, inappropriate. I suggest that an estrangement exists between the tactics and logics of LGBTQ women in the rural Midwest and those of gay rights movements, which celebrate making one's LGBTQ sexuality central to one's sense of self (a concept that is too often reduced to "identity") and relentlessly call for LGBTQ people to be "visible" as LGBTQ. Beyond examining the unbecomingness of visibility politics, I also explore the ways in which calls to be visible function to assist certain subjects in their own *becoming* (legible, authentic, real *or* pitiable, backwards, closeted). Unbecoming is, then, the opposite of becoming, the un-ness of becoming, the undoing of becoming. It is something we can think of as the deconstruction of what it means to become, the interrogating of the ideologies upon which this becoming relies. What possibilities might open up—in our scholarship, in our politics, in our desires—if we reflect on the relationship between that which is largely considered distasteful, disdainful, disgusting, and that which is prevented from coming into existence precisely because of these affects? What possibilities might emerge through taking seriously those affects, beliefs, and ways of life that run counter to that which is generally accepted as unbecoming? How might rethinking dominant ideas regarding what is unbecoming allow us to become differently? While I take up these questions and consider more directly the conceptual utility of "unbecoming" for work outside of queer theory in chapter 6, here I want to focus on its "usefulness," to draw from Sara Ahmed's formulation (2019), for analyses of sexuality: *Visibility Interrupted* argues that a critical examination of contemporary visibility politics can help us to understand how one *becomes* (and might unbecome) a sexual subject and can broaden possibilities for creating and actualizing alternative subjectivities, sexual and otherwise. In short, unbecoming enables us to—or perhaps even requires that we—become differently.

Three words in this book's subtitle—*rural, queer,* and *politics*—might well be understood as unbecoming. That much of the country, and perhaps especially in rural places, looks unfavorably upon "politics" and "politicians"; that the rural is considered anachronistic; and that "queerness" exists in opposition to that which is proper are truisms. At the same time, people *become* through actualizing these positions as well as alternative understandings of these very terms. People organize their lives around engaging in (or hating) mainstream politics while others work to craft and live a set of politics outside of the mainstream; rural ways of life often are rooted in temporalities unlike those of suburban and urban places, and connections to the rural can open up alternative ways of relating that might be read as challenges to neoliberalism, capitalism, and globalization, which, far from backward, provide models for actualizing queer kinship networks for the future. Some who consider themselves "queer" seek to be the type of (proper) people considered worthy of rights while for other queer-identified people, the nonnormativity of queer subcultures is a sustaining life force.

These distinctions point to the contextual character of unbecoming-ness: what one considers unbecoming and how one becomes are spatially, temporally, and politically contingent. They are also mutually constitutive. In other words, the type of subject one becomes relies, in part, on just what one considers unbecoming: Is it LGBTQ politics? The rural? The past? Further, pairings of these words provoke disdain, disinterest, or disbelief in ways that transcend the individual terms. "Queer rurality" might be considered unbecoming at best, and at worst, woebegone, oxymoronic, or even death-dealing. Such ideas about queer rurality circulate both within and outside queer communities and are indicative of what Jack Halberstam termed "metronormativity" (2005, 36), which refers to ideologies that envision "the metropolis as the only sustainable space for queers" (Herring 2010, 14). Metronormative narratives are those that implicitly naturalize urban/rural dichotomies, render the rural backwards, and assign value to rural-to-urban migration patterns—and the "out, loud, and proud" ways of being such moves ostensibly enable. Metronormativity normalizes the metropolitan as the space for gays to the extent that the ethos of the urban functions as unremarkable, as that which need not be marked. Metronormativity makes it difficult to understand why LGBTQ people stay in or move to rural places. Consider the following figures, brought together by Emily Kazyak (2012): From 1990 to 2000, the concentration of same-sex couples in urban areas declined (Rosenfeld and Kim 2005); in 2007, 17 percent of same-sex couples lived in rural areas; and between 2000 and 2007, the number of same-sex couples living in rural areas increased by 51 percent (Gates 2006). These figures speak to the need to push back against the metronormativity that renders the people represented by such figures unintelligible.

Assumptions about visibility are central to metronormative narratives, which simultaneously assign value to and derive value from visibility discourses. Of each of the words in this book's title, *visibility* connotes the least negativity—an irony, perhaps, considering that *Visibility Interrupted* is a critique of visibility discourses. And this is precisely the point: visibility occupies an unduly celebrated place in the cultural imaginary, a place defined alongside and through the ethos of the gay metro. It is impossible to consider the problematics of visibility politics or the lessons that can be gleaned from the ways in which visibility operates in the rural Midwest without engaging with the cultural narratives that compel and attribute value to visibility. One need not look far to find evidence of the value-laden nature of LGBTQ visibility. The dominant narrative goes something like this: You recognize that you are LGBTQ. You work to accept this. You develop an identity. You then orient your life around this identity. You necessarily tell friends, family, and coworkers about this new identification, lest you be an inauthentic liar. Doing so means that you have "come out." Articulating this identity publicly then allows you to have a community. Coming out and becoming visible saves you from the life (and death) of the (community-less) closet and, in the very same moment, pushes society forward.

This rendition of the scripts of gay rights advocates points to the ways in which LGBTQ visibility, identity, and community seem disentangle-able in contemporary logics. Each depends upon and belongs to the other. Within the gay rights trilogy, visibility, identity, and community exist in a one-to-one relation. Rethinking such conflations requires critically examining not just the ubiquity of calls for visibility but also the affirmative affects that have become stuck to LGBTQ community and identity. Other scholars have offered precisely these critiques, outlining the dangers of uncritical and celebratory deployments of LGBTQ "community" (Joseph 2002a) and "identity" (D'Emilio 1983). Dominant LGBTQ discourses suggest that LGBTQ community relies upon people identifying similarly and being willing to be visible around this ostensibly common identity. Such positions are challenged by my interviewees, including Jolene, a lower-middle-class white gay woman in her early thirties from rural Minnesota, who stated that she has a gay community, but "they are just all straight." For Jolene, it is perfectly logical that her straight friends are her gay community because community is made up of people who support you, rather than people who are like you—a far cry from gay rights groups' understandings of gay community.

On Knowing Someone Gay and the Production of the Self

Beyond harnessing LGBTQ community to identity to visibility, gay rights groups also attach progress to these very terms. For the Human Rights Campaign (HRC), there is a straight line from individuals coming out to social progress:

> One of our most basic tools is the power of coming out. One out of every two Americans has someone close to them who is gay or lesbian. For transgender people, that number is only one in 10. Coming out—whether it is as lesbian, gay, bisexual,

transgender or queer—STILL MATTERS. When people know
someone who is LGBTQ, they are far more likely to support
equality under the law. Beyond that, our stories can be powerful
to each other. . . . Every person who speaks up changes more
hearts and minds, and creates new advocates for equality.[5]

For HRC, visibility represents both personal and societal liberation; it
also functions as a means to an end in that visibility allegedly leads to
political rights. That is, visibility is always already evidence of progress
and also will lead to further progress.

Gay rights advocates consistently call for visibility by making this
very point: It works! People who *know* someone gay *do* vote differently!
An article posted on the Pew Research Center website on shifting attitudes toward same-sex marriage notes that, as of March 2013, 49 percent of people in the United States supported same-sex marriage, then
an all-time high. Pew data showed that 14 percent—or approximately
one-third of these same-sex marriage supporters—stated that they had
previously opposed same-sex marriage but had changed their position.
Of this 14 percent, 32 percent claimed that their position shifted as a
result of knowing someone gay. Let's pause here to break this down:
Of the 49 percent of same-sex marriage supporters, then, less than
5 percent stated that they came to their position because they know
someone gay.[6]

Of course, it is plausible that some of those who claim that they
"always favored" same-sex marriage also came to their position, in
part, because they know someone gay. Yet, this is not reflected in the
aforementioned data. The people polled were classified as those who
either had *always* favored the legalization of same sex marriage or had
changed their minds on the issue. It would be strange if those who *came*
to their position because they found out that they "know" someone gay
would report that they had *always* held this belief—particularly when
narratives that claim that knowing gay people changes belief systems
circulate widely. Despite the hegemony of these narratives, 33 percent
of same-sex marriage supporters reported that they had "always" held
this position.

And yet, gay rights advocates continue to praise visibility for its
capacity to change belief systems. This narrative ignores several demographics that exist within this very study: those who claimed their

Pew Research Center: Changing Positions	Pew Research Center: Reasons for Changes

One-in-Seven Have Changed Their Minds in Support of Gay Marriage

Favor

Always favored	Changed mind
33	14 → 49

Oppose

Always opposed	Changed mind
41	2 → 44

PEW RESEARCH CENTER March 13-17, 2013. Q62-63.

Why People Have Changed Their Minds

Asked of supporters who have changed their minds
"What made you change your mind about same-sex marriage?"

What People Said

Know someone who is homosexual	32	"My best friend from high school is a gay man and he deserves the same rights; they are in a committed relationship."
I've grown more open / thought about it more / gotten older	25	
More prevalent / It's inevitable / World is just different now	18	"Old fashioned ignorance, I grew up a little bit."
Everyone is free to choose / Love / Happiness / Govt should stay out	18	"More people are happier if that's how they want to live."
Believe in equal rights	8	"Just the change in society, it's time."
Moral/Religious beliefs	5	"There is one judge and I am not that one judge."

PEW RESEARCH CENTER March 13-17, 2013. Q62a. Open-ended responses.

Images created by the Pew Research Center and published in the Washington Post.

positions shifted for other reasons, those who claimed to have supported same-sex marriage all along, and perhaps most strikingly, the
42 percent of people for whom increased visibility of LGBTQ people
did not shift their anti-same-sex marriage positions. Presumably, many
of the individuals who made up the 42 percent of same-sex marriage
opponents had encountered or knew LGBTQ people. In the context of
the contemporary United States, the increased social and political visibility of LGBTQ issues and people makes it hard to imagine that there
exists a rock big enough to shelter anyone anywhere from LGBTQ issues and people. Indeed, as Suzanna Danuta Walters's book on gay visibility begins, "There is no doubt that gays and lesbians have entered the
public consciousness as never before" (Walters 2001, 3). That nearly half
of the population had not been swayed by increased LGBTQ visibility
ought to give pause to those advocates championing visibility as a political strategy. Furthermore, even if increased visibility did actually
lead to political rights, it is important to keep in mind the personal and
political costs associated with this visibility. It is these costs with which
I am concerned.

The narrative that yokes LGBTQ acceptance to visibility also ignores that social positions do not exist outside of broader discursive
formations. Discourses that suggest that people change their opinions
because they know gay people inform, of course, people's changing
opinions. Within these discourses, if one opposes gay marriage, learns
that a loved one is LGBTQ, and does not shift one's position, one becomes a bigot who cannot love the person in question. If one manages
to retain a relationship with the loved one, but does not shift one's perspective on gay marriage, one becomes a disillusioned hypocrite. None
of these options are particularly compelling ways of viewing oneself. I
am not suggesting that no hypocrites or bigots exist. Rather, drawing
from poststructuralists such as Judith Butler and Michel Foucault, I
am interested in thinking about the ways in which subjects—including
supporters of LGBTQ issues, opponents of LGBTQ rights, LGBTQ
people themselves—*become* through discursive formations. Butler, in
her analysis of how certain bodies come to matter, is worth quoting at
length here.

Th[e] exclusionary matrix by which subjects are formed thus
requires the simultaneous production of a domain of abject

beings, those who are not yet "subjects," but who form the constitutive outside to the domain of the subject. The abject designates here precisely those "unlivable" and "uninhabitable" zones of social life which are nevertheless densely populated by those who do not enjoy the status of the subject, but whose living under the sign of the "unlivable" is required to circumscribe the domain of the subject. This zone of uninhabitability will constitute the defining limit of the subject's domain; it will constitute that site of dreaded identification against which—and by virtue of which—the domain of the subject will circumscribe its own claim to autonomy and life. In this sense, then, the subject is constituted through the force of exclusion and abjection, one which produces a constitutive outside to the subject, an abjected outside, which is, after all, "inside" the subject as its own founding repudiation. (1993, 3)

Butler is not, of course, talking about the abjection of (queer) rural subjects. But her point that all subjects are constituted through their relations to one another is relevant for considering how sexual subjects come to exist in the contemporary moment. That the rural is imagined by urban LGBTQ people, progressives, and gay rights groups as "unlivable" and "uninhabitable" for LGBTQ people, to use Butler's formulation, renders rural queers incomprehensible and in the very same moment marks nonrural LGBTQ people as necessarily liberated. And yet, discursively, each is impossible without the other. We are inside and outside of one another.

Put more simply, discourses create subjects as subjects create discourses. But it is not only particular types of LGBTQ subjects that visibility discourses construct; they also function to create (liberal or conservative) political subjects more broadly. The suggestion that people change their opinion on gay rights issues through learning that someone is gay—or in a particular moment—ignores that visibility discourses circulate much more broadly and have political purchase beyond individual coming out stories. In many ways, the belief that an individual relationship with a gay person could change someone's view points to the ways in which cultural ideologies and discourses are produced to appear natural. It is precisely their unremarkableness that allows the subject to be interpellated by ideology and the state, by what

Althusser termed "ideological state apparatuses" (1971). The subject is never outside of ideology (or the state, particularly in the case of desiring LGBTQ recognition by the state). Instead, we all *become* through these ideologies.

This complexity is precisely what is ignored in the Pew Research Center data. Beyond problems with the deployments of the Pew data, I contend that there are serious flaws with its very logics. If knowing someone gay changes how people vote, as this narrative suggests, we must ask, of course, what it means "to know" someone gay. Is knowing someone *who* is gay different from knowing *that* someone is gay? Or is knowing that someone whom you know is gay enough to shift attitudes? Put otherwise, is knowing that Ellen DeGeneres is gay different from knowing your best friend, who happens to be gay? If not, is there something particular about the prescribed coming out speech act that makes people feel as if they know the person in question to a degree that forces an attitude shift? And what degree of attitude shift would make a difference for LGBTQ politics or queer world-making projects (by which I mean something far beyond that which will appear on a ballot). The data is not clear because researchers have not critically examined, or even operationalized, what it means "to know."

It is not just think tank data that indicates a correlation, even a causation, between knowing an LGBTQ person and political positions on LGBTQ rights. Some academic scholarship has made similar arguments (Herek 1988; Howard-Hassman 2001; Lance 1987; Schneider and Lewis 1984). One scholar argues, "The most important influence on respondents' developing respect for gays and lesbians was actual contact with members of the gay community: having, in effect, gay cousins" (Howard-Hassman 2001, 16). If you don't have "gay cousins," there might still be hope for you. "The new openness of the gay community" means that heterosexual people can see "gays and lesbians a[s] people they know, not merely strangers from a foreign (sexual) landscape" (Howard-Hassman 2001, 16). In this sense, to "know" another, you simply must encounter them. A confessing of one's sexuality may or may not be a part of such encounters (the scholar does not say). The failure to critically examine what it means "to know" has resulted in the conflation of multiple types of knowing, and the subsequent inability to actually know much about knowing, including whether knowing an

LGBTQ person in deep and intimate ways manifests politically in ways that encountering someone who is LGBTQ does not.

I am not the first person to recognize problems with quantitative studies on shifting attitudes toward LGBTQ people. In a review of seventeen studies of university-based interventions geared toward changing homophobic attitudes of students, the authors conclude that "it remains to be seen whether any short-term interventions can create lasting shifts in attitudes that translate into behavioral changes toward LGB individuals" (Tucker and Potocky-Tripodi 2006, 188). This review challenges the efficacy, methods, results, and analyses of studies whose goals include changing "heterosexual prejudices" by either "dispel[ing] myths and stereotypes attributed to homosexuals" or "shar[ing] positive experiences with homosexuals" (Tucker and Potocky-Tripodi 2006, 178). Although these scholars frame their critiques primarily in terms of the studies' methodologies (e.g., lack of operationalizing terms, lack of measuring how much of a change in attitude results in changed behavior), I see their concerns as in alignment with my theoretical critiques of the sloppiness with which visibility discourses, manifesting here as the benefits of "knowing someone gay," are deployed by scholars and activists alike.

This sloppiness is only one of the problems with these studies and related narratives. I am particularly interested in the ways that metronormative ideologies prevail in both the collection and dissemination of this data. The assumption that to know someone gay requires that the person in question "come out," for example, does not capture the ways in which knowledge circulates in rural communities. In many rural places, people know things about people without ever being told by the person in question or by anyone who knows intimately the person in question. Heck, people in my hometown know things about me that I do not know about myself!

Narratives claiming that visibility leads to political rights not only ignore forms of knowledge production and circulation in rural communities but they also reiterate the problematic assumption that in order to "know" someone, you must know about their sexuality. And preferably directly and explicitly. This assumption relies upon viewing the sexual acts in which one engages as necessarily constituting some part of one's authentic identity, a position scholars have heartily critiqued

(Foucault [1978] 1990; Rupp 2009a; Shah 2011). With their alternative understandings of the relevance, value, and meanings of gay identity, community, and visibility, LGBTQ women in the rural Midwest trouble this simplistic suturing. Such understandings—which destabilize the assumed relations among LGBTQ community, identity, and visibility— enable my critical engagement with visibility discourses.

But before I go any further, I will take a cue from rural Midwestern temporalities and slow down long enough to define terms that will remain key throughout my discussion.

Visibility Discourses and Terms of the Debate

In what follows, I explicate how I utilize the terms *rural, queer,* and *Midwestern* as well as how I see the relations between and among *LGBTQ* and *queer,* and *dominant, urban,* and *national.*

Let's start with *queer.* Some activists and scholars use *queer* as an umbrella term that encompasses lesbian, gay, bisexual, trans, and other gender or sexual nonconforming identities and experiences.[7] Others have troubled this usage of the term, arguing that it conflates *queer* with *gay* and disconnects "queerness" from its radical political roots. For many of these scholars, "queerness" refers to a political—rather than (strictly) sexual—orientation and ought to be understood as "an outcome of strange temporalities, imaginative life schedules, and eccentric economic practices" (Halberstam 2005, 1). This focus on queerness as strangeness, imagination, and eccentricity drives the position that queerness "can never define an identity; it can only ever disturb one" (Edelman 2004, 17). In terms of queer epistemologies, the types of sex in which one engages may or may not be relevant. One can have similar-gender and/or wildly nonnormative sex and devastatingly normative politics. Or one can possess radical leftist politics and have quite generic sex. Or some other combination of sexual practices and politics. In short, *queer* operates in opposition to the normative and assimilationist politics gay rights groups have been heavily critiqued for promoting. My use of *queer* is in line with those queer theorists and activists who see "queerness" in relation to political positionalities, rather than strictly sexual acts or identities.

It seems obvious that not all lesbian, gay, bisexual, and trans people live in these imaginative and nonnormative ways, and instead can be characterized as *homonormative*, a term that refers to "a politics that does not contest dominant heteronormative assumptions and institutions, but upholds and sustains them, while promising the possibility of a demobilized gay constituency and a privatized, depoliticized gay culture anchored in domesticity and consumption" (Duggan 2004, 50). Some might even be tempted to characterize the women I interviewed as overwhelmingly "homonormative." Indeed, most had little interest in politics and no desire to "contest heteronormative assumptions and institutions." Yet, at the same time, their disidentification with visibility politics—one key approach through which gay subjects come to be recognizable as those homonormative subjects who desire participation in heteronormative institutions such as the military, marriage, and the capitalist marketplace—suggest that these women also hold certain positions that might best be read as queer. Interviewees simultaneously expressed desires for ways of living that might seem best characterized as homonormative and in the very same moment challenged the very foundations of homonormative logics. This assertion ought to make us rethink the common framing of queer and homonormative as dichotomous, a position that mirrors Cathy Cohen's argument that actualizing queer coalitions requires moving beyond a queer/heterosexual binary as all heterosexual people (such as so-called welfare queens) do not benefit from heteronormativity to the same degree (1997).

Despite my fairly lengthy discussion of the term *queer*, my interviewees overwhelmingly did not identify with this term. They largely considered themselves gay or lesbian and some even balked at or interrogated my use of "queer" in both my call for interviewees and also in my answering their questions about my own (epistemological, political, and sexual) identifications. Genie, one interviewee, told me that she almost did not do the interview because the call I circulated included the word *queer*. But then, as Genie told me, she thought otherwise, explaining, "Oh, it's just Carly, and she is at the university, and she lives in California."

Inspired by Genie's insights, I avoid describing those who did not identify as queer with this term, although I may suggest that their ideologies and practices are, in fact, queer. Further, the rural occupies a queer location in the cultural imaginary and, as such, rural lesbians are, within the hegemony of metronormative logics, culturally queer. Therefore, I find it most useful to think of gay/lesbian/bisexual/trans positionalities and queerness as relations, rather than either as if one term possesses the power to accurately supplant another or as an oppositional dichotomy. I often use *LGBTQ*, an intentional move that points to the relations among the letters of this acronym and also reflects the most common iteration of letters gay rights groups use at this time to describe their imagined constituency. On the other hand, I have little interest in encouraging the conflation of terms represented in the LGBTQ acronym and use more specificity when doing so is possible and desirable. In general, I use *gay* or *lesbian and gay* to refer to national organizations, whose normalizing politics have primarily served white, upper-class, gay men, and to a lesser degree lesbians, rather than bisexual, trans, or queer identified people. At other times, I use *LGBTQ* to point to the ways in which the discourses, expectations, and strategies of these very organizations traverse their boundaries and inform those with an array of political, gender, and sexual identifications.

Much like the term *queer,* the terms *rural* and *Midwest* evade simplistic definition. Scott Herring suggests that "something in excess of empirical geographic specificities or the faulty logic of population density governs the urban/rural divide that informs U.S.-based queer studies" (2010, 8). Following Herring, I am not interested in viewing urbanity and rurality as dichotomous and instead see that "any 'urban/ rural' distinction is as much context-specific, phantasmatic, performative, subjective, and . . . standardizing as it is geographically verifiable" (2010, 8). In examining the "sexual imaginary" that drew people to San Francisco in the 1970s and early 1980s, Kath Weston noted something similar: that one can study the rural through the urban (1995, 255). Time and time again, my interviewees spoke to the necessarily blurry boundaries between the urban and rural. One interviewee who currently lives in Sioux Falls, a city of 160,000 people that comprises 28 percent of South Dakota's population, suggested that the city feels rural because so many of the people who live there are from rural places.

Considering that Sioux Falls is *the* city in the state—the place where people living in smaller nearby or not-so-nearby towns visit for groceries, shopping, movies, and special occasions—this characterization of Sioux Falls as rural may seem surprising. Such a position, I suggest, is as informed by the culture and aesthetics of the town, as Herring might emphasize, as it is broader geographical imaginaries. "The Midwest" is understood as rural and, therefore, its urban areas are rural too—both for some of the people who live there and also for those who imagine it from afar, a point that gestures toward the complex ways in which "the rural is always present in the urban and vice versa" (Manalansan et al. 2014, 4).

On to *the Midwest.* According to the U.S. census data that Herring so astutely critiques, the Midwest is composed of twelve states: Illinois, Indiana, Iowa, Kansas, Michigan, Minnesota, Missouri, Nebraska, North Dakota, Ohio, South Dakota, and Wisconsin. In some "Midwestern" states, such as Ohio and Missouri, certain people think of themselves as Midwestern, while others do not, depending, in part, on their geographic (and urban) location within that state. Beyond signifying a geographic location, "the Midwest is also a perspective, a way of positioning oneself in the world" (Osborne and Spurlin 1996, xxi), both a "geographic entity and . . . a discursive formation" (Manalansan et al. 2014, 1). At the very least, these scholars urge us to see that the Midwest—the largest (and most academically ignored) geographic region in the United States—deserves to be viewed as complex, contradictory, and worthy of critical attention.

My use of the terms *queer, rural,* and *Midwestern,* then, should not be read as totalizing, homogenizing, or essentializing. I am not interested in producing a homogenous rural LGBTQ woman, nor am I making claims about how LGBTQness works in all rural places (in the Midwest or more broadly). Following Scott Herring, I resist setting up strict boundaries around these terms, which are always already performative, relational, and subjective (2010).[8] *Visibility Interrupted* approaches the rural Midwest, and specifically South Dakota and Minnesota, as simultaneously particular geographic locales and imagined sites—that is, as places *and* spaces. Yi-Fu Tuan examines the relationship between conceptions of place and space, suggesting that "place" connotes pause and familiarity while "space" gestures to movement, spaciousness, and freedom. This distinction is evident, Tuan argues, in statements such as "There is no place like home" or "There is no space here" (2011, 3). Kathleen Kirby describes the draw to thinking about subjectivities in relation to space, arguing that space connects us with the material in a fluid and mobile way that is consistently open to negotiation and reshaping (1993, 175). We might view "rural" and "Midwestern" as containing the types of possibilities for fluidity and continuous shifting evident in other markers of social location, including those along the lines of class, gender, race, disability, sexuality, and so on.

Recognizing the ways in which gay rights activists often use the terms *urban, national,* and *dominant* interchangeably may create possibilities for actualizing such epistemological shifts. Consider, for instance, HRC's story of itself:

> The Human Rights Campaign is a force of more than 3 million members and supporters *nationwide.* As the *largest national* lesbian, gay, bisexual, transgender and queer civil rights organization, HRC envisions a world where LGBTQ people are ensured of their basic equal rights, and can be open, honest, and safe at home, at work, and in the community. (emphasis added)[9]

This two-sentence description of HRC points to the slipperiness of *dominant, urban,* and *national.* The group uses the words "national" and "largest" to connote HRC's dominance. Although the urban location of the group is unmarked in their self-description, their urban-centric nature is present in their urban Washington, D.C., address, the kinds of work that they do, and the make-up of their board of directors, foundation board, and board of governors, as listed on the organization's website. In 2010, for example, just five of the 201 individuals serving on HRC's various boards listed a rural place as their location.[10] When I did a similar type of accounting eight years later, the boards' composition had changed slightly. Of HRC's 170 listed board members, twenty-one claimed to live in a rural place. However, the seventeen rural towns represented by these board members were restricted to just seven states, and only one of these states is in the Midwest (Ohio).[11] HRC does not, of course, acknowledge its metronormative underpinnings as doing so would point toward the myopic manner in which the group has conceptualized the "national." While I do not desire to contribute to the presumed interchangeability of these terms, I view this slipperiness as symptomatic of the social and spatial location these groups occupy: national gay and lesbian rights groups are urban based and they dominate LGBTQ rights discourses and approaches.

In the following section, I situate this project in relation to the various bodies of academic literature to which it is indebted and upon which it seeks to build, which include most prominently feminist and queer theory and rural queer studies. Although I also draw from and contribute to debates in transnational queer, critical race, critical geography, queer Marxist, and disability studies in the subsequent chapters, here I point to those texts that provide the intellectual scaffolding for the entire project.

Queer Reflections on Visibility

While LGBTQ activists call for and celebrate gay visibility, scholars have taken up a variety of positions on the topic. In *Epistemology of the Closet*, largely considered one of queer theory's foundational texts, Eve Sedgwick points out that visibility is treated as the binary other to invisibility, which functions as the abjection that visibility must work against ([1990] 2008). In a long footnote in the book's introduction, Sedgwick speaks to the conundrum of visibility: "the damages of . . . intensive regulatory visibility on the one hand, of discursive erasure on the other" ([1990] 2008, 6). Sedgwick sees this dichotomous pairing as flawed and incommensurable, arguing that "the most significant stakes for the [LGBTQ] culture are involved in precisely the volatile, fractured, dangerous relations of visibility and articulation around homosexual possibility" ([1990] 2008, 18). For Sedgwick, questions of visibility must be examined in regard to possibility *and* regulation; that most supporters of LGBTQ issues have come to ignore the latter part of this equation—celebrating visibility as possibility while ignoring its regulatory and surveilling functions—is precisely what *Visibility Interrupted* seeks to counter.

The arguments I advance here build upon scholarly analyses of the ways in which regulatory regimes are furthered through visibility, LGBTQ and otherwise. In his well-known analysis of the panopticon, a prison with a tower at the center from which a guard could always view all prisoners, Foucault suggests that visibility creates the possibility of additional surveillance. Visibility is, as Foucault succinctly puts it, "a trap" (1977). In her discussion of state power and regulation, Wendy Brown argues that claims to a victimized identity, expressed through making this identification publicly visible, further victimize those marginalized by the state by framing them as so helpless they inherently require state protection. Through this process, according to Brown, the state's power is increased (1995). Moyukh Chatterjee suggests that the spectacular and public nature of anti-Muslim violence in India—its explicitness and ability to be witnessed—is precisely what allows Hindu nationalists to utilize violence as a "form of government" (2017, 127). In short, such violence is "visible but unaccountable" (2017, 127). And Leila Rupp, in her discussion of what scholars have termed "romantic friendships" in the late eighteenth and early nineteenth centuries, suggests that we know less about men's romantic friendships than women's because the "greater visibility of male same-sex sexuality in the urban subcultures" meant greater surveillance of men (1999, 87).

Other scholars have focused less on state surveillance and formation in their critical analyses of visibility. In perhaps the most pointed polemic against visibility, performance studies scholar Peggy Phelan argues that "the risk of visibility . . . is the risk of any translation—a weaker version of the original script" (1993, 97). Avery Gordon, in theorizing ghosts and haunting, draws from Ralph Ellison's *Invisible Man* to consider the relations among hypervisibility and *un*-visibility, suggesting that "the dialectics of visibility and invisibility involve a constant negotiation between what can be seen and what is in the shadows" ([1997] 2008, 17). Queer disability studies scholar Robert McRuer terms such a dialectic "relations of visibility," arguing that "visibility and invisibility are not, after all, fixed attributes that somehow permanently attach to any identity" (2006, 2). Collectively, these analyses, while not necessarily about *LGBTQ* visibility, strike at the heart of the logics of contemporary LGBTQ visibility politics. These politics are problematic because they rely on an understanding of LGBTQ subjectivity as inherently victimized (it is through our personal and cultural visibility that we move from marginalized to liberated, after all); view visibility as a fixed place at which one arrives and stays; and rarely conceptualize visibility in terms of risk—aside from the potential risk of being out in "unsafe" (read: rural and non-Western) places.

In her critical analysis of gay visibility, Suzanna Danuta Walters grapples with, to draw from Sedgwick's language, the regulation and possibility that visibility politics enable. Walters seeks to identify which forms of visibility "shake up the world and which ones just shake us down" (2001, 15) and suggests that "new visibility creates new forms of homophobia (for example, the new good marriage-loving, sexless gay vs. the bad, liberationist, promiscuous gay) and lends itself to a false and dangerous substitution of cultural visibility for inclusive citizen-ship" (2001, 10). What is, perhaps, most important for my analysis of the relationship between visibility politics and the production of place is how metronormativity tempers Walters's otherwise trenchant critique. Consider, for instance, her discussion of the 1993 March on Washing-ton for LGBTQ rights:

> It is probably no overstatement to claim that thousands now live *more open* lives than they did prior to that weekend. And, this was, importantly, not simply an urban festival. *Small towns are beginning to produce the same sorts of gay enclaves* once only found in the larger metropolitan areas such as New York and San Francisco. Gay people have—obviously—always existed in small towns and rural regions. But the *new visibility and politi-cal power of gays has given momentum to the development of real communities in those previously isolated areas,* many of whom were represented at the march. (2001, 48, emphasis added)

Walters's claim that people live "more open" lives as a result of this march is clearly value laden; it is meant to point to the benefit of the march, a benefit articulated through spatial discourses. For Walters, it is important that the event had social relevance beyond the urban—an especially notable concern two decades ago, far before the existence of rural queer studies as a subfield and when acknowledging rural LGBTQ life was rare. Evidence for this relevance includes both that the movement's "new visibility" reached gay people in "previously isolated" rural areas, allowing them to develop "real communities," and also that LGBTQ people from rural areas attended the march. Such descriptions rest upon broader cultural beliefs that visibility marks progress, as-sumptions that rural life is characterized by isolation, and tendency to subsume the rural into the urban. Rural queer studies scholars writing in the years since Walters's book was published, by contrast, argue that what we understand today as evidence of LGBTQ identities or desires have long existed, and continue to exist, in rural places in ways that *differ* radically from those in urban areas. These experiences are in-comprehensible within narratives that link a particular type of political visibility to living "more open" lives.

That such a framing of visibility peppers a text that sets out to examine (in part) the *limits* of visibility politics points to the difficulty in conceptualizing visibility as regulation in a cultural landscape in which visibility is, as Walters aptly puts it, "all the rage." Such a point helps to make sense of those queer theoretical texts that sharply critique mainstream LGBTQ movements but leave intact cultural assumptions regarding visibility, as is the case in Alan Sears's analysis of the commodification of gayness (further discussed in chapter 6): "In many of the most developed capitalist countries, lesbians and gays are heading towards winning full civil rights, including anti-discrimination legislation, the recognition of same-sex relationships, legal marriage and an unprecedented cultural visibility" (2005, 92). Sears presents visibility as something that, like marriage and antidiscrimination legislation, is won. Visibility, as these scholars underscore, is understood almost solely through the lens of possibility—indicating that all is right in the world of gayness (or at least moving in this direction). This rightness is, of course, always already spatialized: it is of those "developed capitalist countries"; it is of the urban West.

Visibility and the Politics of Place

Transnational and rural queer studies scholars have critiqued those ideologies that reinforce such metronormativity and orientalism. Those readers well versed in queer studies, particularly queer anthropology, transnational queer studies, and queer of color critique, will recognize as familiar the position that the approaches of mainstream Western gay rights groups do not work for _____ group in _____ place. (Go ahead, fill in the blanks!) In many ways, the arguments made by scholars writing about sexuality in non-Western places and in the rural United States are remarkably similar: both tend to argue that dominant ways of understanding sexuality, and the social movement strategies that emerge out of them, do not capture the nuances of those non-Western (Boellstorff 2005; Currier 2012; Essig 1999; Massad 2008; Puar 2007; Rupp 2009b; Russo-Garrido 2020; Shah 2014; Swarr 2012) or nonurban places (Gray 2009; Herring 2010; Howard 2006; Stein 2002) about which they write. Scholars also have noted that contemporary ways of understanding gay identity—and, by extension, the visibility that somehow both enables and emerges from proper identification—do not work for those who experience marginalization along more than one axis.

They may not capture the experiences of LGBTQ people of color, poor and working-class LGBTQ people, and LGBTQ people who live in the non-West.[12] My goal is not to add rural LGBTQ women to a list of those marginalized by gay rights strategies and logics, but rather to jump off from the insights of transnational and rural queer studies and rural LGBTQ women to take on the cultural logics of visibility directly.

Considering the epistemological overlaps in the scholarship on rural and transnational LGBTQ sexualities is particularly generative for an analysis of visibility because visibility politics emerge out of particular spaces and, perhaps even more importantly, *produce* place and space, as well as the people who live there—a point I make in different ways in each of the chapters that follow. Here, I outline how this project builds upon the work of rural queer studies scholars who have critiqued the metronormativity of LGBTQ studies and activism, and have provided counternarratives in which rural queer lives are not defined by violence, fear, and reclusiveness. These scholars urge us to rethink the cultural narratives that pair closeted, violent, and homophobic with the rural and liberated, safe, and tolerant with the city, challenging the idea that same-sex sexual desires and experiences in rural spaces are rare, invisible, dangerous, or isolated.

Historical accounts of rural queerness reveal the depths of the inaccuracies of these narratives. In *True Sex: The Lives of Trans Men at the Turn of the Twentieth Century*, Emily Skidmore tells the story of "unexceptional" trans men who, between 1876 and 1936, sought to pass as ordinary men and, in so doing, lived in alignment with the values of their small town communities (2019). The story of men who desired men and lived in rural Mississippi told by John Howard starts just a decade later. In *Men Like That: A Southern Queer History*, Howard shows that, from 1945–1985, these men's sexualities flourished in precisely the kinds of small town institutions where one likely imagines they would be repressed: church, work, farms, and sports facilities (1999). Brock Thompson's analysis of twentieth-century gay life in a neighboring Southern state extends many of Howard's interventions. In *The Unnatural State: Arkansas and the Queer South*, Thompson demonstrates that drag shows and other forms of small town entertainment emerged in rural churches and schools decades before they took place at bars (2010). In *Just Queer Folks: Gender and Sexuality in Rural America*, Colin Johnson points out that the first Kinsey Report, published by sex researcher Alfred Kinsey in 1948, noted that the "highest frequencies" of homosexual behavior the researchers found were in rural and remote areas. Attitudes that "sex is just sex . . . irrespective of the nature of the partner," Kinsey suggested, were bred by rural backgrounds, a point that the sex researcher noted "contradicts the theory that homosexuality in itself is an urban product" (2013, 1–2). Johnson reads Kinsey's framing of his finding as a "contradiction" as evidence that the historical amnesias upon which contemporary metronormativity rely were in circulation by the middle of the twentieth century. Johnson makes the case that these collective forgettings are rarely arbitrary and are always political (2013). Indeed, as Johnson argues, metronormativity is fostered by ignoring both the historical materiality of rural life, including the "mannish women" and cross-dressers who lived in rural America in the early decades of the twentieth century, and also the *similarities* between rural and urban places in any particular period. Johnson shows, for example, that "the heteronormalization of American culture" that transformed ideas about gender and sexuality in rural areas during the second half of the twentieth century was also at work in urban places (2013, 3).

The metronormativity central to the "sexual imaginarium" (Weston 1995, 255) necessitates that we selectively forget unbecoming things that transpire in urban areas while amplifying those that take place elsewhere. In what scholars have described as the text that "inaugurated the subfield of queer rural/regional studies before it named itself as such" (Tongson and Herring 2019), Kath Weston analyzes stories told by those who moved to San Francisco in the 1970s and early 1980s as part of what she calls the "great gay migration" (1995). One of Weston's interviewees, who left Mississippi after witnessing the abuse of his effeminate male peer, had not "considered the antigay violence that has flourished in tandem with gay visibility in urban areas" (287). For new arrivals hoping to have found a gay haven, "It sometimes became difficult," Weston notes, "to sustain the vision of the city as a space of liberation from sexual restrictions and surveillance" (287).

While these scholars challenge metronormativity by accounting for the richness of rural queer life throughout the nineteenth and twentieth centuries, or by upending myths associated with urban LGBTQ life in the late twentieth century, others do similar work by turning to the contemporary moment. In an analysis of survey data, Emily Kazyak and Mathew Stange show that Nebraskans support employment non-discrimination acts at rates similar to the rest of the nation, although they—incidentally, like leftist queer studies scholars and activists!—are less supportive of same-sex marriage and adoption rights (2016). The undoing of metronormativity enabled by quantitative analyses of the similarities between metropoles and the countryside—and everything in between—is bolstered by stories of LGBTQ people who *want to stay* in rural places. In collecting and analyzing these stories, rural queer studies scholars and LGBTQ activists have shown us how "rurality—at once a geographic and performative space that has often been shunned, mocked, and discarded by the metropolitan-minded—can be a supreme site of queer critique" (Herring 2010, 13). Mary Gray, the only other queer studies scholar to focus explicitly on questions related to rurality and visibility, offers an example of how this queer critique might manifest. In examining how mostly men-identified LGBTQ youth in rural Appalachia negotiate the politics of visibility—politics that are central to the framing of rural queers as "out of place" (2009, 4)—Gray posits that the goals and strategies of rural LGBTQ people differ dramatically from those of urban LGBTQ folks. Gray further suggests that rural queers prioritize solidarity and loyalty to the familiar over public declarations of difference (2009, 91) in ways that "render them ill-suited to strategies of visibility currently privileged by the priorities of the United States' predominantly middle-class, urban-focused gay and lesbian social movement" (2009, 30). I focus on a radically different demographic and place than does Gray, and in so doing, extend her analyses of the contextual nature of visibility; what it means, what it looks like, and how it operates are deeply contingent upon one's (gendered) place in this world. To be clear, I do not seek to show here that Gray's positions do or do not play out among a different demographic (LGBTQ women rather than queer and mostly male youth) or in a different rural area (the Midwest versus Kentucky). Gray's assertions regarding the limitations of strategies of visibility for rural queers are in line with my analyses of my interviewees' narratives. Indeed, Gray's work serves as my point of departure, the point from which I begin in order to examine heretofore unexplored problematics of visibility politics: their enabling of metronormativity, producing of post-racial and post-spatial logics, and obscuring of labored processes. Understanding how visibility works for one demographic in one rural locale, it turns out, is inadequate to the task of examining—and challenging—the ubiquity of both visibility politics and metronormativity.

One reason that dominant cultural narratives cloaked in metronormativity persist is because alternate modes of being queer and articulating queerness—including those based in the rural or outside of "out, loud and proud" discourses—are not recognized as legitimate modes of queerness. Rethinking the centrality of metronormative narratives to mainstream gay cultural imaginaries requires rethinking dominant discourses and strategies that assume that visibility and "outness" constitute the only path toward liberation, strategies that are not only deeply placed, but are also deeply gendered. Indeed, the aforementioned omission of LGBTQ women in queer studies scholarship has been explained through the lens of visibility. Drawing from the work of Julie Podmore (2001), the editors of *Geographies of Sexualities,* for example, state, "lesbians have very different means of making themselves visible (to each other) than gay men and that to properly explore these practices, geographers need to (re-)integrate the domestic sphere into their interpretations of urban space" (Browne, Lim, and Brown 2007, 7). Although I am fond of the editors' call for scholars to integrate both gender and space into their analyses of sexuality, this suggestion falls devastatingly short. It reproduces problematic public/private splits and implicitly places women in the domestic sphere. Furthermore, understanding LGBTQ women's lives, I argue, requires not just rethinking spatial assumptions (including the value of the urban or the danger of the rural), but also a radical rethinking of the value of visibility.[13] While the scholarship on rural LGBTQ lives typically achieves the former, the dominant ideas about visibility I deconstruct here even, at times, find their way into otherwise critical work on sexuality and space. In her discussion of the performance of masculinity among lesbians in the rural Midwest, Emily Kazyak suggests that visibility is something that is "achieved" (2012, 843). E. Patrick Johnson notes that "the art of black queer women is not always visible or celebrated, especially in the South" (2018, 323). In her analysis of the ways Namibian and South African LGBTQ activists utilize visibility and invisibility strategically, Ashley Currier suggests that "invisibility involves withdrawal from public interactions, whether intentional or not" (2012, 9). In her chapter on lesbians, Currier argues that "invisibility was an attractive cloak to some black lesbians who survived or feared being the targets of antilesbian violence" (2012, 55).

Invisibility, for Currier, involves isolation and may result from violence. Approaching invisibility as negative is in line with elevating visibility to an achievement and conflating lack of visibility with lack of celebration. These moves, which leave the logics of metronormativity intact, are also evident in the work of both mainstream gay rights activists and those queer and trans activists positing their work as decidedly oppositional.

Assimilation, Normativity, Visibility

Queer studies scholars and leftist queer activists have heartily critiqued gay rights activists for their normativity—that is, their focus on gaining rights that are largely in line with, rather than disruptive to, broader ideas about gender and sexuality (Conrad 2010; Duggan 2004; Warner 1999). I suggest here that calls for visibility are one mode through which such normativity is compelled; indeed, the kind of gay person at the center of rights-seeking approaches is not only visible as such but is also presented as mostly similar to respectable heterosexuals: job holding, coupled, and desiring a family. Despite leftist scholars' and activists' critiques of normativity, the centrality of visibility politics to broader assimilationist projects largely has gone unexamined. Campaigns for marriage equality epitomize such widely critiqued assimilationist goals of gay rights groups. Here, I briefly outline queer critiques of same-sex marriage campaigns to make clear the ideologies that inform mine and to further explicate how my examinations of visibility advance queer critiques of the normativity driving gay rights work.[14]

Long before queer theory had a name, feminists asserted that marriage is an institution rooted in and perpetuating patriarchy (De Beauvoir 1949; Greer 1970; Millett 1971). In a more recent feminist analysis of marriage equality, Nan Hunter asks if making same-sex marriages legal has the potential to disrupt the patriarchal understandings of gender that underpin the institution of marriage (1991). Overwhelmingly, leftist queer activists and scholars suggest that the answer is an emphatic "No!" Additionally, critics suggest that marriage equality campaigns ignore ongoing racial oppression through their narratives of social progress (Farrow 2010), reiterate partnered monogamy (and thus a narrow family structure) as the norm (Bornstein 2010), and ignore those for whom marriage is an impossibility or will not lead to rights (Nair 2010). If neither partner is a citizen nor has health insurance, for instance, marriage will not increase access to citizenship or health care. For critics, same-sex marriage is not the problem; it is merely a symptom of the broader issues with contemporary LGBTQ rights movements: the quest for inclusion via normativity (Nair 2010; Spade 2015; Warner 1999). Expanding who might be able to squeeze into "the norm" or making more diverse the norm, these scholars argue, does little to create a world that accepts—or encourages!—deviation from norms.

Calls to come out and be visible have been central to the work of marriage equality activists. In an article entitled "Visibility Key to Repealing Gay Marriage Ban," posted on Michigan-based LGBTQ news outlet *Pride Source, Detroit News* columnist Deb Price argues that the first five years of a broader ten-year plan to repeal Michigan's gay marriage ban should focus on a "massive coming out project."[15] Scholars writing on the same-sex marriage debate similarly yoke visibility to marriage, arguing that marriage reflects desires for "visibility and recognition of . . . partnerships and families" (Bernstein and Taylor 2013, 5). In both of these cases, assumptions about the value of visibility and of marriage inform one another. Here, as elsewhere, visibility is so sutured to what counts as the political that it becomes nearly impossible to imagine a politics outside of this framework.

Beliefs in the value of visibility are not limited to the assimilationist projects of mainstream gay rights groups. Visibility discourses also have found their way into activism that frames itself as queer and trans, activism that claims to work in opposition to various cultural norms—a paradox considering both that calls for visibility are one approach through which lesbian and gay rights groups compel normativity and also that scholars and activists often critique mainstream groups for ignoring the concerns of the BTQ of the LGBTQ. We ought to think about what it means that those fighting for queer and trans justice often, in the case of visibility in particular, utilize discourses and approaches quite *similar* to those of the very mainstream gay rights groups they critique. In fact, the ubiquity of visibility discourses challenges the production of queer and mainstream gay rights projects as fundamentally distinct.

The LGBTQ activism at the University of California, Santa Barbara, my beloved alma mater, serves as but one example through which we can see visibility discourses deployed to describe projects articulated as queer. A blog post detailing the history of "Queer Organizing at UCSB" describes how the iconic "queer bombing" came to be a part of campus activism.[16]

> Queer Bombing arose [from] the need to heighten queer visibility in and around UCSB and to reclaim hetero-dominated spaces for our community to connect and celebrate. . . . [Students] found an activist/improv group called Guerilla Queer bar whose sole mission was to infiltrate traditionally heterosexual social venues and bomb/overwhelm it with Queer Fabulousity. [Students] decided to use the iconic "Queer Bomb" T-shirts to actively engage the UCSB community and to celebrate our Queer identity at events ranging from bowling nights to queer bombing UCSB's graduation ceremony. Queer activism has always had a heritage of being in-your-face, media-savvy, and effective. We Queer Bomb because in a hostile world, our civil rights and our access to space are constantly attacked, we refuse to take it lying down because we're not "gay" as in "happy," we're Queer as in "FUCK YOU."[17]

Notably, the group does not mention working to address any of the issues driving contemporary mainstream gay rights work. Instead, they founded an improv group, held social events, and sought to disturb public spaces. The "fuck you," which speaks to the antiassimilationist and antinormative perspectives that motivate the "queer bombing" project, was actualized through visibility. But visibility was not only the Queer Bombers' method. It was the reason for their founding; it was their political goal. The Queer Bombers' fight was against invisibility. Those who wore the black T-shirts decorated with the classic neon pink "queer bomb," and, thus, were "heighten[ing] queer visibility," *became* the political projects.

Such a reliance on visibility politics is also evident in contemporary trans rights activism. #GirlsLikeUs, a movement started by well-known Black transgender activist Janet Mock, "encourages trans women to live visibly."[18] In its discussion of the International Transgender Day of Visibility, GLAAD states: "The need for visibility is incredibly important, as it fosters the understanding needed to gain acceptance. Positive visibility humanizes trans folks, which is crucial when 40% have attempted suicide and 4 out of 5 trans students feel unsafe at school."[19] Trans

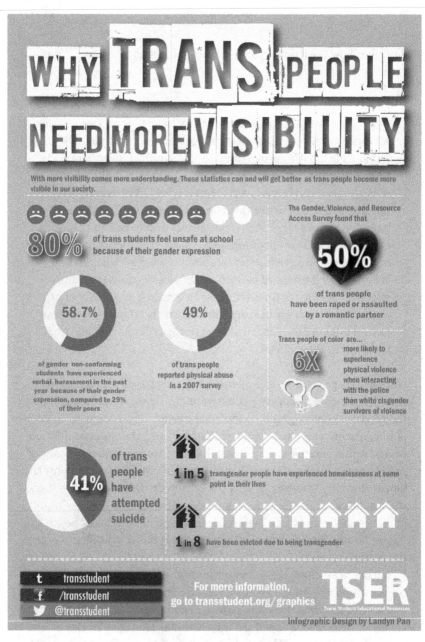

Infographic on trans visibility created by Trans Student Educational Resources, a trans-youth-led organization that addresses educational issues and policy.

Student Educational Resources utilizes similar figures in its "Why Trans People Need More Visibility" infographic. Trans people, they assert, need more visibility because 41 percent of trans people have attempted suicide, 50 percent of trans people have been sexually assaulted by a romantic partner, 80 percent of trans students feel unsafe at school, and 1 in 8 trans people have been evicted from their homes due to being transgender. Such harrowing figures demand that we critically examine the strategies by which we attempt to address the issues that produce such figures. The significance of visibility is so taken for granted that LGBTQ advocates suggest that increased visibility will decrease sexual assault rates and fix our schools, policing crises, and housing laws. We ought to be asking how *exactly* increased visibility would address any of these problems.

This brief discussion of calls for trans and queer visibility suggests that visibility discourses animate the work of those fighting for trans and queer issues in ways that are remarkably similar to homonormative gay rights groups. Put otherwise, queer and trans visibility discourses can operate in the service of precisely those sorts of normalizing projects that queer and trans politics have long attempted to disrupt. Trans studies scholars have both spurred and critiqued such commitments to visibility politics. In what is now a classic (and debated) text, Sandy Stone urged "transsexuals" to be visible as such because, for Stone, the visibility of alternatively gendered bodies holds the promise for gender transformation; the (visible) trans body is, Stone suggests, itself a site from which we can gain a better understanding of the relationship between gender and the body (1991).

Other trans studies scholars have critiqued this linking of trans bodies to transgression, suggesting that such conflations place representational burdens on trans people (Halberstam 1998; Namaste 2000; Stryker and Whittle 2006) and ignore that many trans people manipulate their bodies precisely so that they do not appear to be transgressing gender expectations. Dan Irving suggests that calls for the visibility of trans bodies reproduce individualistic, neoliberal, rights-based notions of subjectivity and liberation. Irving notes that academic and activist obsessions with the visibility of trans bodies have precluded analyzing the ways in which class and capitalism operate in order to produce trans subjects who are visible, and, therefore, intelligible as workers (2008). Beyond this, expectations for visibility can be especially fraught for trans people, for whom passing—and not "living visibly"—might be desirable for many reasons, including but not limited to material need. Trans studies scholars and cultural producers most directly addressed these paradoxes in the aptly titled *Trap Door: Trans Cultural Production and the Politics of Visibility* (Gossett, Stanley, and Burton 2017), in which the editors note that the "doors" many trans people are offered—to visibility, to recognition, to resources—are also "traps" (xxiii), the same term, incidentally, that Foucault used forty years prior to describe visibility. What, we should ask, are the politics of championing trans visibility when—even after "gaining unprecedented representation in the mass media" (xxv)—trans people continue to face extreme violence? Answering this question requires thinking beyond visibility, because, as Abraham Weil notes, regardless of whether Black and trans bodies work to "becom[e] visible or [to] remain invisibl[e]," their subjection to "biopolitical management strategies" does not change (forthcoming). In a moment in which LGBTQ visibility has become the political project for mainstream gay rights groups as well as activism that positions itself as queer and trans, the task of deconstructing the regulatory regimes attached to visibility politics is particularly pressing.

Methodology of the "Out There"

This book began when the story of Jene Newsome, a lesbian in South Dakota, made it onto the national stage. Rarely does South Dakota appear in the national spotlight, particularly in regard to LGBTQ issues, and I—a first-year graduate student in California at the time—quickly became enthralled with the case. I followed all traces of Newsome in the news and subsequently recognized that South Dakota's press covered the story in ways quite distinct from both LGBTQ organizations and press outside of South Dakota (discussed further in chapter 1). Newsome, a Black Air Force Sergeant stationed in South Dakota, was discharged from the military in 2009 under Don't Ask, Don't Tell— the former policy that allowed lesbian, gay, or bisexual individuals to serve in the military so long as the military remained unaware of their sexuality—after local police officers informed the military that Newsome was married to a woman. Outrage ensued among gay rights advocates who utilized Newsome's story to critique Don't Ask, Don't

Tell, ignoring that Newsome herself made clear her disinterest in critiquing the military and its policies.

In my quest to understand what appeared to be, at best, an estrangement between the approaches and concerns of Newsome and gay rights groups, I attempted to locate additional cultural representations of and news stories about rural LGBTQ women. Following the largely unquestioned narrative that online platforms are enabling rural LGBTQ people to find one another, I scoured the internet for any trace of rural LGBTQ women. When I began this project in 2010, I found very few, many of which have been deleted in the decade since. Today, in 2021, cultural representations of rural LGBTQ women, online or otherwise, remain rare—especially those that do not position the rural as inherently more backwards and homophobic than cities. Still, I remain committed to following these traces. Such media objects are, as Karen Tongson and Scott Herring discuss, responsible for forging what Kath Weston famously termed the "imagined gay community" (2019, 53). My objects included Flickr accounts, Facebook pages, Instagram accounts, gay rights campaigns, and journalistic coverage of various events and moments—a web, so to speak, mediated by the web.

At the same time, Newsome's case, along with the general absence of cultural representations of rural LGBTQ women, especially at the time, raised questions that I could not answer through an analysis of cultural texts alone. This realization drove my decision to engage in participant observation at LGBTQ social and political gatherings and to conduct interviews with fifty LGBTQ women in rural South Dakota and Minnesota. Between September and December 2011, I drove more than seven thousand miles to learn about these women's lives. The interviews I conducted were semistructured, lasted between one and four hours, and were audio recorded and transcribed. My sample is quite diverse: interviewees ranged in age from 18 to 73. Eight are women of color. Many interviewees have disabilities or are intimately connected to people who do. Interviewees identified with a range of class positions, from poor to upper middle class to "wealthy in the heart, poor in the pocket," as one woman joked. Annual incomes ranged from $2,400 to $80,000. Interviewees included women connected to, disconnected from, and indifferent toward LGBTQ causes.

I chose to focus on South Dakota and Minnesota for both practical and intellectual reasons. I spent the first twenty-five years of my life in these two states, where I was born and raised, attended college, and first worked with progressive nonprofit organizations, including the White Earth Land Recovery Project and Central Minnesota Citizens for Choice. Because I have friends, family, and mentors in this region—some of whom are part of my feminist and queer networks and some who are not—I accurately predicted that this meant I would have entrée, which might otherwise be difficult to gain. Beyond this, South Dakota and Minnesota exemplify the types of rural places overlooked in the metronormativity of both LGBTQ rights activism and academic scholarship. They are also very different neighboring states, a diversity that is lost in disparaging references to the country's "flyover zone" (a term to which I was first introduced while attending graduate school in California).[20] South Dakota is, in general, extremely rural and consistently politically red, while Minnesota is a mix of rural, suburban, and urban and regularly votes Democratic-Farmer-Labor Party on both state and national levels. LGBTQ organizations are active, easy to locate, and well-organized in Minnesota, and the state's college campuses boast developed and long-standing LGBTQ and women's centers. In contrast, not a single university in South Dakota has an LGBTQ or women's center. These distinctions speak to the rich and complex differences in Midwestern states and disrupt the homogeneity of representations of the Midwest.

That one of the first questions I often am asked when discussing my research is how I managed to find interviewees *out there* speaks to the hegemony of metronormative logics; such questions assume implicitly that LGBTQ people do not live out *there,* and if we do, we cannot possibly be *out* there. Locating interviewees in either case would be difficult. In fact, identifying interviewees and conducting interviews was an easy and enjoyable part of writing this book. I accurately predicted that I would have little trouble locating interviewees in Minnesota because I am connected to networks of feminist, LGBTQ, and racial justice activists in the state. I began by contacting my friends and colleagues in Minnesota—all of whom I knew through our mutual connections to campus-based women's centers, academic gender studies programs, and feminist, queer, and indigenous activist groups—and asking them to share my call for interviewees with their networks. This approach generated many interviews.

I began in a similar manner in South Dakota, but without prior political and affective ties to those I contacted. First, I emailed faculty members connected to gender studies departments at South Dakota universities. No university in the state has a gender studies major or an LGBTQ studies major or minor, but the state's two largest universities both offer gender studies minors.[21] I also contacted various campus-based LGBTQ and feminist student groups through email and Facebook. The dozens of emails I sent went unanswered, with a single exception. While the emails in my sent folder acquired virtual dust, I tried two other approaches: I posted an ad to Craigslist under "Women Seeking Women," making clear my desire to identify interviewees for research purposes. I also reached out to Equality South Dakota, an LGBTQ political organization in the state, despite my initial plan to find interviewees without drawing from the resources of LGBTQ organizations.[22] Based on information on the nonprofit's website, two women appeared to serve as board members. I emailed the director to ask if he would forward my request to the organization's listserv and also connect me with the women on the board. He replied that both women had resigned from the board, making it crystal clear that he had no interest in supporting my research. These efforts did not result in a single interview—though they were generative failures. Posting to Craigslist led me to see that at the same time my ad was the sole post under "Women Seeking Women" for the entire state of South Dakota, there were 94 ads under "Men Seeking Men" and 77 under "Men Seeking Women"—which suggests that men are using the internet in ways that women are not. And when I expressed earnest confusion over Equality South Dakota's response to my inquiries, my interviewees consistently laughed, sighed, and rolled their eyes, making clear they did not find the organization's response surprising. Apparently, the group was understood locally as the gay men's group and women tended to connect with another LGBTQ organization that organized more potlucks and socials. Had I not attempted to connect with Equality South Dakota or to utilize Craigslist, I would have missed out on a gendered aspect of LGBTQ life in South Dakota.

Such insights did not, however, produce interviewees. After my success identifying interested interlocutors in Minnesota using similar methods, I was shocked that my approaches were falling flat in South Dakota, my home state! In desperation, I turned to my (mostly heterosexual) network of South Dakotans. My hometown friends, some of whom I had not seen or communicated with since high school, re-posted my call on Facebook and sent me personal messages to let me know they were sharing the information in other ways, as well. My mother printed out my call for interviewees and put it on the table in the breakroom at the elementary school at which she worked. High school acquaintances who now were involved in South Dakota's progressive political circles connected me with their networks. Friends of my friends, strangers to me, went out of their way to connect me to people in their networks.

The ease with which this process evolved once I reached out to my networks speaks to the cultural politics of the region; the materiality of what we upper Midwesterners refer to as "Minnesota nice"—the belief that you should always put on a nice face, help those around you, and treat others with kindness, regardless of whether you actually want to—meant that I had an incredible amount of support. In South Dakota, it just did not come from where I assumed it would: those overtly connected to feminist and LGBTQ issues. As it turns out, the cultural politics of the rural Midwest make the region quite conducive—*for those considered locals*—to identifying research participants and to utilizing "snowball sampling," a method through which referrals from interviewees generate additional contacts. I met eighteen of my interviewees via my (mostly heterosexual) contacts in Minnesota and South Dakota or via (the mostly heterosexual) people in the networks of my contacts. Twenty-six of my interviewees were referred to me by other women I had interviewed. I also interviewed one close friend, one woman I met at a Pride festival, one woman who reached out to me after seeing the call for participants in a newsletter put out by a local LGBTQ group, and three women who were employees or board members of LGBTQ nonprofits.

I was open to interviewing anyone who answered the call in which I expressed interest in interviewing women in rural South Dakota and Minnesota who love or desire women. I intentionally did not demarcate boundaries to any of these terms: LGBTQ, women, rural, South Dakota, Minnesota. In fact, I interviewed one person who identified as a transgender man; one person who had spent significant parts of her life in South Dakota but who lived in the very northwestern corner of Iowa (not far from Sioux Falls) at the time of the interview; a couple who previously lived in Minnesota but recently had moved to Fargo,

North Dakota; and several women who now live in Midwestern cities, including Minneapolis and Sioux Falls. Despite this, all interviewees had some connection to rural South Dakota or Minnesota and nearly everyone considered themselves to be "from" a rural place. As I mentioned in my discussion of terms, I have no interest in policing the boundaries of terms that are, as Scott Herring suggests, phantasmatic, fluid, and performative. If a person who did not appear to fit within the confines of the call as circulated expressed interest in being interviewed, I accepted that they must know their lives, experiences, desires, and identifications better than I could, and I worked to understand through the interview what about my call spoke to them. I accepted that people "are" what they claimed to be, both in terms of their sexuality and geography. Although few people would question the methodological decision to accept outright participants' articulations of their genders or sexualities, some have expressed confusion at my decision to define space and place through a similarly capacious model. Following rural queer studies scholars, the "rural" and "the Midwest" mark ways of living, thinking, and being simultaneously connected to and disconnected from geography—a point made evident through the various people who contacted me who did not "fit" perfectly with my call.

I conducted interviews, in part, because I believe we can access information that does not circulate otherwise through conversations. Heeding Joan Scott's warning that approaching experience as evidence or as unmediated truth can result in an undertheorization of the structures that shape our experiences and our understandings of these experiences (1991), I analyze the relationships among institutions, discourses, cultural representations, and individual experiences, to avoid, as Scott suggests, reproducing individual identities and experiences as that which is true, natural, or unproblematic. Interviewees' remembering, constructing, and sharing of their experiences, desires, and pains—as well as my (re)interpreting of their lives here—is, of course, mediated and political. How we tell stories matters (Hemmings 2011). My viewing of my interviewees as interlocutors is crucial, and influences the story I can craft here: I refuse to fetishize interviewees, to view them as any more "real" than other cultural representations, to uncritically share their stories, or to occupy a type of maternal subject position from which researchers often claim to protect their "informants." To be clear, any critique I launch here is not directed at my interviewees; I have no interest in chiding interviewees for drawing from available cultural discourses and ideologies. Rather, I consider what emerges when interviewees' stories are considered in relation to one another and to broader ideologies and epistemologies.

To be able to consider the contours of these relations, I created what is a decidedly queer archive. I did so out of necessity—no other archive of rural LGBTQ women in contemporary times exists—but also out of a desire to *do* queer theory via "queer methods" and via queering methods (Ghaziani and Brim 2019). Such an approach—which scholars have also described as "dyke methods" and "trans* . . . as methodology"—includes celebrating those "failure[s] to adhere to stable classificatory systems or be contained by disciplinary boundaries" (Ward 2016, 71; Weil 2017a, 644). Indeed, this "messy" archive, to utilize Martin Manalansan's description, might rightly raise questions regarding my method, archive, and even the disciplines of feminist and queer studies (2014): What happens to our work when our queer method is our archive, our queer archive our method? What happens to our method and to our archive when they are so mutually constituted they become one? When is an archive a method? Viewing mess as "a route for funking up and mobilizing new understandings of stories, values, objects" makes clear the value of a queer archive, a queer method (Manalansan 2014, 99)—an archive/method I have constructed with the dual goals of sharing the insights of LGBTQ women in rural South Dakota and Minnesota and providing tools to deconstruct dominant and subcultural ideas about LGBTQ visibility.

Working in the service of such an endeavor does not require a comparative analysis, and I do not provide one here. I do not compare women and people of other genders. I do not compare the rural upper Midwest with upper Midwestern cities. I do not compare interviewees in South Dakota and Minnesota. And I do not reflect at great length on the differences between women. The reason for this is simple: the very real differences between interviewees did not manifest as different positions on visibility politics. The women in South Dakota, a red state, did not feel less supported or accepted than those in Minnesota, a blue state, despite greater LGBTQ political organizing in the latter. While Native and white women, working-class and middle-class women, women with and without disabilities, and women living in extremely rural areas and midsized towns experience the world in profoundly different ways, these differences did not result in differing ideas about LGBTQ visibility (even in cases where their positions on other topics were notably different). Interviewees' insights form the heart and soul of this book, and they drive my analyses even when I discuss evidence far afield from their words.

At the same time, my audience is less LGBTQ women in the rural upper Midwest than it is LGBTQ studies scholars and students, LGBTQ activists, and people who live in urban places and think of themselves as members of the LGBTQ community—the very people, of course, who are likely to both celebrate LGBTQ visibility without so much as a slight pause and also to pity rural queers. I hope, of course, that my interviewees and other LGBTQ women in the rural upper Midwest will find warmth, joy, and pride in having their perspectives shared, valued, and taken seriously. But the thrust of my intervention lies elsewhere. As such, each chapter of this book deliberately fronts the metronormative and pro-visibility discourses and ideas it deconstructs by focusing on LGBTQ women in the rural upper Midwest. Over the past decade, I have found that most people with whom I converse about this project initially assume that I must be critiquing rural places and highlighting the resilience of LGBTQ people who manage to live in these ostensibly horrific areas. They assume that the book's intended audience is ignorant rural people to whom rural queers have something to say. The hegemony of metronormativity has made it such that the very people in need of this message find it impossible to believe that rural LGBTQ women have something interesting to teach *them,* particularly around their thinking about sexuality, but also about place. The task at hand, then, is to spell out the ways in which the pro-visibility strategies that contribute to urban liberal self-righteousness, which are rooted in and perpetuate metronormativity and sexism, are deeply unbecoming.

Mapping This Queer Terrain

In chapter 1, I conduct a close reading of media associated with two cases of queer rurality that entered into the national spotlight, although to substantially different degrees, and in different times and places. Of the two people at the center of these stories, just one is likely to be familiar to readers. I begin here, examining the narratives circulating around *the* person many associate with queer rurality: Matthew

Shepard, a young white gay man who was murdered in 1998 while a student at the University of Wyoming. Shepard, whose death has long been understood as the result of an antigay hate crime, has had an ongoing impact on the work of gay rights activists, who advocated for the passing of hate crimes legislation in Shepard's name. Chapter 1 considers the responses of gay rights activists and the liberal media to a journalist's alternative account of Shepard's murder, one in which Shepard's death did not result from homophobia, but, rather, from his involvement with a methamphetamine ring. I am less interested in whether this account is true and more interested in what liberals' responses to it can tell us about metronormativity and visibility politics. I begin *Visibility Interrupted* by reflecting on Shepard's case because its ubiquity represents one significant moment in the consolidation of imaginings of queer rurality, and, further, because the interventions this book makes require a willingness to rethink those widely accepted stories that have shrunk conceptualizations of LGBTQ life in rural places. The second part of the chapter focuses on the more recent and less known case of Jene Newsome, the aforementioned Black lesbian who, in 2009, was discharged from the military under Don't Ask, Don't Tell—an event that took place in western South Dakota, just five hours from where Shepard had lived and died more than a decade earlier. Chapter 1, "Metronormativity as Legacy: The Cases of Matthew Shepard and Jene Newsome," explores the social and political ramifications of the metronormativity inherent in gay rights groups' discussions of these cases, including their contribution to racism and classism.

Chapter 2, "(Be)coming Out, Be(com)ing Visible," draws from my interviewees' insights to critically examine the relationships among coming out, being out, and (personal and political) visibility, which are, I argue, simultaneously distinct and overlapping phenomena. Interviewees shared stories that speak to the complex relationships among coming out, being out, and various forms of visibility. They suggest that one can *be* out, but not have *come* out, particularly if the only way to be (authentically) out is to explicitly tell those with whom one is (expected to be) affectively close. Further, their insights suggest that one might come out and still not be visible in prescribed ways. Beyond disrupting the coming out = being out = being visible formula, my interviewees' observations challenge the related assumption that LGBTQ people must be visible in order to live their sexualities, be who they feel they are, and engage in the political sphere more broadly. In outlining the geographically contextual nature of visibility—the ways in which the values attached to it, what it looks like, and what it means are rooted in place-based specificity—I aim to give texture to my claim that LGBTQ women in the rural Midwest live their lives in ways that do not align with gay rights groups' demands for visibility. In chapter 2, I argue that we might read this lack of alignment as a form of what José Muñoz terms "disidentification," and, in so doing, expand a theory that emerged in relation to queer of color performance artists to consider practices and epistemologies associated with rural queerness.

Extending the theoretical scaffolding I provide in this introductory chapter as well as the insights of chapters 1 and 2, chapters 3, 4, and 5 each make a theoretical intervention into the interdisciplinary study of visibility. In chapter 3, "Post-Race, Post-Space: Calls for Disability and LGBTQ Visibility," I consider the ideologies that emerge when disability and LGBTQ rights advocates' ubiquitous calls for visibility collide. I argue that contemporary visibility politics enable the (re)production of post-racial and what I term post-spatial logics. In demanding visibility, disability and LGBTQ rights advocates ignore, ironically, visible markers of (racial) difference and assume that being "out, loud, and proud" is desirable transgeographically. Put more colloquially, the idea that visibility promotes progress is racist; it necessarily ignores that those whose minoritization is visible as such on their bodies experience oppression precisely because of their visibility. Chapter 3 brings together disability, critical race, and rural queer studies—fields that have engaged in remarkably little dialogue—to analyze the ideologies that animate calls for LGBTQ and disability visibility, making clear that the analyses of visibility that I advance here have relevance far beyond LGBTQ studies and politics.

In chapter 4, "Queer Labors: Visibility and Capitalism," I explore the *work* of the production of legible sexual subjectivities and examine the ways that visibility discourses enable an erasure of that labor. Drawing from queer Marxist thought, I analyze activists' calls for LGBTQ visibility at work as well as interviewees' refusals of these calls. Considering how demands for visibility inform the experiences of LGBTQ people at work, in particular, allows us to explore the work of the production of legible LGBTQ sexual subjectivities in new ways. Doing so opens up possibilities to consider the state of being visible as laborious, and indeed, as work itself. In short, I am concerned with how labor is compelled of us without our even recognizing it, and, as frighteningly, under the guise of authenticity. Chapter 4 suggests that becoming recognizable as an authentic LGBTQ subject occurs through labored processes so insidious that they are illegible as such, and, further, that calls for LGBTQ visibility, which relentlessly demand constant laboring (even as they obscure this very laboring), reflect and extend capitalist relations.

In chapter 5, "The More Things Change, the More They Stay the Same: Metronormativity on the Move," I reflect on what we might learn about the relationship of metronormativity to visibility politics through a retrospective look at how representations of and concerns related to rural queerness have changed over the course of the last decade and how they have stayed the same, despite the appearance of change. In the last ten years, the rural queer has come to occupy the concerns of LGBTQ groups in ways that were unimaginable when I began this project. In chapter 5, I reflect on these changes by examining the first campaigns and events that major gay rights groups launched related to rural place: the Rural LGBT Summits organized by the U.S. Department of Agriculture and the National Center for Lesbian Rights, the Human Rights Campaign's "Project One America," and a rural LGBT event held at the White House. In so doing, I analyze how the rural is produced by national gay rights groups conducting outreach *in rural areas* as well as those liberal supporters of this work. Doing so allows me to reflect on the relationship of visual representation to visibility politics, or, more specifically, on how the increase in visual representations of queer rurality might inform my arguments regarding visibility politics more broadly. I examine this relationship by putting into conversation two snapshots of representations of rural queer life captured a decade apart: imagery shared in the "Suburban and Rural Gay Life" Flickr group in 2010 and rural gay Instagram accounts in 2019. Ultimately, I argue that a stated focus on rural place may do nothing to shift perceptions about place or inspire a more nuanced approach to understanding differences that manifest along spatial lines.

In chapter 6, the concluding chapter, I reflect on what I have learned through the process of producing and directing *In Plain Sight,* a documentary short through which I translate some of the arguments in this book and also make new arguments better suited to a visual medium.

The first step in doing so was to return home, five and six years after initially conducting interviews, to reinterview on film some of the women whose interviews I analyze throughout this book. Informed by several years of reflections on the interview material and excitement by the opportunities offered by a nonprint medium, I asked interviewees questions that were more pointed than those I had asked several years prior. These include: How do you imagine that LGBTQ people in Los Angeles, San Francisco, or New York City imagine your life? What three adjectives would you use to describe your life? Why did you agree to be interviewed on film? By way of concluding, I share interviewees' answers to these questions. In so doing, I revisit some of the arguments I make throughout this book, elongating my discussion of the relationship between visual representation and visibility politics. Through Sara Ahmed's formulation of "use," which anchors my discussion, I reflect on the queer potential of both *In Plain Sight* and *unbecoming* as conceptual shorthand—that is, of queer theory on the move.

Throughout each of these chapters, I analyze the ways in which LGBTQ women in rural South Dakota and Minnesota relate to the cultural templates that construct the rural, the queer, and the rural queer. In so doing, I expand upon queer theoretical examinations of intimacy and public life (Berlant 2000). Lauren Berlant, for example, asks how what she calls an "intimate public" came to be viewed as a (personal and cultural) "achievement":

> Whether linked to women or other nondominant people, it flourishes as a porous, affective scene of identification among strangers that promises a certain experience of belonging and provides a complex of consolation, confirmation, discipline, and discussion about how to live as an *x*. One may have chosen freely to identify as an *x*; one may be marked by traditional taxonomies—those details matter, but not to the general operation of the public sense that some qualities or experience are held in common. (2008, viii)

For Berlant, the desire to construct a common intimate public "means that people participate in it who may share nothing of the particular worlds being represented in a given magazine, book, film, or soap opera venue" (2008, ix). For many scholars and activists, the problematic in need of addressing has become precisely this: a lack of (social, institutional, political, popular) representation of the marginalized group in question, which, it is assumed, both contributes to and reflects a broader lack of social belonging. These various cultural representations construct the intimate publics that, in turn, make clear how one is to "live as an *x*." It would be quite easy to argue that LGBTQ rural women "share nothing of the particular worlds being represented" and that we are not represented within discourses and cultural texts that collectively construct those intimate publics that let one know how one is to live as an *x*, particularly when that *x* is an LGBTQ person. For Berlant, this variety of argument is symptomatic of a much larger issue: "Even when people speak out against the terms the intimate public sets out as normative, they are still participating in the promise of belonging that it represents insofar as they are trying to recalibrate whose experience it can absorb so that they can feel included in the mass intimacy that has promised to include them" (2008, ix).

My goal here, then, is not to attempt to make more "visible" those (rural women's) experiences that LGBTQ intimate publics have rendered irrelevant or obsolete so that rural queers might come to be included in these LGBTQ public spheres. It is, rather, to recalibrate LGBTQ politics and discourses by critically examining the ideologies undergirding and ramifications of one aspect of what makes the public intimate (for LGBTQ people and otherwise) in the first place: contemporary visibility discourses and politics. I do so with the belief that the insights of LGBTQ women in the rural upper Midwest contain possibilities for this social and political recalibration. If, as Avery Gordon argues, "We need to know where we live in order to imagine living elsewhere. We need to imagine living elsewhere before we can live there" ([1997] 2008, 5), *Visibility Interrupted* suggests that knowing, too, *where* those who are not the "we" live might illuminate aspects of where we live that make it difficult to imagine living elsewhere, both literally and figuratively. Indeed, our imagining of living elsewhere and otherwise might be enhanced by knowing where those framed as *others* live now.

Ultimately, I contend that this analysis is crucial for feminist, queer, and trans studies and related activism because it offers new possibilities for understanding the depths to which sexuality and gender are understood, experienced, and framed as spatial. It also provides new opportunities for challenging the visibility-laden foundations of the metronormative logics that prevent us from recognizing the spatially contingent nature of gender and sexuality. The articulation and actualizing of more capacious sexual and gendered subjectivities, then, is intimately harnessed to broadening the limited cultural understandings of the queerness of the rural and to questioning the political utility of visibility politics. In the pages that follow, I argue that new epistemological and political approaches could be enabled by asking and trying to answer two wildly simple questions: What does it mean to be (in)visible? What political possibilities are foreclosed when becoming visible is the political project?

Answering these questions is urgent in a moment in which visibility is represented as personal and social liberation, as that to which we ought to aspire. If we are to turn that which is represented as "a shadow of a life into an undiminished life" (Gordon [1997] 2008, 208), we must question the terms by which rural LGBTQ women have come to be understood and represented as (living in the) shadows. We also might consider what we would need in order to resist the hegemonic push to occupy the space of the nonshadows and, instead, engage in a revaluing of the shadows themselves, and the shape-shifting, trickery, and queer ways of being that such shadows enable.

Metronormativity as Legacy

The Cases of Matthew Shepard and Jene Newsome

WHEN I TELL URBAN-BASED feminist and LGBTQ studies scholars and activists, self-identified liberals, and even random strangers about my book on LGBTQ women in rural South Dakota and Minnesota, they often respond with a look of pity and a reference to Matthew Shepard. Never mind that Matthew Shepard was not a woman and that Wyoming is a Mountain West, not Midwestern, state. Such responses are symptomatic of the lack of knowledge about the Midwest, the dearth of positive cultural referents for rural LGBTQness, and gay rights groups' ongoing refusal to address sexism and the related issues that LGBTQ women, in particular, face. Beyond this, such responses also speak to Matthew Shepard's remarkable legacy, particularly in terms of shaping both contemporary gay politics and conceptualizations of LGBTQ rurality. Indeed, there is no story of rural LGBTQ life more pervasive than that of Matthew Shepard's. As such, I start the first nonintroductory chapter of this book with a discussion of Matthew Shepard's case. In the second part of this chapter, I consider the more recent and less well-known case of Jene Newsome, a Black woman who, in 2009, was discharged from the military under Don't Ask, Don't Tell—an event that took place in western South Dakota, just five hours from where Shepard had lived and died more than a decade earlier. In this chapter, I conduct a close reading of media representations of each of these cases, through which I analyze how gay rights groups' discussions of both Shepard and Newsome reflect their metronormativity as well as the social and political ramifications of this metronormativity, particularly as it contributes to racism and classism.

If gay rights activists' responses to journalism that questions the most commonly told story of Matthew Shepard are any indication, rethinking Shepard's story may be difficult for some readers. A wide array of people experience deep affective attachments to Shepard, attachments developed, in part, through the affectively charged nature of representations of his case as well as the story's ubiquitous circulation. Shepard's murder has been the subject of emotionally moving plays, dramas, documentaries, books, 20/20 exposés, and a plethora of academic scholarship from an array of disciplinary locations.[1] Indeed, we might think of the circulation of such texts as part of what comprises the "Matthew industry," as Jack Halberstam described that which emerged in relation to the death of Brandon Teena, a transgender teenager who was raped and killed in Nebraska five years prior to Shepard's death (2005, 16). What I add to the "Matthew industry" so to speak, to the seemingly saturated discussions of Shepard, is a close read of Stephen Jimenez's account of the murder in *The Book of Matt: Hidden Truths About the Murder of Matthew Shepard* and LGBTQ rights advocates' angry and dismissive responses to the text.[2] As these responses show, questioning that which we think we know and also that to which we are affectively connected can be challenging emotionally and intellectually. It can also present political challenges, something activists know well. At the same time, and far more importantly for my purposes, rethinking stories that have become dominant and critically considering our affective responses to doing so can open up epistemological and political *possibilities.* Indeed, the contention of this book is that developing more capacious queer politics requires pausing—and pushing back!—in moments in which rurality is homogenized and LGBTQ visibility naturalized. I begin *Visibility Interrupted* by reflecting on Shepard's case because its ubiquity represents one significant moment in the consolidation of imaginings of queer rurality, and further, because the interventions this book makes require a willingness to rethink those widely accepted stories that have shrunk conceptualizations of LGBTQ life in rural places.

Matthew Shepard and *The Book of Matt*

I remember the exact moment I first heard Matthew Shepard's name. My high school German teacher, an alumna of the University of Wyoming in Laramie, cried as she informed our class about Shepard's hospitalization and the homophobic violence that led to it. At the time, in October 1998, I was a junior in high school in Huron, South Dakota, a town one-third the size of Laramie, where Shepard lived and died. Huron is a mere nine hours from Laramie, not far by Midwestern standards; it can take as many hours to cross the state of South Dakota. The story of Matthew Shepard's tragedy moved from Laramie to the international and back to rural South Dakota in fewer minutes than it takes hours to drive across my home state. It is a story that most LGBTQ people of my generation, among many others, know well.

On the nineteenth anniversary of Shepard's attack, the Matthew Shepard Foundation shared the widely accepted version of the story of Shepard's death on their Facebook page:

> On the night of October 6, 1998, Matthew met Aaron McKinney and Russell Henderson at the Fireside Lounge in Laramie, Wyoming. McKinney and Henderson decided to give Shepard a ride home. They subsequently drove the car to a remote, rural area, and proceeded to rob, pistol-whip, and torture Shepard, tie him to a fence, and leave him to die—all because he was gay.[3]

It is a story that circulated immediately after Shepard was found and before the commencement of the crime's investigation. It is also a story that, in the years since Shepard's death on October 12, 1998, rarely has been challenged. Until, 2004, that is, when a *20/20* episode on the case was aired, and again in 2013 when Stephen Jimenez's controversial *The Book of Matt: Hidden Truths About the Murder of Matthew Shepard* was published. Jimenez questions widely accepted accounts of Matthew Shepard's death and crafts an alternative narrative of the murder. In short, Jimenez argues that Matthew Shepard was beaten as part of a methamphetamine deal gone awry, and that the violence inflicted on Shepard had nothing to do with his sexuality.

Jimenez's argument is based on information he gathered via interviews with more than one hundred people connected to the case in an investigation that lasted thirteen years. He argues that Shepard and McKinney were not strangers on the night of the attack; according to Jimenez's sources, the two knew one another through doing and selling meth, and, further, they had engaged previously in sexual acts with one another. Jimenez also claims that McKinney, who regularly had sex with men, created the "gay panic" defense as a cover-up for his involvement with meth, and then convinced Henderson as well as both of their girlfriends to go along with the story he crafted. In an interview with Jimenez, Kristen Price—who was, at the time of the trial, a teenage mother to an infant son fathered by McKinney—admitted that she went along with McKinney's concocted story in hopes that it would keep her boyfriend out of prison. Apparently, it seemed to McKinney, who was just twenty-one years old and coming off a methamphetamine binge, that constructing this lie would be his best defense. At the very least, it would protect his suppliers. Had meth been considered a significant factor in the case, a different kind of investigation might have taken place, one with the potential to implicate many people beyond McKinney, including local police officers involved in the drug trade. Jimenez suggests that McKinney knew he would be killed if such an investigation took off.

Gay rights activists, organizations, and supporters responded to Jimenez's provocative claims with outrage, disdain, and disbelief. In the first part of this chapter, I conduct a close reading of *The Book of Matt* itself, noting the ways in which it relies on metronormativity even as it provides tools for upending it. Next, I examine the cultural commentary surrounding *The Book of Matt*, including gay rights organizations' (lack of) engagement with Jimenez's arguments as well as comments posted in response to journalistic coverage of Jimenez's claims. I argue that gay rights advocates' refusal to engage with criticism of the story of Matthew Shepard is rooted in and perpetuates metronormativity, and further, that one of the most significant and ongoing legacies of Matthew Shepard's death is the normalizing and bolstering of metronormativity. I then consider what rethinking the dominant narratives of Shepard's death might make possible for LGBTQ movements. To be clear, I am less interested in debating the veracity of Stephen Jimenez's account than in what we might learn from the cultural circulation of his claims. I ask: How might Jimenez's account—itself mired in metronormativity—help us to rethink dominant conceptions of queer rurality, and in so doing, expand what José Muñoz describes as the "potentialities" of queer politics (2006, 11)?

Metronormativity and *The Book of Matt*

Throughout *The Book of Matt*, Stephen Jimenez references media coverage of the Matthew Shepard case. In their analysis of "the visual technologies of Shepard's iconicity," E. Cram notes that metronormativity is evident across this media coverage (2016, 268). More specifically, Cram argues that metronormative optics resulted in Shepard's murder being discussed in radically different ways than violence inflicted on LGBTQ people in urban areas; in short, in many accounts of Shepard's murder, violence became an *effect* of rural place (2016). While Jimenez's book serves as an archive of the metronormativity that drove representations of Shepard's case, he does not explicitly question the characterization of rurality in the media coverage he references. Instead, Jimenez reproduces the very metronormativity that I see as responsible for the primary problematic with which he grapples: the ignoring of the role of meth in Shepard's case. In this section, I conduct a close read of *The Book of Matt*, reflecting on several key instances in the text through which metronormativity is reproduced: the discussion of the fence to which Shepard ostensibly was tied; the characterization of Shepard, Henderson, and McKinney; the use of textured imagery related to rurality without discussing the place of rurality in representations of the case; and reflections on the role of meth in the case in a way that disconnect it from broader place-based issues.

Jimenez begins *The Book of Matt* with a sampling of quotes from the earliest journalistic reports of the attack. The final quote in this introductory section, which comes from the *New York Times*, states, "While some gay leaders saw crucifixion imagery in Mr. Shepard's death, others saw a different symbolism: the Old West practice of nailing a dead coyote to a ranch fence as a warning to future intruders" (2013, 5). In what follows, Jimenez works to undo the assumption to which the first part of this sentence refers: that Matthew Shepard was tied to a fence. Jimenez states that this rendition is inaccurate and, that, instead, Shepard's hands were tied loosely behind his back and he was found near a fence. For Jimenez, this distinction is crucial because the image of Shepard tied to a fence informed the public perception of Shepard as Christ-like, angelic, and a martyr, both in life and in death.

Never once in the 348 pages that follow this quote does Jimenez analyze the assumptions that make possible this "different symbolism"— that unrelated to Christian imagery, Jimenez's concern with the fence—referenced in the *New York Times* quote: "the Old West practice of nailing a dead coyote to a ranch fence as a warning to future intruders." The imagery conjured up in this quote is decidedly rural—"The

Old West," the "practice of nailing a dead coyote to a ranch fence" and "a warning to future intruders." Walt Boulden, Shepard's friend who was quoted by many media outlets, stated, "They hung [Matt] to that fence as a very clear message for the rest of us that *this isn't a place that you're supposed to be if you're gay. . . .* They displayed him like some kind of trophy. You don't do that to a robbery victim" (2013, 245, emphasis added). This image of Shepard and characterization of Wyoming, which circulated nationally, are mutually constitutive; the fence, in other words, was central to the construction of both Shepard and Wyoming. In reflecting on the case later, prosecuting attorney Cal Rerucha pointedly stated, "The fence and where we are [geographically] also had a lot to do with how people viewed this" (245). The image of the wooden fence on the desolate prairie, then, functioned to frame Laramie as rural. With a population of nearly 32,000, Laramie is the third largest city in Wyoming—though one would never know this from representations of Shepard's case. Jimenez's refusal to take on assumptions about the "where we are," as Cal Rerucha put it, when such assumptions were furthered through the image of the fence—the ubiquitous circulation of which Jimenez does address—speaks to the ways in which Jimenez's book furthers metronormativity.

To underscore this point, the fence was not exactly "in the middle of nowhere" or in a "remote" area, as it was often represented. It was, by Jimenez's own description, "bordering the subdivision" (2013, 51) where Aaron McKinney grew up. For Jimenez, this appears to be a passing thought, something he describes as "a strange coincidence" without extrapolating further (51). Much more than a mere coincidence, this point—that the fence bordered a subdivision, and that McKinney grew up there—has the potential to challenge the antirurality that drove representations and understandings of Shepard's life and death. Subdivisions evoke suburbia, rather than rurality, and Aaron McKinney, "the redneck," grew up in such an environment.

While the media presented McKinney and Henderson as "rednecks," they described Shepard as educated, upper class, and worldly, a characterization Jimenez suggests was in "glaring contrast" with the "chilling ordinariness of McKinney's and Henderson's small-town backgrounds"—Jimenez's own description (2013, 5). This framing of Henderson and McKinney on the one hand and Shepard on the other as radically different types of people is also evident in the prosecution's approach. In his opening statement, Cal Rerucha, the prosecuting attorney, stated, "Mr. Shepard paid in bills [at the Fireside bar]. . . . he was immaculately dressed, he was polite, his shoes were shined, he had the air of someone who was educated and someone who was wealthy" (326). By contrast, Henderson and McKinney "spilled dimes and quarters to pay for a pitcher of beer, and they asked for the cheapest. Their manner is rough. They're not polite . . . and they look across the bar at Matthew Shepard. They could see he is . . . an easy mark" (326–27).

As much as Jimenez subtly calls into question such overtly classist and metronormative descriptions—and gestures toward their effects, particularly in terms of Henderson's sentence—he also invokes similar characterizations of Shepard, McKinney, and Henderson. The "lurid tales" he had encountered about Laramie led him to wonder "how it might have looked to Matthew—a petite, twenty-one-year-old freshman *who had attended a Swiss boarding school*" (2013, 21, emphasis added). He expresses a similar thought just twenty pages later: "I thought of Matthew again and how Laramie might have looked to him as a *smart* and *worldly* yet confused twenty-one-year old" (41, emphasis added). Here, Jimenez seems to forget that Shepard was born and raised in Wyoming. He attended elementary, middle, and most of high school in Wyoming, prior to attending boarding school in Switzerland his senior year. Laramie, then, likely would have looked quite familiar to Shepard. Yet, Jimenez produces him as out of place, in ways that are remarkably similar to the media representations that Jimenez critiques.

Although largely unnamed, rural America operates as an interesting character in Jimenez's book. It is both the backdrop and the center, cliché and surprising, familiar and foreign. It is also consistently simple, as that which simply is, rather than something that has been produced to be as it is. The simplicity of the rural is precisely what allows Jimenez to forego examining how the rural has been produced—by gay rights organizations and the mainstream media, sure, but also by broader economic and political forces that contribute to rural poverty and lead people, for example, to sell meth, a point to which I return below.

Indeed, Jimenez never uses the word "rural" himself, although his descriptions rely on characterizations and imagery associated with rurality. He calls Laramie a "friendly but frightening college town" (2013, 21), "a tight-knit, somewhat incestuous town" (117), a "netherworld" (21). "True to its hometown character," Jimenez says, "Laramie is a community where more often than not everyone knows everyone else" (124). Jimenez describes Wyoming as "an expanse of rugged, hilly plains" (352), "pristine high-desert" (30), as having a "cloudless sky" (30). It is a place where people "mountain bike" and "hit the dirt trails" on the same property where livestock roam (25), a place with "boundless solitude and a quiet disrupted only by the lowing of cattle and the bleating of sheep or the occasional truck rumbling along Highway 14" (7). It is a place where a judge, "a bearded old-school conservative . . . carr[ies] a loaded pistol under his judicial robe while hearing cases" (23). It is where the customers at a breakfast joint are "mostly men in thick flannels and work clothes packing in a big breakfast to start the day" (38). It is a place of Carhartt-wearing men with "rugged" looks, an adjective Jimenez uses to describe at least three men, including "the best cop in the county" (25), whose "rugged physical presence said *rancher*. A hankering for the vast emptiness of the high plains seemed to emanate from him head-to-toe" (25, emphasis in original).

Just in case these descriptions do not make clear what Jimenez— who was "coming from [his] native Brooklyn" (2013, 7)—sees as "bona fide Wyoming" (7), he defines it for his readers:

> Ice cold longnecks. An old jukebox stacked with Hank Williams, Vince Gill, and Loretta Lynn. Well-worn pool tables. And on Saturday nights a live musician or band cranking out pure honky-tonk. Fresh-faced cowboys and cowgirls barely old enough to drink thought nothing of driving forty or fifty miles for what had to be the sexiest two-stepping in the world. (7–8)

The descriptions of Wyoming as place and the people of Wyoming are completely inextricable here. Indeed, Wyoming is composed of "starkly beautiful landscape *and* bighearted locals" (8, emphasis added). Jimenez's framing of the two-steppers—who were dancing at Porky's, a "homey" bar and gas station combination—as thinking "nothing of driving forty or fifty miles" to dance functions to describe both the place (desolate, with nothing around) and the people (who do not recognize what a burden this is!).

In this 353-page, painstakingly detailed book, the word *rural* appears twice, both in quotes by gay rights activists. Its debut, 258 pages in, is from a post on the website of conservative gay politico Andrew Sullivan: "The real problem in the gay male epidemic right now is the use of crystal meth (it is hurting the health of people already HIV-positive just as much as it is contributing to the infections of people who are HIV-negative). This drug has rampaged and is coursing through straight rural America and parts of gay urban America" (2013, 258). Here, the rural is the place of straight people and the urban is the place of gays, and meth is equally a problem for both (gay) urban and rural (straight) communities.

Later in the book, however, Jimenez draws from an interview in which meth is framed as a rural issue; this is the second appearance of the term *rural*. Jimenez asked Jason Marsden, one of Shepard's friends who became the executive director of the Matthew Shepard Foundation several years after Jimenez interviewed him, about the place of methamphetamine in Shepard's death. Marsden responded:

> It was very clear ten years ago . . . that [meth] was going to become a scourge in Middle America, *in our rural communities*. . . . It dominates life for a lot of people in our state. . . . I remember thinking at the time that the Matt Shepard case would forever go down in history as . . . one of the saddest examples of gay bashing, but what it also was, was one of the saddest examples of the desperate lengths people on methamphetamine will go to. (2013, 284; emphasis added)

For Marsden, meth was a distinctly rural problem. Jimenez never addresses the tension between the quotes of Sullivan and Marsden—Is meth a rural problem or equally a (straight) rural and (gay male) urban problem?—or the rural aspect of Marsden's comment. He also does not problematize Sullivan's comment, through which Sullivan places gay people squarely in the urban. Instead, he uses these quotes simply to reassert Shepard's involvement with meth.

What are readers to make of Jimenez's lack of engagement with the place of rurality in Shepard's case alongside his consistent deployment of rural imagery—especially when meth commonly is attached to rurality and when LGBTQ people are not? Examining one (meth) without the other (rural) is utterly bizarre, especially considering that rurality is crucial to the story Jimenez crafts: that crystal meth, not homophobia, was the root of Shepard's murder. Dominant ideas about methamphetamine locate it firmly in small-town America, after all. Beyond this, assumptions about rurality are precisely what made Shepard a kind of pitiable, knowable, and mourn-able gay subject. Jimenez's position that the cover-up of Shepard's drug use by the mainstream media, prosecution, his family, and gay rights groups made possible his martyrdom, in other words, misses the influence of place on how people understood and continue to remember the case. Metronormativity is precisely what allowed Shepard to be always already known and grieve-able when so little information about Shepard circulated. As Jimenez argues, in part by drawing from journalist JoAnn Wypijewski, Shepard was conspicuously absent in representations of Shepard. Speaking to this point, Wypijewski states that "the mythologizing of Matthew . . . has left him oddly faceless. No one has seemed interested in publishing the details of his life—as if they would detract from his martyrdom" (Jimenez 2013, 65). For Jimenez, gay rights groups' desire to produce Shepard as a martyr prevented us from knowing "the real Matthew Shepard" because "the real" Shepard was involved in the use and selling of meth and this does not a martyr make (64). However, it is not as if Shepard's use of meth erased all other interesting things about his life; details of his life could have circulated that had nothing to do with his drug use. Details did not circulate because they did not need to; people felt as if they knew Shepard by knowing his final plight—which stood in for the horror of his life and the lives of all LGBTQ people in rural places. Jimenez's suggestion that Shepard's martyrdom required obscuring details about his life ignores the ways in which metronormativity renders these details unnecessary.

Had Jimenez considered any factors other than the role of meth in Shepard's case, his book would have been radically different. Simply put, metronormativity runs deep. It is evident in Shepard's becoming a martyr and in Jimenez's telling of what he presents as an alternative account of Matthew Shepard's story. It is also evident in gay rights supporters' responses to *The Book of Matt* and discussions of Shepard's legacy.

Gay Rights Politicos

Gay rights activists have attempted to intervene in the circulation of Jimenez's claims in a variety of ways over the course of, at least, the last fifteen years. In 2004, approximately a decade before *The Book of Matt* hit the shelves, Jimenez's research led to the aforementioned *20/20* episode. Prior to its airing, gay rights advocates contacted the show's executive producer in an effort to kill the story (Jimenez 2013, 123). When they were unsuccessful, employees of GLAAD and HRC tried to intervene editorially. *20/20* denied their requests. In response, GLAAD, HRC, and the Matthew Shepard Foundation crafted a collective statement in which Joan Garry, the then-executive director of GLAAD, stated, "This simply is not a credible piece of journalism."[4] Garry's response captures the approach of gay rights groups in 2004: attack the credibility of the journalism. They did so primarily through the production of a "viewers' guide" for watching the show.[5] The guide outlined ten reasons for dismissing the *20/20* exposé—all of which can be dismantled easily or are implicitly addressed in *The Book of Matt,* although Jimenez does not respond to the viewers' guide directly. Three of the guide's ten points question the credibility of sources, including Kristen Price and Aaron McKinney. Importantly, these same activists found Price and McKinney credible when they were saying things that made possible the soundbites gay rights activists desired. Others were deemed noncredible for the following questionable reasons: having known Shepard for a short time, being "a former drug-using associate of McKinney's," and because *20/20* did not include the last name of a witness, who GLAAD described as "an anonymous bartender." The ease with which gay rights activists wrote off interviewees for being a bartender or a former drug user speaks to broader classism among these gay rights groups.

The 2004 viewers' guide marks gay rights groups' last substantive engagement with Jimenez's claims. Their response to *The Book of Matt* a decade later was decidedly different, both in quantity and content. In response to journalists' requests for comments on *The Book of Matt,* the Matthew Shepard Foundation stated, "We do not respond to innuendo, rumor or conspiracy theories. Instead we remain committed to honoring Matthew's memory, and refuse to be intimidated by those who seek to tarnish it."[6] GLAAD and HRC both refused to comment. Such (non)responses to Jimenez's book run counter to gay rights activists' attempts to intervene in and engage in damage control around the *20/20* episode nearly a decade earlier. In much of the media coverage of the book, gay rights groups' declining to comment became part of the coverage itself.

While no gay rights organizations made a public statement regarding *The Book of Matt*, the gay press did cover the story. *The Advocate*, for example, published two pieces about Jimenez's book. In one, the author accurately portrays Jimenez's ideas, but, curiously, still concludes that Shepard's death was the result of a hate crime. The other, an op-ed written by Neal Broverman, the magazine's executive editor, is entitled, "Why I'm Not Reading the 'Trutherism' about Matt Shepard." Broverman leads with a question: "A new book aims to get the real story behind Matthew Shepard's murder, but is emboldening the right wing and sullying Shepard's image worth a still-unclear 'truth'?"[7] For Broverman and other gay rights activists like him, the book could only serve the right wing and hinder LGBTQ movements, particularly around their work related to passing hate crimes legislation.

Four years earlier, in 2009, President Obama signed into law the Matthew Shepard and James Byrd Jr. Hate Crimes Prevention Act. While mainstream gay rights groups—as well as many supporters of LGBTQ rights—celebrated the passage of this legislation as a victory, leftist scholars and activists have been less enthusiastic about attaching LGBTQ rights to the U.S. prison system (Stanley and Smith 2015). In a statement expressing its opposition to hate crimes legislation, the Sylvia Rivera Law Project (SRLP) outlines many of the critiques in circulation of this variety of legislation. First, SRLP draws from evidence that suggests that punitive laws do not deter violence to argue that this legislation similarly promises to do nothing to prevent hate crimes. Second, they argue that the prison system has long criminalized same-sex acts and gender nonconforming behaviors and continues to target, and disproportionately arrest and detain, transgender people; as such, LGBTQ people should be wary of that which produces the state as a concerned ally. Third, they point out the problems with legislation that expands the authorization of and funding for the so-called Department of Justice, an apparatus that targets poor people and people of color. Black people are "six times more likely to be incarcerated than white people" after all.[8] In an analysis of the transnational circulation of discourses related to hate crimes and related hate crimes activism, Jin Haritaworn speaks to this latter point regarding the racialization of such laws. Haritaworn argues that the fight for hate crimes legislation in Germany coincided with racialized fear of ostensibly homophobic Arab migrants from whom white Germans needed protection. Put otherwise, such legislation was always already racialized and racist (Haritaworn 2010–2011, 11). In short, queer studies scholars and leftist queer activists give us tools with which we can question the desire for such laws—desires that continue to stimulate discussions of Shepard's case. Importantly, neither McKinney nor Henderson was charged with a hate crime, although Shepard's murder is consistently described as "one of the most notorious anti-gay hate crimes in American history."[9] It was, instead, according to Jimenez, "the national media, special interest groups, and politicians—and hence the court of public opinion— that rendered the decision" (2013, 125).

The Advocate's editor's refusal to engage with Jimenez's claims is as rooted in his belief in the value of hate crimes legislation as it is his metronormativity. Broverman makes clear that he does not "want to know if Matthew Shepard had a three-way in a limo 15 years ago or dabbled in meth dealing or was HIV-positive. It doesn't change the fact that he's dead and that being an out gay man contributed to that death." Jimenez's entire point is, of course, that Shepard's "being an out gay man" did *not* contribute to his death. Broverman's metronormativity manifests here as a refusal to believe that a gay man in rural America died for any reason other than being gay. Such metronormativity is evident across the liberal media's engagement with Jimenez's book, to which I now turn.

An Argument for Reading the Comments

The liberal press covered the publication of *The Book of Matt* in several ways. The vast majority of press was wildly dismissive, often focusing on the (lack of) credibility of Jimenez's sources and/or attacking Jimenez himself, strategies gay rights groups had used when responding to the *20/20* episode a decade earlier. In her *Think Progress* article entitled "'The Book of Matt' Doesn't Prove Anything, Other Than the Size of Stephen Jimenez's Ego," Alyssa Rosenberg argues that "the real subject" of the book "is Jimenez himself."[10] Furthermore, when *The Guardian*, a liberal news site, engaged with the ideas published in *The Book of Matt*, it was attacked by Media Matters, a liberal media watchdog that works to correct what it calls "conservative misinformation in the U.S. media."[11] Media Matters slammed *The Guardian* for covering the book and critiqued Jimenez for being interviewed on anti-LGBTQ right-wing radio shows.[12] Simply engaging Jimenez's claims proved to be, for the liberal press, too risqué.

The reader comments left in response to journalistic coverage of the publication of *The Book of Matt* both mirror and depart from the broader cultural commentary regarding Jimenez's claims. Of the 705 comments posted on *The Guardian* article critiqued by Media Matters, for example, the overwhelming majority exhibit the same lack of willingness to engage with Jimenez's ideas and general disbelief evident across gay rights advocates' responses.[13] Examples include that this case never should have been brought up again; there is no way that this is true; the author, who wrote the book for fame and riches, should die. The vast majority of such comments do not engage with evidence presented in the book or in *The Guardian*'s coverage. Commenters simply do not believe the claims and feel no reason to justify their positions, ignoring evidence that operates in opposition to their positions.

Ideas about rurality figure in the comments in particularly interesting ways, especially because the journalists writing the articles upon which people are commenting do not tend to yoke Shepard's death to rurality in the egregious manner evident in the immediate aftermath of Shepard's murder. The rural operates in this coverage in much the same way as it does in Jimenez's book—there, but unnamed, unremarkable. Here, I focus on the twenty-nine (of 705) comments posted on *The Guardian* article that raise the issue of rural place; although these comments do not comprise a large percentage of the comments posted, they are some of the most substantive and work to counter what commenters view as metronormativity in the refusals to engage with Jimenez's ideas.

One commenter, Magneticnorth50, posted: "This murder had more to do with a drug lifestyle than a gay lifestyle. It is because [of] WHERE it happened that made it NOTORIOUS. The Media and Gay Rights activists took the ball and ran with it." In another comment, Magneticnorth50 expanded on this position: "The point of the book was not to 'defrock' Matthew, but [to] describe the circumstances surrounding his death, and contradicting the view, which is evident here—Wyoming=Redneck=Hate mongering State full of homophobes."

While I do not agree with Magneticnorth50's suggestion that "the point of the book" was to contradict the view of Wyoming as homophobic (a point on which I expand in the following section), I do find accurate their assertion that the widely held assumption that Wyoming is homophobic is evident among the comments.

Others responded to the metronormativity within the comments by referencing their own experiences as gay people living in rural areas. Sehome shared the following story:

> As a gay man quite familiar with the stereotype about the "rural west" being so bigoted (I live in it) I never have found that to be the case at all—more of a "live and let live" society, and when it was noised around that I myself was gay, people became even more friendly and accepting (after a lot of jokes and some laughter) and one of the most "macho" men in our little town of 900 came up to me on the street and hugged me. I was embarrassed.

WeAreNumberOne also shared a personal story, through which they work to counter negative depictions of Wyoming evident in the comments:

> The broad brush painting of Wyoming bothered me too. . . . I regard Wyoming in the same way that I regard every other place I've spent more than a little time: as a mixed bag. It's a physically beautiful state, wide open and remote in places, with a lot more diversity of people and attitudes than was portrayed at the time. I never thought there was anything "Wyoming-specific" about what happened to Shepherd [*sic*]. I was gay bashed outside of a gay bar in Madison, Wisconsin while alone and doing nothing more than leaving by myself to walk home. I have a friend who was hurt very badly in similar circumstances in Denver.

Some commenters critical of Jimenez's book or *The Guardian*'s coverage of it suggested that it does not matter why Shepard was killed, that he was still dead, and that dredging up this story was in poor taste. Commenter threesixty responded to this sentiment directly, stating:

> I think it does matter whether this was a hate crime or a normal drug dealer one. The connotations are quite different. For a start if "any" gay person can be brutally killed for no reason other than their sexuality then that must have been a pretty scary time in the

Wyoming of the late 90's. If it wasn't the case that it was a homo-phobic crime and you are a gay man in Wyoming at that time who was not involved in the drug trade then you can feel pretty safe doing what you're doing without that type of fear. So "why" an actual crime occurred is always important because it can be a sample of what a society is about at a particular point in time.

Several commenters locate the problems with how the case was portrayed in the approaches of the media and gay rights activists. Magneticnorth50 stated, "This was made a Cause Celebre by the Media and gay community, at a time when there were other disturbing inci-dents involving harassment of gay people. So Wyoming is sacrificed by stereotype on the altar of PC." WeAreNumberOne similarly argued:

> For the gay establishment, and the media, the fact that it hap-pened in Wyoming made for the perfect, simple story of rural hatred. Not one in 50 of those who pontificated at the time had ever spent any time there. The reality is different than what was portrayed: The problem for gay people in places like Wyoming isn't nearly as much the gay bashing as it is the simple numbers, and the distances.

Others were more concerned about the responses of contemporary gay rights leaders to Jimenez's claims than they were about the role of gay rights groups in shaping narratives about Shepard's death in the imme-diate aftermath of the murder. Sehome commented:

> As for the horror of Mathew Shepard's murder, afterward many good things were achieved, and now the (apparent) facts about his drug use and prior relationships including sex with one of his killers does not take from that, and I applaud the writer for his careful but painful research. . . . I am ashamed for the so-called Gay Leaders and PC people who reject this book. They seem as narrowminded as those they often criticize.

Unlike Sehome, threesixty views the work of gay rights groups posi-tively and asks if the cost to Wyoming's reputation might be worth the increased awareness of homophobia enabled by discussions of Shepard's case:

> I suppose the real question is whether using something that is false (like this appears to be) to justify something positive is a good thing. . . . Does the end always justify the means? Maybe in the great scheme of things in this instance it did (greater awareness of homophobic crime around the world etc.) but it probably always comes at a cost (i.e. the reputation of Wyoming). Maybe that's a good price to pay in this instance.

Each of these commenters recognizes and works to counter the metronormativity perpetuated in Shepard's name, evident both in the comments and in the articles upon which people commented. In so doing, they express positions not evident elsewhere in discussions of Jimenez's claims. Catchee does so, perhaps most explicitly, pointedly asking, "Why spoil a progressive's dream narrative? Saintly LGBT man, victimised by white working-class men from a rural town? Can't have the truth getting in the way of a good story." In the following section, I offer a response to Catchee's provocative question: Why, in other words, would it behoove those committed to LGBTQ justice to spoil progressives' narratives? What good might come of challenging dominant iterations of Shepard's life and death?

"Why Spoil a Progressive's Dream Narrative?": Lessons for Scholars, Activists, and LGBTQ Rights Supporters

Those critical of *The Book of Matt* have questioned why Jimenez would write such a book, expressing concern over its potential negative political consequences. Here, I discuss what I see as the incongruities between Jimenez's stated goal and what his text accomplishes. I suggest that lessons for those of us committed to living a queer life exist in this gap, and further, that we can access these lessons through engaging critically with both *The Book of Matt* and also gay rights groups' responses to the text.

In response to journalists' questions regarding his reasons for embarking on this project, Jimenez stated:

My principal reason for writing *The Book of Matt* stemmed from my discovery that the tragedy of Matthew's murder was bigger and more complicated than most people understood at the time. . . . As a gay man who survived the AIDS epidemic— who experienced the death of so many friends—I was stunned by the devastating impact of the crystal meth epidemic in *our community, as well as in parts of rural America.* Once I learned of Matthew's previously unreported involvement with this drug, I felt the moral imperative to investigate and report that part of the story. If we're serious about preventing similar tragedies, we need to understand what really happened—and why—which means coming to terms with Matthew in all his human complexity and not merely as a symbol. (emphasis added)[14]

Jimenez was similarly quoted in an interview with the *Bay Area Reporter,* an LGBTQ publication, as stating, "A full portrait of who Matthew was as a person, as a human being, was missing from the public narrative."[15] In his "Author's Note" to the book, Jimenez states, "We have enshrined Matthew's tragedy as passion play and folktale but hardly ever for the truth of what it was, or who he was—much to our own diminishment" (2013, vii). How would learning about "Matthew in all his human complexity" prevent "similar tragedies"? How would our collective diminishment be reduced by knowing "the truth" about the case? How does Jimenez's account help to construct a "full portrait" of Shepard?

The short answer to the latter question is: it doesn't. In fact, Jimenez does not provide answers to any of these questions, either in *The Book of Matt* or in his comments to the media regarding the book. Rather, Jimenez's framing of the gay community as separate from rural America ("I was stunned by the devastating impact of the crystal meth epidemic in *our community, as well as in parts of rural America.*"), which mirrors Andrew Sullivan's aforementioned comment, contributes to an inability to "know" Shepard, as well as other LGBTQ people living in rural areas (or those places imagined as rural). Despite Jimenez's claims that he offers a fuller portrait of Shepard, he simply swaps one superficial version of Shepard for another. In Jimenez's account, Shepard appears as little more than a damaged soul who did drugs to cope with trauma. Jimenez paints Shepard as what journalist Andrew

Gumbel called "far from angelic," through tracing Shepard's "history of depression, of heavy drinking, of crystal meth and heroin use and a lurid series of sexual misadventures including episodes of rape and molestation."[16] This sentence—which includes one of the few mentions of molestation I have found in journalistic coverage of Jimenez's book—is written in such a way that it does not make clear who was doing the raping or molesting. (Incidentally, it also suggests that being raped or experiencing depression can be part of what makes one less "angelic.") Gumbel is gesturing here toward Jimenez's claims that Shepard was gang raped in Morocco and that Shepard had been both the victim and perpetrator of molestation. Jimenez notes that as a teenager Shepard "was arrested for molesting two eight-year-old boys in his Casper neighborhood" (2013, 349). Jimenez cites a court motion in which the prosecution requested "that the defense be barred from reference to or testimony regarding any information . . . which may be contained in police reports regarding Matthew Shepard, obtained from the Casper Police Department as well as juvenile [court] records" (349).

Throughout *The Book of Matt*, readers learn about the ostensibly less-than-savory activities Shepard engaged in—selling drugs, falsely reporting a rape (a different rape than that which he experienced in Morocco), molesting young boys, and so on. Jimenez goes to painstaking lengths to detail these aspects of Shepard's life. As a result, readers actually learn little about what made Matthew Shepard Matthew Shepard: What were his favorite foods, bands, and books? What did he most value in his friendships and in his romantic relationships? What did he most often eat for breakfast? What jobs did he have? What was his relationship like with his brother? Did he desire alone time? If so, where did he go for solitude? What were his favorite things about himself? In the book's epilogue, readers learn that Shepard loved Nelson Mandela and dreamed of doing human rights work (2013, 352). Had Jimenez included more of these kinds of details—nearly nonexistent throughout the book—his claim that he desired to create a more complete portrait of Shepard would be corroborated. Such a portrait would necessarily include anecdotes about Shepard's compelling characteristics, daily life, and his dreams for his future, along with the ostensibly less likeable aspects of Shepard upon which Jimenez focuses. Jimenez's approach is, then, not much different from those he critiques for making Shepard "faceless" in their desire for a martyr.

Despite his claims to the contrary, Jimenez's primary concern appears to be neither Shepard nor LGBTQ politics; it is Russell Henderson and the fairness of Henderson's fate. Jimenez asks if Henderson's trial would have had a different outcome had the jurors known "that Matthew was part of an interstate meth-trafficking circle, and that the buying and selling of crystal meth was only one of the activities he and Aaron shared" (2013, 331). Jimenez cites legal experts who "agreed almost unanimously that Russell's chances of receiving the death penalty for his role as an accomplice were slim to none" (306). Although McKinney knew Shepard prior to the attack, Henderson first met Shepard on that fateful night, and according to Jimenez, his role in the events has been exaggerated grossly. Henderson's lawyers advised him that he should accept a plea bargain to avoid the possibility of the death penalty, and Henderson acquiesced. As such, his story was never in the public sphere—or at least not a version he crafted. The courts and the public alike conflated Henderson and McKinney; we did not learn, for example, that Henderson never hit Shepard and that, when he expressed that McKinney should stop beating Shepard, McKinney turned on Henderson and hit him in the face with the same pistol that killed Shepard, leaving Henderson with a scar that matches Shepard's laceration. In an interview with Jimenez, McKinney stated, "It's really hard for me to talk to Russ, to see him in this situation, knowing that I'm the one that put him here. . . . I ruined that guy's life. He was a good kid. Squeaky clean . . . He didn't do nothing. The only thing that man's guilty of is keeping his mouth shut" (2013, 94).

Jimenez draws from interviewees who, like Jimenez, question Henderson's lifelong imprisonment. A former lover of Shepard's, for instance, blames the series of events that led to Shepard's death entirely on McKinney and since has developed a friendship with Henderson. Others reference the much lighter sentences given for similar crimes, including to the man sentenced to serve just four years in prison for raping and murdering Henderson's mother while Henderson was awaiting trial for Shepard's murder. Regarding this discrepancy, a Laramie woman asked Jimenez, "What's wrong with this picture?" (2013, 307).

Several things, to be sure—none of which can be addressed with the current discourses surrounding Shepard that either position Shepard as beyond critique or that recharacterize Shepard as Jimenez does. "What is wrong with this picture" neither begins nor ends with the discrepancy in the prison sentences for Henderson and McKinney and for the man who killed Henderson's mother. In fact, this picture cannot be addressed without engaging critically with the prison system and the notion that trials can be fair (a position that ignores the ways in which the prison system relies on and reproduces racism, as well as sexism, classism, homophobia, transphobia, and ableism); addressing sexism and sexual assault and the relationship of LGBTQ justice to feminism; taking seriously class, classism, and political economy; and paying careful attention to the ways in which rural life did and did not contribute to Shepard's life and death, as well as the public memory of him. Each of these issues—classism, sexism, racism, metronormativity— has been largely ignored by mainstream gay rights groups.

These are the issues that need to be addressed if Shepard's death could possibly prevent "similar tragedies" in the future. Might Jimenez's account—in which homophobia had nothing to do with Shepard's death—open up alternative and more capacious possibilities for queer politics? In dismissing outright Jimenez's claims, gay rights activists squash possibilities for extending what we conceptualize as LGBTQ issues. The level of engagement—both on the right and the left, by those who support Jimenez's claims and those outraged by them—with Jimenez's ideas rarely goes beyond whether people are willing to imagine that Shepard's death was informed by anything other than homophobia. Put otherwise, most cultural commentary focuses simply on whether people *believe* Jimenez's claims, beliefs that appear to be based almost entirely on the political commitments commentators otherwise hold. Conservatives support Jimenez's claims because they are skeptical of the need for LGBTQ rights. Liberals oppose Jimenez's claims because they worry about their potential to influence hate crimes legislation. Furthermore, engaging seriously with Jimenez's claims requires a willingness to challenge metronormative beliefs, which many liberals hold. This wholesale belief or dismissal without engaging with evidence should frighten all of us. For those on the political left, we ought to be concerned with the ways in which such approaches foreclose conversations regarding how critiquing our own narratives might open up new ways to approach queer politics. The comments I shared in the previous section, which disrupt the metronormativity evident in liberal media as well as responses to it, serve as rare (and refreshing!) examples of people engaging with ideas otherwise.

As a couple of commenters noted, Shepard's death may not have been a result of a hate crime but still could have been informed by homophobia. Rebel7 asked: "How many gay men ended up as addicts because they wanted an escape from intolerant parents, schools, churches, and society? That in itself is a tragedy and has been overlooked by far too many concerned that Shepard will loose [*sic*] his victim status." Matthew Shepard was, according to statements made by his mother and shared in Jimenez's book, someone who used drugs to escape the pain the world had caused him, including being raped in Morocco. It is certainly plausible that meth and heroin became a part of his self-medicating. It is also plausible that Shepard was a target for rape, as he had been for bullying, because of his small 105-pound body, which survived premature birth to experience a host of other physical and mental health issues over the course of its life. In this case, Shepard's involvement with drugs might have been connected to homophobia and ableism. Other factors also may have influenced Shepard's involvement with drugs. It is possible that Shepard was unable to find work because of the lack of economic development increasingly common across rural America. Selling meth might have been one of few options for earning an income. Laramie has a 29 percent poverty rate, but just a 3.1 percent unemployment rate, after all, which suggests that there are not many jobs to be had, and that many of the jobs already held by people are not particularly lucrative ones.[17] Perhaps Shepard was unable to work for a variety of reasons related to mental health or his physical embodiment, which may have made him undesirable for many of the jobs that are gendered masculine in rural areas and beyond. It is possible that any or all of these factors contributed to Shepard's involvement with meth; meth, then, would need to be considered a symptom of broader problems, rather than a problem that, if addressed on its own, could save lives. Alternatively, Shepard simply may have enjoyed doing drugs and being a part of circles of similar people; perhaps Jimenez's production of Shepard as an addict might better reflect broader antidrug discourses (which position all drug users as addicts and abusers at constant risk) than Shepard's own drug use. We do not know what factors did and did not contribute to Shepard's drug use.

What we do know is that hate crimes legislation would not have prevented Shepard's death. We know that many LGBTQ people—disproportionately transgender people of color—have been targeted and killed for being LGBTQ since the passing of this very legislation. We know that rural economies have not improved in the last two decades. We know that people—90 percent of whom are women—continue to be sexually assaulted at rates no different from those in the 1990s, when Shepard was assaulted. If gay rights supporters, including Jimenez, want to prevent the kinds of violence that killed Shepard, we are going to have to do far more than pass hate crimes laws and address drug use. In this sense, Jimenez and the gay rights supporters refusing to engage with Jimenez's claims are both short-sighted. We need to question why gay rights supporters and organizations view Jimenez's claims as dangerous, or even worse, unbelievable and unworthy of engagement—an irony given that the book shares many of the same limitations as the approaches of gay rights groups, namely in terms of metronormativity and a refusal to engage with the structural causes of crime. We also need to critique the critique Jimenez launches—which we cannot do without recognizing the role of rural place in Shepard's life and the place of metronormativity in his becoming a martyr, two things Jimenez ignores. It was metronormativity, after all, that made Shepard a perfect mourn-able subject, finally legible to urban audiences—and thus gay rights organizations and liberal politicos—in his death.

If Shepard's murder was a meth deal gone awry, and homophobia may have led to the conditions in which he found himself using drugs, one could argue that homophobia informed Shepard's death, without his death resulting from a hate crime. In many ways, this is a much more powerful position, and one with fewer simple solutions. It is a position that does not allow the rural to be scapegoated and two working-class men barely old enough to purchase alcohol to stand in for the horror of the rural; there is homophobia everywhere, after all (although it manifests differently along spatial lines, of course). It is a position that would force gay rights groups to question what makes Shepard the perfect martyr. It is a position that would allow us to recognize that social justice issues far beyond those typically considered LGBTQ issues are, in fact, LGBTQ issues. It is a position that would encourage us to reckon with the limits of the approaches of gay rights groups, particularly in this case, their work to pass hate crimes legislation and reliance on metronormativity—which manifests here as a refusal to believe that Shepard's murder might have possibly been informed by factors other than his visible gayness and the geographic location in which it occurred. Questioning that which we think we know about Shepard allows for a broader rethinking of rural place and the ways in which metronormativity is furthered via visibility politics, as ideas about Shepard's supposed visibility as a gay man have informed our understanding of Shepard's life and death in profound ways. As gay rights activist Neal Broverman asserted, it was Shepard's being an "out" gay man in "rural Wyoming" that led to his death.

More than a decade after Shepard's death, Jene Newsome, an Air Force sergeant stationed at Ellsworth Air Force Base in western South Dakota (which is just a handful of hours from where Shepard lived and died), found herself in the national spotlight. The same metronormativity that inflects narratives of Shepard's death is also evident in discussions of Newsome's case. Beyond this, Newsome's case allows us to consider the ongoing and contemporary illegibility of the rural LGBTQ woman as well as related racial politics in ways that Shepard's does not. Let's turn to Newsome now.

Newsome in the News

Jene Newsome didn't tell. And no one asked. Until November 2009, that is, when members of the Rapid City Police Department visited Newsome's home looking for her partner and spotted through the window a marriage certificate on her kitchen table. Just a month or so earlier, Newsome married her partner, Cheryl Hutson, in Iowa, the only Midwestern state to have legalized same-sex marriage at the time. The officers were looking for Hutson, who was wanted on theft charges in Alaska, and although they did not find her, they did see the couple's marriage certificate. They subsequently reported this piece of information to the military, essentially "outing" Newsome, who was honorably discharged in January 2010 under Don't Ask, Don't Tell, the military's former policy that dictated that lesbian, gay, or bisexual individuals could serve in the military so long as the military remained unaware of their sexual orientation.[18]

With assistance from ACLU South Dakota, Newsome filed a complaint against the city of Rapid City in which she asked for $800,000 in damages, a policy change that would prohibit police officers from releasing personal information to the military in the future, a reprimand for the officers involved with her case, and a formal apology. Despite the applicability of Don't Ask, Don't Tell and same-sex marriage rights—two issues that were dominating the efforts of national gay rights groups at the time—to Newsome's case, she continually aimed her criticisms at the Rapid City Police Department, rather than commenting on either of these federal issues or the governmental institutions responsible for such policies. Newsome filed a complaint against the Rapid City Police Department, stating, "I played by 'Don't Ask, Don't Tell.' . . . I just don't agree with what the Rapid City police department did. . . . They violated a lot of internal policies on their end, and I feel like my privacy was violated."[19]

Despite Newsome's position, various liberal media sources, as well as national gay rights organizations working to abolish Don't Ask, Don't Tell, used Newsome's story to express and foment opposition to the policy. The *Washington Monthly,* one such liberal news source, wrote, "Meet Jene Newsome . . . The repeal of 'Don't Ask, Don't Tell,' pending in Congress, can't come quickly enough."[20] The remainder of this report argues for the need both to completely do away with Don't Ask, Don't Tell and, in the interim, make the policy less stringent so that third-party "outings"—such as the one that occurred in Newsome's case—would not lead to the dismissal of military service members. Of course, readers did not actually "meet" Jene Newsome in this article, as its opening line promised. Instead, her story was co-opted to support a broader fight against Don't Ask, Don't Tell, despite Newsome's own refusal to critique the policy.

The vast majority of local and regional press coverage of Newsome's case, by contrast, focused on the Rapid City Police Department, with little mention of same-sex marriage rights or Don't Ask, Don't Tell. Of the thirteen articles published in the *Rapid City Journal* regarding Newsome's case, none focuses primarily on Don't Ask, Don't Tell or even mentions marriage. An editorial written by the *Journal*'s board begins, "The Rapid City Police Department has changed its policy on sharing information with Ellsworth Air Force Base officials. The new policy states that only the department's records custodian can turn over official documents to the military."[21] The editors go on to describe this policy change, which emerged out of Newsome's encounter, as "sensible," without addressing the national policies responsible for making Newsome's case notable in the first place; the word *marriage* is absent, and Don't Ask, Don't Tell is mentioned just once. Much like

Newsome's own approach, the editors work to decouple Newsome's story from both national politics and from her sexuality, stating, "We don't see how the case would have been handled any differently regardless of Newsome's sexual orientation." It seems obvious that the case would have been handled differently had Newsome's partner been a man—in fact, there would have been no case. Had Newsome been married to a man sought by local police, officers still may have contacted the military as part of their search, but reporting Newsome as married would have had no repercussions. In suggesting that Newsome's sexuality was extraneous to the officers' decisions, the editors depoliticize the case's connections to national debates over same-sex politics and shift the focus to the politics of policing in the context of the local community—repoliticizing the case in ways that mirror Newsome's concerns, as I discuss below.

By contrast, Newsome herself was tertiary in the coverage of her story by urban non-Midwestern news sources and national gay rights groups, both of which used her story in order to argue for same-sex marriage rights and repealing Don't Ask, Don't Tell, framing these issues, rather than the Rapid City Police Department, as the roots of Newsome's problems. Even in a *San Francisco Chronicle* article titled "Military Discharges Sergeant After Cops Out Her," which one might reasonably assume would focus on the outed sergeant, national gay political issues occupy at least as much space as does Newsome's actual story.[22] The article ends with a statement from Nathaniel Frank, a researcher at the Palm Center, a University of California, Santa Barbara, think tank dedicated to research regarding LGBT people in the military: "Even though 80 percent of 'Don't Ask, Don't Tell' discharges come from gay and lesbian service members who out themselves, third-party outings are some of the most heinous instances of 'Don't Ask, Don't Tell.'" That the article ends by referencing a national political issue, rather than Newsome's story, marks a significant departure from the framings of the case by the local and regional press and by Newsome, who said very little about third-party outings, Don't Ask, Don't Tell, or same-sex marriage, and refrained from intertwining her narrative with discourses and positions evident in national political debates.

The complexity of Newsome's story is not captured, however, by viewing her case as a simple co-optation of rural stories for the fulfillment of urban goals. In fact, it is certainly possible that Newsome's

desires could be in line with the goals of mainstream gay rights organizations; she is, after all, both married and a former military employee. Furthermore, her demands for compensation included *public*
reprimands of the officers and a *public* apology. However, even in this
case, Newsome's desires were never for her own visibility and were not
intended to gain rights or further a movement, pointing to the distance between Newsome's approaches and those of national gay rights
organizations.

Justice for Jene! and the Politics of Race

These distinctions are nowhere more evident than on the "Justice for
Jene!" Facebook page, launched on March 13, 2010, by Newsome's sup-
porters. The anonymous creator of the site, who goes by the name
Justice for Jene!, posted forty-eight messages between the day of its in-
ception and June 3, 2010.[23] The group's first wall post, which mimicked
the group's mission, stated, "Jene Newsome was outed by the Rapid
City Police Department for no apparent reason to the United States
Air Force. Because of the outing Jene, a nine year service member, has
been removed based upon the military's 'Don't Ask, Don't Tell' policy.
Let's end DADT and get justice for Jene!" Although Justice for Jene!'s
initial post called for ending Don't Ask, Don't Tell, and implied that
doing so would result in local recompense, none of Justice for Jene!'s
future posts, nor any of the posts of the group's 5,135 fans, even reference the policy. During the time in which the Facebook page was active,
Congress considered legislation regarding Don't Ask, Don't Tell and
the policy consistently appeared in the national spotlight. But neither
Newsome herself nor her Facebook supporters conceptualized Jene's
justice in relation to national gay politics and, thus, challenging this
policy was not the intended purpose of the page. That Justice for Jene!
never again mentioned Don't Ask, Don't Tell in any of their forty-seven
subsequent posts—but that the ban is referenced in the page's initial
post and mission statement—speaks to the difficulty of discussing
Newsome's case outside of the logics of mainstream gay politics as well
as the desires of rural LGBTQ women to do so.

The function of the "Justice for Jene!" Facebook page was to generate
support for Newsome's battle against local authorities and institutions.
Forty-one of Justice for Jene!'s forty-eight wall posts commented on

the Rapid City Police Department, Rapid City Council, or Rapid City Mayor. In one such post from April 6, 2010, approximately one month after the page launched, Justice for Jene! wrote

> The Rapid City Council discussed the situation with Jene last night but they are still not taking any official action. It's been three weeks since Jene's story went public and the Rapid City Council has not made a single statement. It looks as if they are simply going to allow the Rapid City Police Department to act and do what they want too [*sic*].

Such posts are reflective of Newsome's public statements documenting her frustration with the police officers' violation of what she viewed as a set of unspoken local norms that functioned to allow her to presume that her marriage was a private matter, rather than with local politics that might appear to preclude her from being "out" or visible. In many ways, Newsome was "out"; her family and friends knew about her sexual orientation, and she is married, something scholars have argued "forces people to be out" (Bernstein and Taylor 2013, 18). But the assumptions regarding the value of visibility that inform such assertions do not resonate with those posting to the "Justice for Jene!" Facebook page nor with Newsome, who is married and out, but exists in ways that cannot satisfy the demands of calls for visibility. As Newsome said, "I'm not an activist. I hadn't planned to be changing my life. . . . If I hadn't been discharged I'd be making the Air Force my career."[24] In discussing her case, Newsome refused to criticize the military or the federal government, a discursive move that makes clear her lack of desire to work to change these institutions so that she might be allowed to exist in alternative (more visible) ways.

Despite Newsome's stated disinterest in politics, the "Justice for Jene!" page serves as one site through which Newsome's supporters comment on an otherwise overlooked and highly political dimension of the case: the politics of race. Newsome is Black and part of an interracial couple, two points rarely mentioned in deployments and coverage of her case. By contrast, Justice for Jene!'s final two Facebook posts addressed racism directly. On June 2, 2010, Justice for Jene! wrote, "Continued race problems haunt policing in Rapid City," and included an accompanying link to an article in the *Rapid City Journal* that describes a march protesting the Rapid City police department's refusal to punish an officer for killing a young Native man exactly one month earlier. The following day Justice for Jene! posted a link to a 1963 report on the racism of the Rapid City police department, stating

> Rapid City, South Dakota has a fairly extensive past of racial discrimination. In 1963 the United States Government investigated allegations of racism against African-American Airmen from Ellsworth Air Force Base and found systemic racism. Racism continues to be an issue that haunts Rapid City.

Such posts simultaneously work to historicize contemporary instances of racism against Native people and to suggest that racism was involved in Newsome's case—a marked difference from the approaches of gay rights groups, which ignored Newsome's race in their attempts to increase opposition to Don't Ask, Don't Tell via deploying Newsome's story, and often, ironically, her photo. Similarly, the ACLU never publicly addressed Newsome's race or the influence it may have had on her case. Although Newsome's concerns—her critique of the Rapid City Police Department rather than the U.S. military or government—directly reflect the history of police brutality against Black communities, Newsome also refrained from explicitly addressing how her race may have impacted her case, framing her situation as one in which local police officers violated her privacy.

As it turns out, marriage and intimacy are, for Newsome, private matters. In many ways, desires for privacy exist in fundamental opposition to calls for certain (homonormative) intimacies to be made visible. While Newsome's deployment of privacy discourses reflects the ways in which the contemporary neoliberal moment compels individualization, privacy also becomes the mode through which Newsome both expresses a distancing from national gay rights groups and also carves out a place through which she can connect her case to histories of police brutality against communities of color without explicitly addressing the role her race played in her case.

These discursive and material complexities are flattened when sexuality is not examined in relation to race or when race goes unacknowledged altogether. Such a problematic is especially evident in South Dakota, a state largely imagined as white, but with particular racial dynamics that require serious consideration: American Indians comprise 9 percent of the state's population; the state's history of radical Indian activism continues to influence how race is understood and experienced within the state; Indian leaders such as Cecilia Fire Thunder have made national headlines by discussing race in relation to contemporary political issues, including abortion and land rights; and Huron, South Dakota, (my hometown) has recently received international attention for its "embracing" of Karen refugees, many of whom work at a Hutterite-owned turkey processing plant.[25] These dynamics inform race relations within the state and region and, when acknowledged, also can inform how South Dakota is imagined more broadly. The framing of the Midwest as white allows for such intricacies to be left out of analyses, resulting in the further marginalization of racialized subjects. In ignoring Newsome's race, gay rights organizations, the ACLU, and local, regional, and national news unintentionally participated in constructing the Midwest as white and its racial minorities as inherent "others." In Newsome's case, the representation of the Midwest as white likely informed the ignoring of race common in deployments of Newsome's story. Racialized subjects are always already outside of hegemonic representations of what constitutes both the (good) gay and the (good) rural Midwesterner—and yet Newsome was (even if temporarily) both.

The ignoring of Newsome's race, then, informs and is informed by the metronormative narrative that constructs the rural as backwards, homophobic, and stifling, always lacking the glamour, lights, and diversity of the big city. Metronormativity depends upon and benefits from dominant constructions of the rural as white, which come to stand in for the ostensible safety and backwardness of the rural. The relation of whiteness to both safety and backwardness is, of course, contextual; the presumed whiteness of the rural will feel safe to some and dangerous to others and many conflate rural whiteness with conservative anachronistic beliefs. Those with liberal political commitments, including those reminiscent of the gay rights movement, who desire to be understood as what Robert McRuer calls "flexible subjects," require various forms of (racial, gendered, sexual) otherness in order to perform their ideological flexibility (2006). While metronormative narratives require that race in the rural must be erased, race remains central to narratives of Western-global and urban-global relations. In many ways, non-Western LGBTQ subjects who move to the urban United States are compelled to retain their "otherness" in order for urban liberal subjects to assert a (nationalist) progress narrative and present their own flexible subjectivity. The rural's failure at multiculturalism, then, comes to represent the inability of its people to be "inclusive," and thus, its backwardness—narratives that appear to be concerned with race, but, in fact, disappear the people of color who make the rural Midwest home.

Looking Back, Looking Forward

In many ways, Jene Newsome's story has been more foundational to the arguments I craft in this book than any other. Indeed, it was through my following of Newsome's case that I first perceived and became interested in what I viewed as an estrangement between the discourses, ideologies, and strategies used by dominant gay rights organizations and those embraced by rural LGBTQ Midwesterners, epitomized here by Newsome. Through additional research and subsequent interviews, which I share in the chapters that follow, I came to recognize Newsome's estrangement as indicative of a broader disidentification with gay rights groups—and particularly their reliance on visibility politics—among LGBTQ women in the rural upper Midwest. My reflections on Newsome's case are, thus, central to my examination of the ways in which visibility discourses produce the rural LGBTQ woman as illegible.

When I started this project, I could not have predicted that Matthew Shepard might come to occupy a place in it. I initially found well-meaning liberals' mentioning of Matthew Shepard in response to learning about my research curious and even interesting. Over the years, I have come to find interlocutors' recentering of a white gay man in a story about rural women's pushing back against political strategies that were largely created by and for urban white gay men quite unbecoming. Despite my aggravations and reservations, I began to recognize that the consistency of this response suggested that I would need to address the ghost of Matthew Shepard in order for this project to *become* anything at all. I would need to take on what exactly I found unbecoming about the afterlife of Shepard, including the metronormative slippages that led people to yoke Shepard to a project on LGBTQ women in the rural upper Midwest, as well as the use of his case to stand in for the horrors of the rural. Throughout this chapter, I have examined the unbecoming aspects of media coverage of Matthew Shepard alongside that associated with Jene Newsome. I am less concerned with the lack of visibility, so to speak, of Newsome's case—although, of course, LGBTQ studies scholars and gay rights activists' consistent deployment of Shepard and disinterest in Newsome reveals unbecoming things, as I've suggested here[26]—than I am with the ways in which putting the cases in conversation exposes fissures in the logics of gay rights activists, particularly in relation to visibility.

In narratives of Shepard's murder, he was always already visible as gay. His gayness was apparent to strangers who met him at a bar, in fact. Shepard's hypervisibility—and in a rural place, no less!—is central to his representation as a quintessentially good young gay man and to his becoming a martyr. Paradoxically, it was also Shepard's visibility that, according to these same narratives, led to his death. By contrast, Newsome's desired relationship to outness was ignored in gay rights advocates' discussions of her case. It had to be, of course, because her lack of interest in prescribed outness worked against gay rights groups' production of Don't Ask, Don't Tell—and its prevention of workplace outness, a topic I discuss further in chapter 4—as Newsome's fundamental problem. Newsome did not care about being able to be out at work, but she certainly cared about having a job, something taken from her by what she viewed as the unethical practices of local police officers. Nonetheless, gay rights groups used Newsome to advocate for legislation that is fundamentally rooted in a belief in the value and necessity of LGBTQ visibility. In fact, the legislation that gay rights groups attached to both Shepard and Newsome relies on assumptions about visibility. The hate crimes legislation passed in Shepard's name assumes that victims of hate crimes are always already visible as LGBTQ, while Don't Ask, Don't Tell assumes that people want to be out, at work or otherwise. In both cases, gay rights groups assume that visibility is desirable and politically valuable across geographic locales, illuminating the centrality of visibility politics to metronormativity.

The approaches of Jene Newsome and her Facebook fans, and also of Stephen Jimenez and those commenting on the journalistic coverage of *The Book of Matt*, complicate this metronormativity, as well as the broader ideologies of gay rights groups that rely on and reproduce this very metronormativity. Such partings might best be understood as disidentificatory practices, which, as José Muñoz argues, allow marginalized people to simultaneously work on, within, and against dominant ideologies, neither assimilating into nor dogmatically opposing such structures (1999, 11). Newsome and her supporters at "Justice for Jene!" and the commenters responding to the metronormativity in their fellow commenters' posts neither reproduce the discourses and strategies evident within national gay rights groups nor engage in oppositional approaches that would place themselves outside of struggles for gay rights. If Newsome and her supporters at "Justice for Jene!" identified with the logics of gay rights groups, they likely would have blamed federal policies for Newsome's problems. If they counteridentified with such groups, they might reject the logics of the dominant system, and criticize the military, the government, and marriage as oppressive institutions. Newsome and her Facebook fans disidentify, working on, within, and against dominant logics, power structures, and institutions. In the chapter that follows, I extend this discussion of Muñoz's theory of disidentification to examine the relationships the LGBTQ women I interviewed have to ideas about outness and visibility, suggesting that their approaches, like Newsome's and the commenters we heard from here, might best be read as disidentificatory.

2

(Be)coming Out, Be(com)ing Visible

THE HEADLINE OF A 2017 ARTICLE posted on Bustle, a website that is a part of a digital group with the "largest reach and engagement of any Millennial and Gen Z focused publisher,"[1] reads "What Is National Coming Out Day? Celebrating Visibility in the LGBTQ Community Is More Crucial Than Ever."[2] A 2015 article on Odyssey, a website that has "more than 15,000 millennial content creators,"[3] is succinctly titled "On 'Coming Out' and Gay Visibility."[4] In 2014, the Human Rights Campaign posted a "Transgender Visibility Guide" on their "Resources: Coming Out" web page.[5] Each of these examples gestures toward the cultural conflation of coming out, being out, and being visible. For gay rights advocates, *being* out is simply impossible without *coming* out. Being visible is, similarly, inconceivable without coming *and* being out. And, as the Introduction to this book outlines, coming and being out are understood as always already politically and socially relevant. In this chapter, I draw from the insights of the LGBTQ women in rural South Dakota and Minnesota whom I interviewed to critically examine the relationships among coming out, being out, and (personal and political) visibility, which are, I argue, simultaneously distinct and overlapping phenomena. Interviewees shared stories that speak to the complex relationships among coming out, being out, and various forms of visibility. Collectively, they suggest that one can *be* out, but not have *come* out, particularly if the only way to be (authentically) out is to explicitly tell those with whom one is (expected to be) affectively close. Further, they suggest that one can come out and still not be visible in prescribed ways.

Such assertions require critically examining what visibility itself means. This chapter extends Mary Gray's argument—rooted in her ethnographic examination of LGBTQ youth in rural Appalachia (2009)—that visibility does not have the cachet in rural places as it does elsewhere by considering the relationships of LGBTQ women in the rural Midwest to outness and visibility. The LGBTQ women in rural South Dakota and Minnesota who I interviewed generally viewed themselves as "out," but many had explicitly "come out" to very few people. In fact, many of my interviewees would be considered "closeted" according to dominant cultural narratives regarding what it means to "be out": that one has *explicitly told* one's coworkers, friends, family, and, most importantly, parents about one's sexual orientation.

Yet, they do not feel inauthentic, stuck in some spider-web-filled closet, or unknown. Indeed, those (affectively and geographically) close to the women I interviewed *know*. Beyond disrupting the coming out = being out = visibility formula, I also draw from interviewees' stories to challenge the related assumption that LGBTQ people must be visible in order to live their sexualities, be who they feel they are, and engage in the political sphere more broadly. The LGBTQ women with whom I spoke are living their sexualities, feel as if they are completely themselves, and are engaged in politics on their own terms, while simultaneously disidentifying with visibility politics.

In outlining the geographically contextual nature of visibility—the ways in which the values attached to it, what it looks like, and what it means are rooted in place-based specificity—I aim to give texture to my claim that LGBTQ women in the rural Midwest live their lives in ways that do not align with gay rights groups' demands for visibility. My interviewees' experiences demonstrate how rural queerness exists in a disidentificatory relationship with mainstream visibility politics, through which they reconfigure its vocabulary to validate their authenticity, living one geographically contingent version of "outness" while simultaneously dismantling its central commitment to the confessional performance that such politics insist is at the heart of liberation.

In what follows, I first outline José Muñoz's theory of disidentification, an important contribution to queer of color critique, and spell out how I utilize Muñoz's insights as scaffolding for my analyses here. I then engage scholars' discussions of "coming out" and "the closet," with the intention of highlighting how a focus on rural LGBTQ women's understandings of outness and visibility speak to what Steven Seidman views as the limitations of the trope of the closet in the contemporary moment (2002). Doing so sets the stage for my analyses of how and why the women I interviewed disidentify with demands to come out and be visible. I highlight interviewees' lack of identifying strongly with an LGBTQ identity, as well as their broader disinterest in the ways in which gay rights groups politicize sexuality. I close by sharing examples of what I describe as their quiet forms of resistance to this very politicization.

Disidentificatory Practices

In what has become widely recognized as a key queer theory text, José Muñoz examines how those marginalized because of their race and sexuality negotiate majoritarian culture (1999). It is short-sighted, he suggests, to think that queers of color would either align themselves with or exist entirely outside of exclusionary (racist and homophobic) mainstream cultures. Muñoz calls for recognizing that those marginalized by racial and sexual norms work "on, within, and against" these norms simultaneously, neither assimilating into nor dogmatically opposing them. Muñoz terms this approach "disidentification" and argues that developing a disidentificatory position is one way that marginalized people negotiate engaging with that which alienates them (1999, 11). Still, by focusing on queer of color performance artists putting on what Muñoz reads as politicized performances, he makes clear that disidentification refers to practices of resistance that are "deeply indebted to anti-assimilationist thought" (1999, 18).

In many ways, Muñoz's disidentification might seem a strange theory for framing the experiences and desires of those LGBTQ women in the rural upper Midwest I focus on here. Their queerness and their forms of resistance are understated, quiet, and modest; they are rural and Midwestern, after all. The queer of color performance artists about whom Muñoz writes are decidedly over-the-top, campy, and based entirely in urban places (Berlin, London, Los Angeles, Miami, New York City, and Toronto). Furthermore, considering his focus on the visual and visuality, Muñoz says remarkably little about visibility—at least in part it seems because, as he notes, "the erosion of gay civil rights is simultaneous with the advent of higher degrees of queer visibility in the mainstream media" (1999, 99). Still, there are moments when Muñoz uses the language of visibility to analyze the variety of antiassimilationist and disidentificatory art with which he is concerned. In a chapter on autoethnographic performance, for example, Muñoz examines the work of queer Chinese Trinidadian cultural producer Richard Fung in terms of postcoloniality, hybridity, and queerness. Muñoz suggests that we should read Fung's work "as a making visible of the mediations that attempt to render hybridity invisible and unthinkable . . . Fung works to make hybridity and its process comprehensible and visible" (1999, 79). Here, Muñoz conflates invisibility with unthinkability and visibility with comprehensibility. Just twenty pages later, in his analysis of modalities of drag, Muñoz gestures toward the spatial assumptions that underpin his analysis of such disidentificatory art. He sets up mainstream commercial drag, which he says "presents a sanitized and desexualized queer subject for mass consumption" by liberals, against that which he terms "queerer drag" performed by queer performers in queer spaces for queer consumption (99). The place of the problematic and apolitical "mass commercialization of drag" is, unsurprisingly, "suburban multiplexes," which Muñoz differentiates from that which includes possibilities for disidentificatory resistance: the metropolitan (99).

Still, Muñoz's rich theory provides crucial tools for making sense of the complexity of my interviewees' lives. Some of my interviewees discussed their desires for marriage and children or their participation in the military, and those who did not were not explicitly critical of the assimilationist goals of those mainstream gay rights groups working to advance marriage equality or gay and lesbian inclusion in the military. And they were certainly not concerned with the variety of antiassimilationist thought that drives the queer of color performance artists' work as well as Muñoz's theorizing of it. However, their expressions of what might appear to be assimilationist desires operate, I argue, in a markedly different manner from those of gay rights groups. Put more directly, even when the desires of some of my interviewees—for things such as marriage equality—aligned with the work of gay rights groups, they often pushed back against the assumption that they ought to be visible. Drawing inspiration from Muñoz, I read such moves as disidentificatory: interviewees did not avoid visibility discourses entirely and were rarely explicitly critical of gay rights groups, but they also described their lives in ways that gesture toward a radically different understanding of what visibility means to the degree that their positions reflect a refusal of visibility politics. In other words, interviewees often utilized visibility discourses, but did so with a difference—and to the extent that their deployments of such discourses constitute challenges to the logics of gay rights groups, including those views of visibility as necessary for or equivalent to liberation. Muñoz describes the practice of desiring the cultural ideal (which here manifests as the variety of normativity shepherded by gay rights groups) but "desiring it with a difference" as the type of negotiation central to disidentification (1999, 15). For Muñoz, these negotiations work to resist, empower, rethink, and ultimately create something new.

> The process of disidentification scrambles and reconstructs the encoded message of a cultural text in a fashion that both exposes the encoded message's universalizing and exclusionary machinations and recircuits its workings to account for, include, and empower minority identities and identifications. Thus, disidentification is a step further than cracking open the code of the majority; it proceeds to use this code as raw material for representing a disempowered politics or positionality that has been rendered unthinkable by the dominant culture. (1999, 31)

The cultural texts that I deconstruct and reconstruct throughout this book allow us to ask new questions about the ideologies buttressing visibility discourses, as well as their ramifications. In this chapter, I center interviewees' narratives to expose the exclusionary machinations and encoded meanings of these discourses. My hope is that my interviewees' stories and my interpretations of them might break "open the code of the majority" and create possibilities for thinking through those politics and positionalities "rendered unthinkable by the dominant culture": both queer rurality and queerness beyond an out, loud, and proud frame.

Disidentification, then, operates in this chapter on two distinct but interwoven scales. In reading interviewees' thoughts, experiences, discourses and desires as disidentificatory, I, too, participate in a disidentificatory process via "recycling and rethinking encoded meaning" (1999, 31). The encoded meaning that interviewees rethink and recycle, is, I suggest, that of dominant gay rights groups, while the codes I rethink and recycle are those of both gay rights groups and interviewees' stories themselves. A researcher's deployment of interviewees' stories is necessarily a recycling, and I intend to use this recycling in the service of imagining new epistemological possibilities and political positionalities regarding rurality as well as visibility—in short, to disidentify.

My examination of interviewees' narratives, as well as my subsequent recycling of their stories, is informed by Judith Butler's analysis of the discursive production of the subject. As Butler argues, "the real task is to figure out how a subject who is constituted in and by discourses then recites that very same discourse but perhaps *to another purpose*" ([1990] 1999, 165 emphasis added). In an interview with Vicki Bell, Butler draws from Althusser to ask: "What does it mean to appropriate the terms by which one is hailed or the discourses in which one is constituted?" (Bell 1999, 164). Just as Muñoz calls for recognizing the complex ways that people resist majoritarian culture even as they participate in it, Butler's question suggests that we take seriously the ways in which people appropriate dominant terms in order to create something different. Taking seriously these complexities—which we ought to read as just that, rather than as contradictions—is central to recognizing what Avery Gordon terms "complex personhood."

> Complex personhood means that the stories people tell about themselves, about their troubles, about their social worlds, and about their society's problems are entangled and weave between what is immediately available as a story and what their imaginations are reaching toward. . . . Complex personhood is about conferring the respect on others that comes from presuming that life and people's lives are simultaneously straightforward and full of enormously subtle meaning. (Gordon [1997] 2008, 4–5)

This chapter considers that which may appear to be straightforward about interviewees' stories in an attempt to grapple with the "enormously subtle meaning" of their lives and how this subtlety illuminates the falsities and fissures of hegemonic visibility politics. Such an analysis of the specific ways in which LGBTQ women in rural South Dakota and Minnesota disidentify with traditional ideas about visibility is enriched by critically considering the trope of "the closet" and what it means to "come out."

The Closet

LGBTQ studies scholars have complicated the typically celebratory understandings and deployments of "coming out" of "the closet" that have driven gay rights activism for the last half century—and that remain evident across almost every sector of contemporary social life, including in the work of medical professionals, politicians, student affairs workers, religious leaders, and journalists alike (Esterberg 1997; Phelan 1993; Rust 1993; Schweighofer 2016; Sedgwick [1990] 2008; Stein 1997). Mignon Moore, for example, critiques those who present "coming out" as a linear process that happens in predictable stages and culminates in the "acceptance of a modern gay identity in which the subject has merged her private self-understandings with the public self she reveals to others" (2011, 21).[6] That the height of gay identity development is presented as "coming out" from people as diverse as gay rights activists, medical professionals, and religious leaders gestures toward the deep links between visibility and identity politics as well as the institutionalized structures through which visibility has come to be viewed as valuable.

LGBTQ studies scholars have long critiqued this "coming out" model for the ways in which it renders individual processes that are quite complex and socially enacted, overlooks the often circuitous paths by which people might come to view their experiences and develop their identities, and ignores examples of alternative ways of understanding sexuality—geographic, cultural, and historical—that would challenge its very premises. Joseph Massad, for example, argues that same-sex sexual acts have long been widely accepted in the Middle East and that more recent increased homophobia in the region resulted in response to the strategies of what Massad terms the "gay international"—including demands to develop a gay identity and to organize one's life around that identity (2008). Mignon Moore similarly suggests that the linear models for making sense of coming out processes do not apply to Black women in New York City, whose acting on their same-sex sexual desires is better understood as "coming into" a community (2011, 22). George Chauncey provides evidence that the approach Moore witnessed among her interviewees has deep historical roots. Gay people in New York City in the pre–World War II years, Chauncy says, "did not speak of coming out of what we call the 'gay closet' but rather of coming out into what they called 'homosexual society' or the 'gay world,' a world neither so small nor so isolated, nor, often, so hidden as 'closet' implies" (Chauncey 1994, 7). In fact, the phrase "coming out of the closet," according to Chauncey, was not in circulation until the 1960s. If coming out has meant, and for some people in some places continues to mean, coming *into* a group (of LGBTQ people), rather than coming *out* of a group (of presumably heterosexual people)—the latter being the contemporary model—then what it means to "come out" or to be "in the closet" is historically and culturally specific.

The pressures, dangers, benefits, and value associated with (not) coming out are, by extension, also contextual. From the 1890s to 1940, the decades Chauncey examines, joining a community of other lesbians or gay men—"coming out," if you will—could lead to arrest (as well as the expression of one's desires, of course). Being known as lesbian or gay during the AIDS epidemic in the 1980s was also extremely dangerous (and, in other contexts during the same period, pleasurable). The dangers, perhaps much like the various pleasures, associated with "coming out" in the prewar era or in the 1980s, were, then, quite different than they are in 2021. Today, the hegemony of visibility discourses makes it quite dangerous to *not* come out—for precisely the reasons I outlined in the Introduction: one is assumed to be unknowable, thwarted in their realization of who one "is," and, perhaps worst of all, an inhibitor of social progress. In an age when identity politics and gay rights reign, ostensibly lacking an authentic gay identity or impeding the gaining of rights (which come to stand in for progress) marks a type of social illegibility akin to social death.

In a moment in which "gay visibility . . . in popular culture is not viewed as exceptional but speaks to broader changes in the social status of lesbians and gay men," we must, Steven Seidman argues, question the continued relevance of the trope of the closet (2002, 1). Seidman did precisely this, examining contemporary manifestations of the "psychological and social texture of the closet," by interviewing thirty people who considered themselves closeted (7). Seidman concluded that "many gay Americans today live outside of the social framework of the closet" (9). Strikingly, Seidman came to this conclusion by interviewing people who considered themselves "closeted." Seidman found that his interviewees tended to frame their past—rather than present—lives as closeted. Part of this contradiction is definitional: what Seidman's interviewees described as "closeted" (hiding particular details of their lives from particular individuals) Seidman decidedly argues against. The closet, for Seidman, refers to an individual's making "life-shaping decisions in order to pass" rather than what Seidman sees as an "episodic pattern of concealment" that had little bearing on one's life (7). Not sharing that one is LGBTQ with a stranger on an airplane or a coworker, for instance, does not necessarily make one closeted. "If the concept of the closet is to be useful in understanding gay life," Seidman argues, "it should describe a *'life-shaping'* social pattern" (8).

But, as Seidman points out, many LGBTQ people—even those who consider themselves closeted—no longer conceal their desires, experiences, or identities in a manner that allows this omission to shape their lives *significantly*. Such statements accurately characterize my interviewees' descriptions of their lives. So, while I agree with Seidman's assertion that the framework of "the closet" no longer captures the experiences of many LGBTQ people in the United States, I am resistant to the implicit suggestion that this renders the closet analytically obsolete. It is certainly not obsolete for those who live in (rural and/or non-Western) places that serve as the proverbial closet of the urban and/or West. LGBTQ women in the rural Midwest can never be outside of the "country-as-closet construct," as Katherine Schweighofer terms it, regardless of how (out) they live their lives (2016, 223). They live there, in the closet, after all. That both my own and Seidman's interviewees viewed themselves as closeted if they conceal their sexuality in *any* moment speaks to the continued relevance of the closet in dominant and LGBTQ subcultural imaginaries, even as it can no longer capture the complexity of the material experiences of LGBTQ people and, therefore, its usefulness—indeed, its very meaning—must be questioned. My goal here is not to further complicate what it means to come out[7] (I have drawn substantially in this chapter from scholars who convincingly do so), but rather to consider how my interviewees' ideas regarding LGBTQ identity as well as their geographic positionalities manifest in their disidentification with dominant conceptions of visibility.

In what follows, I analyze my interviewees' articulations of their relationships to visibility, their appropriation of terms and logics that they undermine even as they deploy them. I begin by considering why it is that these women expressed a disinterest in visibility, focusing on their lack of identification with their sexuality and the role of rurality in shaping their positions. In the following passages, it will become evident that the women with whom I was in conversation craft their identities in ways that neither centralize nor ignore their sexualities. This form of crafting implicitly rejects mainstream gay rights advocates' assumption that visibility is the key to self-actualization. Based on the testimonies of these LGBTQ women in rural South Dakota and Minnesota, it is evident that in some cases acquiescing to demands to be visible would actually interfere with their ability to be themselves, live their sexualities, and engage politics in ways that feel authentic to them.

Identity, Community, Visibility

Claudia, a lower-middle-class, white, disabled woman in her late twenties who lives in central Minnesota and is in an interracial relationship, pushed back against the idea that her sexuality ought to define her.[8] In regards to relating to an LGBTQ identity, Claudia stated:

> I think that it's really interesting that people . . . want people to identify and even in the LGBT community people want people to identify. And I know I've always kinda resisted identifying as anything. And so even calling myself a lesbian doesn't feel accurate. Even calling myself bisexual doesn't feel accurate either. I don't feel that my identity is in my sexual orientation. . . .
> In the LGBT community, a lot of people put their identity in their sexual orientation probably because its marginalized. . . . But I've always kinda resisted that and so I don't necessarily see . . . myself as an LGBT person. I just see myself. I identify as a woman pretty strongly. You know because it's always been there. But I'm more. You know I just see myself as a person who fell in love with a person. . . . I feel like it's very strange to go from . . . a privileged status to an oppressed minority status just like that. [After] I came out in college, I didn't really identify as anything. . . . People would ask you in grad school . . . what your orientation is. And it always made me uncomfortable. . . . I was never really sure how to answer that because I didn't identify as straight, lesbian, or bi. Anything. Or even as queer. You know some people would say, "Oh, well then you're just in the queer category." No. You know, I just feel like why do I have to pick an

identity all because I have something that is a difference? But it doesn't have to be my identity. . . . We don't identify. We don't have identities based on other differences between us. You know. I'm aware that it's very socially constructed, this whole identity thing. Probably because I studied it.

Claudia made clear that her identity is not located in her sexual orientation. As a former graduate student in sociology, Claudia said that she understands identity labels based in difference as products of social construction, explaining that she is not comfortable allowing those constructions to define her. Beyond this, she is concerned about what it means to identify strongly with an aspect of yourself that is oppressed and, further, that doing so positions you as different from others. At the same time, Claudia stated that she identifies as a woman "pretty strongly." Claudia's signaling to a distinction between the roles of gender and sexuality in terms of her understanding of herself extends what we might think of as the feminist stakes of this project, as I detailed in the introduction.

Eileen, a lower-middle-class white woman in her late twenties who lives in southeastern South Dakota, also views her sexuality as just one small part of who she is, noting that it does not dominate or determine how she sees herself:

My mom and I have this conversation all the time. Me being gay does not create who I am. It is a part of who I . . . of my identity and that's something . . . it took me a long time to realize. [In] my Kansas City experience, "Eileen is gay." [The people in my circle] were on the exact same level. . . . I used to have hair down almost to my butt. . . . I went to Pride in Kansas City and went crazy. I shaved my head, I met some girl, we were gonna get married like in two days, forty-eight hours. Like went absolutely crazy because that's who I was, and . . . [now][my partner] to me is number one in my life and there's nothing I would do to hide that, there's nothing I would do to shy away from that subject. . . . That's who I'm going to love for the rest of my life. But I'm also Eileen, I'm also, you know, a full-time employee, I also . . . have my own circle of friends that I can hang out with. . . . Everyone else when I came out saw me as "the lesbian," but it's

almost taken me just as long to realize that there's more to me
than just my sexuality. There's a lot of other aspects to me that are
still just as important. . . . Absolutely it's not everything, or all,
or the most important, it's just, it's there.

Eileen explained that coming out as a lesbian, a process that was marked
by going "absolutely crazy," was just the first step in her self-realization.
For Eileen, there was something about Pride, about her circle of lesbian
friends, that encouraged her to do things she would not normally do.
Eileen "the lesbian" was not actually Eileen, something it took her "a
long time to realize." But when she did, she came into herself as Eileen,
as someone who sees herself as far more than her sexuality.

Both Claudia and Eileen simultaneously used the language of "coming out" and resisted the idea that as an "out" LGBTQ person, their
sexuality ought to be central to how they see themselves in the world.
Others commented similarly, naming the specific pieces of themselves
that make them who they are. As Jody, a lower-middle-class white
woman in her late forties who lives in southeastern South Dakota,
explained:

It's not the biggest thing that I am, it's just something that's
a part of me but it's a small part of me. . . . I hope that people
think that I'm a really good person, and I hope they think that
I'm caring, and kind, and compassionate . . . blue eyed, five foot
eight, 120 pounds. . . . It's a part of me that's no bigger than most
of those other parts. You know, I seriously think that being a gay
is so far down on my totem pole. I'm so much more engrossed in
sports and fantasy football than I ever would be about who's gay.

For Jody, her personality, physical traits, and hobbies are just as important to her as her sexuality. Glenda, a middle-class white woman in her
early twenties who lives in western South Dakota, agreed:

Well, I don't really see my sexuality as . . . who I am, the forefront of who I am. My personality . . . is who I am. And that's
how my friends and family see me, like you're just [Glenda]. I'm
a very big smart-ass. I get it from my father. . . . I'm just like very
loyal, caring . . . love to listen to people . . . always there for any-

body, just . . . very sweet. I'm a very old soul, gentlemen-y kind of person, I guess. . . . I'm a smart-ass and I'm a lesbian.

Glenda's "smart-ass" personality and Jody's love of football are more central to how they see themselves than are their sexualities. Jolene, a lower-middle-class white woman in her late twenties who lives in central Minnesota, offers a pointed critique of the dangers of organizing one's life around a piece of one's identity:

If you have friends [with whom] the only thing you . . . have in common is drinking, well, you know every time you go out, you're just going to get wasted. If you have certain friends that all you guys do [together] is talk about [the TV show] *Twilight*, you're going to get your *Twilight* charts. . . . I think, then, like [focusing on a] certain . . . identifying factor . . . you . . . miss growing because you can be that forever. . . . Regardless of it, you need to grow in other ways.

For Jolene, identifying strongly with one aspect of oneself and surrounding oneself with people who have similar social and political identifications has the potential to thwart personal growth. It is not surprising, then, that none of the aforementioned women build relationships and communities based on ideas regarding shared sexuality. Bobbi and JJ, two middle-class white women who live in central Minnesota and are in their early seventies and early fifties, respectively, speak directly to this point. The two have been partnered for decades. I asked if they use the Internet in search of some kind of LGBTQ community. JJ responded with a laugh and a snicker: "No, for gay. I wouldn't be looking for gay communities . . . because I wouldn't want to identify that way."

I don't relate to somebody based on sexuality because sexuality isn't what it's about for me . . . and so why would [I] go and have the whole basis of a relationship based on something that's kind of irrelevant in my life. . . . What sense does that make? . . . It's like, okay, we just happened to both share the same prejudice . . . that's not something to base a relationship on. When you keep dividing us up into identities, what's left? Ya know, and it, and it

means I'm basically reduced to this identity and that there isn't
something true about me that's beyond all of the identities.

Bobbi chimed in to express that sometimes she thinks "wouldn't it
be nice to have [a gay community] but then as soon as we think of
the reality of that, we say, 'Why would we move into that jungle?'" JJ
agreed, "That's . . . not us." JJ described feeling alienated by feminists
and LGBTQ people who have what she called "a hard line" regarding
feminist and queer politics and approaches. For JJ, building politics out
of identity actually contributes to her feeling invisible, even, or perhaps
especially, within a group of people who share her sexuality:

Where I'm gonna be defined, I'm gonna be more pigeon-holed
by [feminist and queer activists] placing an identity on me. Even
though they're . . . doing it for my purpose . . . *they aren't seeing
me* (emphasis added). They've got much more painting on their
glasses when they look at me than the people around here will.

Each of these women made clear that she is not closeted or not out. As
Bobbi explained, "It's not that we are denying [our sexuality] at all." JJ,
her partner, added, laughing, "No, no we live it." A refusal to hide or
deny one's sexuality does not equate to strongly identifying with it, of
course. For all of these women, rejecting an identity defined exclusively
by sexuality allows them to become the fullest version of themselves,
which includes living their sexuality.

Interviewees' disinterest in centering their sexuality in constructing
their sense of self is accompanied by resistance to politicizing their
sexuality in the ways that gay rights groups demand. In what follows, I
share snippets of interviewees' stories in which they expressed disdain
for the ways in which sexuality has been politicized, and in particular,
those approaches that they see as "in-your-face." While interviewees
rarely explicitly questioned the goals of lesbian and gay rights groups—
and often used discourses in line with those of these groups—they also
resisted (the ideologies informing) their approaches. The following section draws from interviewees' complicating the relationships among
identity, visibility, and the political in an effort to glean a more complex
understanding of what might account for their disidentification with
gay rights advocates' strategies.

"I'm Just Me": On Politics and the Politicization of Sexuality

Across interviews, the women with whom I was in conversation shared interesting ideas about visibility by linking visibility to identity and to the political sphere more broadly. Put more precisely, they expressed their disinterest in politics by disavowing an LGBTQ-centered identity or the "out, loud, and proud" ways of being for which LGBTQ organizations call. Importantly, many women explained their aversion to pursuing a politics based on sexual identity or presumed outness as a function of their general feeling that they belong just fine in their rural communities. Community, then, is a more attractive priority than politically contrived forms of visibility for the rural LGBTQ women I interviewed who live their sexuality but do not define themselves by it.

I asked Nissa, a middle-class Native woman in her late twenties from northern Minnesota, about her relationship to LGBTQ issues. She responded, "I don't really care. I try not to get into that . . . because it gives me a headache." Nissa commented that she does not feel the need to participate in gay rights movements because she does not feel alienated due to her sexuality:

I don't feel you know like "Oh I'm gay, I'm an outsider and I need to." . . . I just feel like me. I don't feel any different than I was before I came out, so I just live my life normal. . . . I don't live it any different.

At another point in the interview, Nissa commented that she wishes that sexuality did not need to be political. Marie, a middle-class white woman in her midthirties who lives in southeastern South Dakota, echoed this point, noting that she does not see sexuality as political. This position informs her disinterest in gay rights activism:

A lot of my friends [are not] the raising-your-fist type. I've never really had . . . a friend that's like, "Let's go on a March!" I just kind of steer clear of all that stuff. . . . Just because I'm gay doesn't mean I have to go out and join every movement. We always laugh like, "I'm not going to carry a damn rainbow flag and have a parade with horns and stuff behind me." No. So I mean just because it's who I am doesn't mean I have to all

of a sudden join a movement. And that's probably most of my
friends. I mean we'll go to . . . Prides probably because they have
beer there. It's probably about 95 percent of why the lesbians are
there: the beer garden! It's not because you're going to sign up
and join a movement. They just want to go have fun. It's a social
thing. Lesbians are very social. They like the social groups and
stuff. And you get beer and other girls there, you're going to have
a good turnout.

Marie pushes back against the expectation that she participate in gay
rights movements just because she is gay. She steers clear of marches
and jokes about gay parades, but also attends Pride—something Marie
disconnects from dominant framings of Pride as necessarily political
through describing it as a fun social event that people attend for the
beer and girls. In another part of the interview, Marie mentioned that
she will "follow [national gay issues] . . . just [to] kind of see what's going
[on] *out there*" (emphasis added), despite her attempts to avoid politics.

In response to my question regarding whether she sees her sexuality
as a political issue, Casey, a white woman in her early thirties who lives
in southeastern South Dakota and marked her class status as "student,"
commented similarly:

No. I don't. I don't. I would be interested in, I think, like the
bullying thing. That's really as far as it goes. I don't really want
to, you know, picket for marriage. I don't need to be doing it
because, for me, it doesn't really make a difference. [My partner]
and I will be fine no matter what the law is.

Casey linked her disinterest in gay marriage to her own life; her relationship with her partner will be "fine" regardless of legal rights to marriage.
At the same time, that she mentions a potential interest in bullying, an
issue that has become increasingly prominent in the work of gay rights
groups, especially post–marriage equality, suggests that she is aware of
the work of gay rights groups.

Leslie, a middle-class two-spirit Native woman in her late forties
who lives on a reservation in northern Minnesota, responded to the
same question by quickly and firmly answering that, "No," her sexuality
is not political.[9] I followed up by asking if she sees her race as political.

She responded without hesitation, stating "Yeah, yeah." After thinking for a moment, she smiled, laughed, and added, "That one threw me off, okay." She continued:

> I was in college . . . and one Native girl came up and said, "We're gonna go and march . . . and say we're gay and all of this, and you better come with us." . . . No, I'm not gonna go. That's not who I am, that's not how I was brought up. . . . You don't stick out.

On our way out of the casino after the interview, Leslie commented that she was still stuck on thinking about whether her sexuality could be politicized in the ways in which race always has been for her. Leslie links her lack of interest in gay marches with her disinterest in sticking out—that is, in being visible as LGBTQ. For Leslie, this disinterest is connected to her Native culture and upbringing.

Nancy, a poor white lesbian in her forties, responded to the question regarding the politicization of her sexuality by stating simply, "I don't. I know a lot of people do. And actually, I'm not very political at all. Like not at all."

> I do try to keep up on . . . the current events, like the Don't Ask, Don't Tell . . . but . . . that's not my purpose in life, and I'm just kind of who I am, and I'll be supportive, and open, and accepting, and affirming . . . but I don't like to go into all that. . . . I'm not real loud, and I never have been, but I am out, and I'm proud of everything about me, and I know that to the people who matter to me, that I am fine, and I don't have to be loud. . . . But I don't go to parades, and do that stuff. . . . I don't know how to explain it.

Like Leslie, Nancy makes clear that she is aware of the demands of gay rights groups, using the "out, loud, and proud" discourses that are commonly associated with gay rights groups. She also references Don't Ask, Don't Tell, noting that she tries to keep up on current events. At the same time, she states that she is not loud in the ways that these groups demand and that she doesn't go to typical LGBTQ events such as Pride parades. For Nancy, these ostensible contradictions make explaining her connection to LGBTQ issues difficult.

Nancy has never been to the gay bar in the town where she lives, but she has taken her daughters to community events focused on LGBTQ issues, such as a screening of *Out in the Silence,* a film about LGBTQ people in rural places. She expressed that she will go to events that are "educational and aren't just about being belligerent and forcing your views on people. . . . It's educational and it's gentle." I followed up by asking if she is connected to any national gay rights organizations or issues. She responded, feeling me out, "No. Should I be? What do you think?" When I responded with, "No, I don't," Nancy immediately relaxed, answering "Okay. Good."

Similarly, Kayla, a lower-middle-class white woman in her late thirties who lives in southeastern South Dakota, commented "I just hate to think about politics, honestly." Her partner, Jody, a lower-middle-class white woman in her late forties, added that she didn't see sexuality "as being related to politics at all." When I asked about their interest in or involvement with any gay rights issues, Jody, Kayla, and their friend Maryam (whom I interviewed at the same time), stared back at me in silence. Considering that this chatty trio had answered every other question with detailed and hilarious stories, the long pause in response to this question compelled a hearty laugh from each of us. Maryam, a lower-middle-class white woman in her midforties who lives nearby to Jody and Kayla, worked to explain their silence, "It's not that we're against . . . rights." Jody added, "Well, we talk about getting married all the time." Kayla added, "But as far as saying marriage is legal for us, I don't really care." Despite the trio's expression of disinterest in mainstream politics, LGBTQ and otherwise, each of them is deeply involved in their local communities in ways we might read as political. All three are active in disability justice activism. They shared stories in which they had challenged people's use of ableist terms and had made themselves known as advocates. Furthermore, all three are involved with a national disability rights group. Kayla, who has a daughter with an intellectual disability, explained this distinction:

> I don't think of myself as a minority [and] that I need to join something, well, for my cause. I would much rather rally for . . . these [disabled] kids than for a gay issue. I think it's selfish. . . . I can see [my daughter] getting picked on a lot faster than a gay or lesbian student.

Kayla explicitly connected a victimized identity to LGBTQ movements and explained that her lack of identification as a victim accounts for her lack of participation in these movements. She also gave a geographic justification, stating:

> I don't think that people in the Midwest really get involved in that kind of stuff. . . . We've got to live our lives, go about our business. . . . I think it's more of a coastal kind of thing where they think they need to be involved and changing the world. . . . We just want to drink beer and watch football.

Jody agreed, providing an additional justification rooted in geography and in generational ties to their rural community:

> How hard we've, how hard our relatives had to work to exist in this environment and part of that is still in us. . . . There wasn't any time to worry about issues up until not so long ago, maybe the '70s.

As Jody, Kayla, and Maryam suggest, interviewees tended to resist gay rights advocates' demands for visibility, explaining their resistance not only through describing their sexuality as not particularly relevant to their identities, lives, or relations with others but also as a reflection of the conditions of rural life.

None of these women see their sexualities as political—but also none of them can accurately be described as "closeted" or "not out." Further, many answered my question regarding the politicization of sexuality by referencing the assumed relationship between the political and the visible. Marie, like Nancy and Casey, tries to keep up on national LGBTQ issues happening "out there," although she does not have any interest in rainbow flags, parades, or movements—those images and events that LGBTQ advocates use to make visible and to politicize sexuality. Leslie has no desire to "stick out" and Nissa said she lives no differently than before she came out. Bethany, a lower-middle-class white woman in her late forties, answered the same question with a bit more trepidation than most others, "I don't know. I don't think I've thought about that. You know maybe if I was more out there. I, I don't know." If only Bethany were more "out there," perhaps she would view her sexuality as political. At the same time, interviewees' lack of inter-est in politics and refusal to politicize their sexualities did not manifest in hiding their sexualities; in fact, interviewees consistently referenced feelings of belonging and acceptance by loved ones who are aware of their sexualities.

Despite their general disinterest in politics, some interviewees an-swered questions that would not require referencing lesbian and gay rights groups by commenting on the politics of these very groups. Genie, a middle-aged, middle-class white woman, has been partnered with women for more than twenty years but refuses to identify with any sort of label in regard to her sexuality, leaving blank the sexual orienta-tion slot on the demographic form I distributed prior to interviews. She shrugged as she explained the blank spot, stating, "I'm just me." I asked if her dislike of labels suggests that her sexuality is not a significant part of how she sees herself.

> You'll never find me in a parade. Guaranteed. Will never be in
> a parade. I'm not gonna advocate for gay, lesbian, any rights like
> that. I will not do it. If I'm gonna advocate for something, it's
> gonna be, ya know . . . you're being an asshole, knock it off!

Although Genie made light of advocating for issues, she is incredibly involved in her local community and she also sits on the board of a national disability rights organization. Of lesbian and gay rights issues, she said, "It's not important to me." She viewed the advocating of gay marriage as a "circus" and described gay rights parades as an "offensive" shoving of beliefs onto others, something she is "turned off by [rather than] motivated [by]." Genie expands upon this stance by referencing her little town with a population of approximately one thousand:

> If you wanted to have a gay rights parade in [the town in which
> I live], not gonna fly. You can't [be] in-your-face [to] people here,
> but if you want to just live your life and be who you are, let's just
> do it.

While Genie offered her take on lesbian and gay politics in response to a question regarding her sexual identity, she also expressed great surprise at my asking, "Do you see your sexuality as political?" This question links the political with personal identification and experience in a way that mirrors the very logics Genie deployed in answering my question about her sexual identity by distancing herself from gay rights activism. In answering my question regarding the place of her sexuality in how she understands her identity, Genie referred to her disinterest in advocating for gay rights and participating in parades. In other words, Genie sutured personal identity to political organizations and their rights-seeking approaches, even as she questioned and pushed back against this very tethering. Genie thought for several seconds before answering:

> Wow. . . . On a national level, I can see where it would be. . . . A personal level? No . . . I've never ya know, I've never been asked that question so I was like wow. . . . Okay.

While it would be easy to view these women's lack of interest in LGBTQ issues as a simple disavowal of the political more broadly, this reading ignores the ways in which these same women engage in and connect with a variety of political issues. Indeed, Marie and her partner talk about marriage, an issue that is widely understood as political. Maryam, Kayla, Jody, and Genie are deeply involved with disability rights issues. And Leslie and Genie have both run for public office. Ideas about visibility are central to how Leslie and Genie described their political positions and approaches to politics (including and beyond LGBTQ issues). When Leslie ran for chairperson of her tribe, she did so as a "silent candidate" who "did not campaign openly," choosing instead to be "just a name on a ballot." When I asked why, she responded:

> Because that's how my life has been actually. Just . . . now . . . I realized that. In silen[ce], we were two-spirited. . . . I just realized [during the interview] that everything was done without saying, and I ran without . . . promoting myself.

When I asked Leslie about her political leanings, she responded that she votes for "whoever supports treaty rights, [or is] leaning toward the positive outcomes of Native American people. That's who I vote for." I followed up by asking if gay rights issues are important to her. Leslie responded, "Sometimes I think so but sometimes, I don't know. . . . It's hard to . . . put a label on your forehead and say 'This is who I am.' So I don't really know." Leslie said that she peripherally follows mainstream gay politics and stays informed via her two-spirit friends who let her know when relevant issues emerge. Leslie's identity as two-spirit, rather than as "lesbian" or another term captured by the LGBTQ acronym, was common among the Native women I interviewed, a point that speaks to their commitment to and prioritizing of traditional Native ways of being.

Like Leslie, Genie has also run for public office. Genie idolized her grandmother, a registered Republican, and followed in her footsteps by registering as a Republican when she turned eighteen years old. Years later, she campaigned as a Republican. When I asked about her political leanings, she responded with a sly smile and a twinkle in her eye, "Honestly? More and more, I'm a closeted Democrat." Genie's use of "closeted" is both an obvious gesture toward gay rights discourses and also speaks to precisely the aforementioned limits of the trope of the closet. Notably, Genie—like each of the women featured here—does not see herself as closeted. She is out about her sexuality, although she is disinterested in attending a gay rights parade. In much the same way, she is politically engaged and also a closeted Democrat. For Genie, keeping her views "closeted" did not manifest as hiding her positions, pretending they are otherwise, or avoiding living her life in ways that are consistent with her values. It meant not being brash or in-your-face in precisely the ways that interviewees tended to view gay rights activism. This disinterest in participating in politics as usual, especially through avoiding standing out, is also evident in Leslie's decision to run as a silent candidate. It is telling that even the two women who had previously run for political office did not see their sexualities as political and that they articulated this position by pushing back against celebratory ideas about visibility.

I suggest that rural ways of being, living, and communicating influence interviewees' positions in at least two ways: the manners in which knowledge circulates in rural communities as well as, drawing from Mary Gray, rural LGBTQ people's prioritizing of similarity rather than difference. These characteristics of rurality are, I suggest, deeply intertwined. Interviewees expressed that they feel not only not closeted but also known and even *visible* because everyone in their communities knows about their sexuality due to the ways in which information circulates in rural spaces; that is, everyone knows everything about everyone. The women I interviewed felt it was rarely necessary to "come out" because everyone already knows. As Leslie said:

> Everybody knows. A lot of people, well, they'll say, "Well, I didn't know that," you know, and it's like oh c'mon. Yeah, I've lived with a couple women, so, yeah, people know. They try to say they don't know, but you know how that goes.

Leslie's friend who was with her during the interview agreed, "The reservation is so small. . . . It would be an impossibility." For Leslie and her friend (who is a lesbian), one would have to completely avoid communicating with others in order to be unaware of the information about community members that is in seemingly constant circulation.

Interviewees felt as if stating what they assumed people already know is unnecessary, a garish manner of imposing one's ways of living onto others, and a harmful way of distinguishing oneself from the community. In regard to this latter point, Jody stated:

> My community is probably pretty small. . . . I have really good friends but not a whole shit ton of them. Our church community, the family is very supportive . . . people at work. I, I can't imagine that it's anything different than heterosexuals. I just, I don't see any distinction at all.

Just as JJ and Bobbi feel more "seen" by people in their rural communities than by feminist and LGBTQ activists, Jody framed LGBTQ people as *similar to* the people in their rural communities; she sees no distinction at all between community for rural LGBTQ people and rural straight people, a point to which I return in chapter 6.

I have suggested here that LGBTQ women in the rural Midwest can feel out and visible without speaking about their sexuality, identifying strongly with it, or politicizing it. The alternative ways of being visible and valuing visibility evident among LGBTQ women in the rural Midwest quietly strike at the heart of the logics of gay rights advocates. In a similar (quiet) fashion, interviewees also challenged local enactments of homophobia. In the next section of this chapter, I consider how interviewees' approaches to LGBTQ visibility (and community and identity, more broadly) inform the production of localized forms of resistance to both dominant LGBTQ politics and local instances of discrimination that exist beyond the out, loud, and proud.

Quiet Resistance

Lavonne, a middle-class white woman in her early thirties, is a university professor in southeastern South Dakota. She responded to my question about whether she feels visible as a lesbian:

> I don't know if I feel like I need to be the one to be this vocal champion of lesbian rights in [my town] in South Dakota. . . . I feel like I'm just kind of doing that . . . by living my life and by teaching and by just meeting other people. Our neighbors have come to our house for dinner. . . . I feel like that's enough championing. I suppose absolutely if I lived in a bigger city with the marches and this and that [and that] had big pride parades, absolutely I would be there.

I followed up to ask Lavonne whether she sees herself as an activist. She replied:

> Um, no. But I think again if I lived in a place where [activism happened] . . . I could totally see myself marching around the capitol or doing something. . . . I don't think I'm an activist in a stereotypical understanding of what it is. But then I'm also . . . not revolutionary by any means, but . . . I'm doing things the way I want to do them. . . . I guess I'm not letting tradition or prescribed rules dictate. So I suppose that's what an activist [does] . . . I don't know!

Lavonne actively displaced activism from the town in which she currently lives; it is something that happens in "bigger cities" and in "capitols." Political activism is not something with which she feels she needs to engage in her current community.

Incidentally, the town in which Lavonne lives has a gay bar, LGBTQ social and political groups, softball teams made up almost entirely of

LGBTQ women, and developed Pride activities. Lavonne knows this, and mentioned that she might join the softball league at some point. Despite this, Lavonne will leave the overt political activism to those elsewhere. Lavonne's activism is covert and includes attempting to inspire students to think about LGBTQ issues in a complex manner *without* her coming out to them. (Lavonne is not out to her colleagues or students, although she is out to her family, friends, and neighbors.)

> [Students] write a big research paper, and the model I give them is a paper [in support of] gay marriage. And I'm like regardless of your feelings on it this is a really good paper because it does this, this, and that. And then they have to read the paper. You know what I mean. So I do all these subtle things to get them to think about rights and equality and diversity and inclusiveness and all that stuff. So I don't know, maybe. . . . It's a maybe. A sneaky, very subtle, quiet activist.

Lavonne frames her classroom assignments as sneaky, subtle, quiet activism, which, notably, takes place in a workplace where she does not see herself as out. Along with her neighborhood dinner parties, she sees this approach as "enough championing." In a geographic region where people and their communication styles tend toward the modest and understated, Lavonne's sneaky, subtle, quiet activism makes perfect sense.

Like Lavonne, neither Mona nor Gladys, two middle-class white women in their midforties who have been partnered for two decades, like the word *activism* and they are not engaged with gay rights groups or activities. Mona and Gladys are "out" and "proud" in ways that are not "loud." Gladys stated, "I feel like we're out to . . . the people in our life that matter." Mona responded, "And we're proud. But we aren't loud about it. I mean, no." They see having children as something that required them to be visible. After working to get to know the other families at their children's elementary school, their older child moved on to middle school. They had to get to know new school administrators, teachers, and parents. They also had to fill out forms. Mona asked rhetorically, "Is it important that we put down both parents? No. But I'm going to write down both parents on this form." I asked if they see these moments as activism or resistance.

Well, it seems that as I'm getting old . . . Yeah, I'm going to tell you your form is screwed up. . . . Yeah, maybe that's my own . . . little South Dakota way of oh! Here.

Gladys added, "Here are changes for you." Mona continued:

You know I kind of enjoy calling up the electric company or whatever and they're like, "Well you're not [the name on the account]." And I'm like, "No, but I would be her wife." And so I kind of like . . . to irritate people over the phone.

Gladys joked, "She likes to do it over the phone." Mona laughed, adding, "Do it over the phone not ever in person with anybody! I think that I would admit to that, yeah!"

For Gladys and Mona, there is political potential in challenging people and institutions that refuse to recognize them. But there is also political potential in preserving various shadows so that people can resist within existing structures without sacrificing the functioning of their daily lives. Gladys and Mona each birthed one child and then they both adopted the child birthed by their partner. According to Gladys and Mona, South Dakota is one of the few states that will allow an unmarried couple to adopt and to have both parents' names on a child's birth certificate—a "loophole" that Gladys and Mona were excited to point out does not exist in New York. They mentioned that they do not actively try to hide this information, but, at the same time, making this information visible would threaten the existence of the loophole. As Gladys said, "We don't want that to be known either so people can continue to do it. If they know about it, then they're going to close that loophole." In this particular case, then, increased visibility related to LGBTQ issues could threaten an important channel through which Gladys and Mona both resisted heteronormativity and made more secure their family.

Aly, a middle-class white woman in her early thirties who lives in South Dakota, works for an LGBTQ organization—one of the few people I interviewed who considers herself an activist. She discussed working to increase the visibility of the organization "because you can't access something if you don't know it's there." Aly's desire for visibility is in regard to increasing the visibility of services to those within a community, not increasing the visibility of their community to heterosexual people with the goal of gaining political rights. While Aly does see her sexuality as political, she said that it is a political issue only "because . . . those that are opposed make it political." Even as an employee of a local LGBTQ community center, Aly claims:

> I don't make a point of talking about it. I also don't make a point of hiding it. . . . If I meet somebody new and they talk about their husband or their wife or their girlfriend or their boyfriend, you know, I'll talk about mine. . . . I won't hide the fact that I'm gay, but I also won't make an announcement, like, "Hey, I'm gay!" You know, it's not the first thing, not even one of the first ten things I tell anyone about myself. . . . But then, because of my position, I'm also sometimes required to essentially be like, hey, gay, very gay. . . . Personally . . . I'm not all about trying to dress in rainbows all the time and announce to the world that I'm gay, but professionally, I mean, there's a rainbow flag right next to you right now.

Aly frames being visible as a requirement of her job, making a distinction between this expectation and her preferred personal approach. Aly also makes a distinction between national organizations and the organization for which she works:

> The national organizations that you tend to hear about are ones that are fighting for political issues, and they're very important, but we're more here to serve all parts of the person. We're definitely interested in equality and rights, and we want those things, and think it's very important to fight for those things. We also think it's very important . . . for a fourteen-year-old gay kid to have a place to go so that they feel safe, or for . . . gay families with children to have a way to come together and show their kids that their families are normal too. There's just a lot of really small things about just being a person, not just a gay person. Being a person . . . gets forgotten in those big agendas that a lot of national organizations can have.

Here, Aly speaks to what she sees as key differences between the efforts of national LGBTQ groups and what happens at her center, differences that she expresses in part through visibility discourses. Personally, she does not always want to be "hey, gay, very gay," but feels as if this is compelled of her as an employee of an LGBTQ organization. This difference opens up the space to consider the other forms of quiet challenges that LGBTQ women in the rural Midwest mount as resistance, both to homophobia and to LGBTQ visibility politics more broadly. Lavonne, Mona, and Gladys, for example, avoid using the word *activism* to describe their actions because they feel they are sneakily, quietly, in a "little South Dakota way" challenging ideologies, and that adopting this tactic, unlike being "visible" in prescribed ways, allows them to be most effective.

But the predominance of metronormativity renders these ways of being LGBTQ—beyond the out, loud, and proud—unintelligible, reducing quiet challenges to visibility politics to little more than fancy ways of being closeted, to evidence of apoliticality or the dangers of queer rurality. This position cannot possibly capture these women's relationships to one another, to their sexualities, or to (those in) their rural communities. The representations, experiences, and narratives of LGBTQ women in the rural Midwest suggest that the simple fastening of identity to outness to visibility to politicality must be rethought, and urge us to see that what (in)visibility means, how it operates, and how it is valued are deeply geographically contingent.

3

Post-Race, Post-Space

Calls for Disability and LGBTQ Visibility

IN JULY 2019, the Movement Advancement Project (MAP)—which describes itself as a "non-profit think tank that provides rigorous research" primarily to LGBTQ organizations[1]—published a report entitled "LGBT People with Disabilities."[2] The four-page report, which was produced in partnership with the National Center for Lesbian Rights, the National LGBTQ Task Force, and the Center for American Progress, lists six "unique challenges for LGBT people with disabilities." Considering LGBTQ rights activists' fetishization of visibility, their listing of "invisibility within both communities" as one such "challenge" is hardly surprising. While "coming out" to be "loud and proud" is language most commonly associated with LGBTQ people and issues, disability rights advocates deploy similar discourses. They, too, call for disabled people—particularly those with "invisible" disabilities—to "come out." Those liberated enough to be "out, loud, and proud" about their (hidden) disability are celebrated as the agents of society's ostensible progress and simultaneously serve as evidence of such advancement. Such ways of thinking, as epitomized in the MAP report, are, perhaps, even most pronounced among those concerned with LGBTQ disability issues. The UCLA LGBT Campus Resource Center's web page on LGBTQ disability issues links, for instance, to a Tumblr page entitled "Queerability," which the center describes as an organization that "seeks to increase *visibility* of LGBTQ disabled people by honoring the intersection of the disability and LGBTQ experience" (emphasis added).[3] Similar impulses are evident in the many personal stories one can find online shared by and about LGBTQ people with disabilities, including but not limited to those with headlines such as "Passing and Disability: Why Coming Out As Disabled Can Be So Difficult,"[4] "We Should Be Natural Allies: The LGBTQ and Disability Communities,"[5] and "I'm Here. I'm Queer. I'm Disabled."[6] Indeed, many discussions of LGBTQ people with disabilities reference the problem of invisibility or the promise of visibility.

In this chapter, I consider moments in which disability and queerness come into contact and illustrate that visibility discourses can compel the erasure of material bodies, and in the process, render certain (spatialized and racialized) experiences obsolete. Through calls for LGBTQ disability visibility, disability and LGBTQ rights advocates ignore, ironically, visible markers of (racial) difference and assume that being "out, loud, and proud" is desirable transgeographically. Ultimately, I argue that contemporary (disability and LGBTQ) visibility politics encourage the (re)production of post-racial and post-spatial logics.

In what follows, I first define terms key to my argument and outline the epistemological assemblages between rural queer and disability studies, fields that have engaged in remarkably little conversation. Next, I turn to my data, putting into conversation two examples of calls for visibility by LGBTQ disability rights activists with three interviews I conducted with LGBTQ women in the rural Midwest who discussed, unprompted, various pieces of their lives in relation to disability.

Setting the Stage: Terms and Assemblages

The argument I set out to make in this chapter, perhaps more than any other in this book, requires bringing together multiple sets of ideas and conversations transpiring across academic and activist spaces. To lay the groundwork for the analysis that follows, I begin by outlining the epistemological connections among things that may not, at first glance, appear to be all that intertwined: LGBTQ and disability visibility politics, race/post-raciality, and rurality/metronormativity/post-spatiality.

Informing my broader argument is the position that post-raciality and what I term "post-spatiality" are deeply intertwined concepts, the ideologies of which are furthered through visibility discourses. My understanding of this entwinement relies upon Sumi Cho's definition of the "post-racial": an "ideology that reflects a belief that due to the significant racial progress that has been made, the state need not engage in race-based remedies, and that civil society should eschew race as a central organizing principle of social action" (2009, 1594). Such post-racial logics are evident in calls for disability and LGBTQ visibility, which situate race and racism in the past, ignore ongoing racial injustices, and insist on colorblindness. These are the features of post-raciality I consider in the analysis that follows.

Just as assumptions about social action and progress are at the heart of post-racialism, they, too, inflect metronormative logics—namely, the idea that the rural is dangerous for LGBTQ people, who cannot live happily, let alone organize, here. What I term "post-spatial" expands upon rural queer studies scholars' discussions of metronormativity. As I outline in this book's Introduction, metronormative narratives naturalize urban/rural binaries, render the rural simultaneously anachronistic and unremarkable, and assign value to the one-directional move from the rural to the urban—as well as the out, loud, and proud ways of being such moves ostensibly enable. When the metaphysics of the metropolis become normative, prescriptive, hegemonic—always already assumed to apply transgeographically—we are, I suggest, imagining post-spatially. Post-spatiality, then, undergirds the metronormativity that inflects and is reflected in calls for visibility. But post-spatiality is not simply another term for describing metronormativity, as practices or analyses that are not necessarily metronormative could still be post-spatial. One can find plenty of examples of academic, journalistic, and activist work in rural places that relies on and advances metronormative assumptions and, further, that ignores processes of rural place making or the influence of rural place on the object of one's analytical or political concerns—especially when those processes or influences are laced with warm affections. (For a discussion of the metronormativity present in gay rights work in the rural South, see chapter 5.) By contrast, metronormativity is necessarily post-spatial. While post-spatiality often works in the service of metronormativity, it also gives us new conceptual tools with which to think about and counter geographic hegemony.

Just as spelling out my use of post-racial and post-spatial is crucial for examining how LGBTQ and disability visibility politics advance such ideologies, such an argument also requires bringing together disability and rural queer studies. While little has been said of these field's shared concerns, scholars in both disability and rural queer studies have made space central to their analyses and, to a lesser degree, have examined the relation of visibility to space. For disability studies scholars, space is central to how disability is understood and experienced: disability is a product of the social and spatial conditions that make living with an impairment difficult; for those who subscribe to the social model of disability, an approach largely considered commonsensical within disability studies and activism, inaccessible spaces *create* disability. Disability, in other words, does not exist prior to (the limits of a) space. Other disability studies scholars have critiqued the assumptions built into the social model, including its focus on visuality and space (Samuels 2003). If space, along with one's recognition of one's own abnormality through another's gaze, creates disability, how can we make sense of those disabilities that seem to be almost entirely disconnected from space (such as chronic pain) or are invisible to others (Patsavas 2014)? Scholars have argued that such approaches simultaneously marginalize those with less apparent disabilities and, in calling for disclosure, target them (Samuels 2003). Others have suggested that disability studies' focus on visibility is masculinist (Corker 2001) and that visibility does not necessarily secure acceptance, particularly for those without racial and economic privilege (Kafer 2013, 46). Despite such critical interventions, disability studies scholars and activists alike continue to discuss the relation of visibility to disability in largely celebratory terms, as that which both represents and ushers in progress. As a result, both the ideologies stimulating and the problematic implications of visibility politics as they relate to disability remain undertheorized.[7]

For rural queer studies scholars, the space one occupies has as great an influence on how we experience and identify in the world—our ways of constructing meaningful lives, as well as our abjection, marginalization, and desires—as other social markers, a position with remarkable similarities to disability studies scholars' and advocates' claims. Rural queer studies scholars suggest that LGBTQ desires, experiences, and identities are value laden in deeply spatial ways, a point that I suggest is epitomized through rural queer disidentification with calls for LGBTQ visibility (see chapter 2). Such visibility-related concerns further tie together disability and rural queer studies. One's sexuality and disability can be both overt and hidden, or sometimes obvious and sometimes hidden, or simultaneously explicit and hidden—evident to some and not to others. Despite the deep intellectual entanglements of rural queer and disability studies, there has been little conversation between the fields, an oversight with potentially significant ramifications for both bodies of thought. Hegemonic representations of the rural as largely able bodied (with its big and strong farmers, mothers, laborers) influence how systems of sexuality are maintained and challenged, a point with which rural queer studies must grapple.[8] In a similar vein, disability studies would benefit from considering alternative conceptualizations of space beyond the built environment—such as geographic location—as significant to how one experiences sexuality or disability.

I bring together and expand upon rural queer and disability studies scholars' work on visibility and space to consider a previously unexamined problematic of visibility discourses: Beyond marginalizing certain (rural) LGBTQ people or perpetuating a simplistic invisible/visible binary that requires disabled people with less overt disabilities to "come out" in ways that are not expected of people with more apparent disabilities (or people without disabilities, for that matter), calls for visibility encourage the production of post-racial and post-spatial ideologies. As critical race studies scholars have convincingly argued, race and space get demarcated together; cultural narratives of place are always already racialized, just as the nuances of race, racism, and racialization will be missed without critically considering the space and place to which such processes are linked (McKittrick and Woods 2007; Lipsitz 2007; Woods 1998). Disability and queer studies scholars have addressed the mutually constitutive nature of race and disability (Bell 2012; Dolmage 2018; Jarman 2012; Puar 2017; Samuels 2014) as well as race and sexuality.[9] My contribution to this scholarship includes examining how visibility discourses *prevent* analyzing the raced and placed nature of disability and sexuality, through which I illustrate the deeply intertwined nature of post-raciality and post-spatiality evident in activists' calls for LGBTQ disability visibility.

"Disabled Access Denied?" and "Disaboom": Activist Deployments of Visibility

In a review of the 2012 gay pride march in New York City, blogger Mia Vayner proposed increased visibility as a solution to social ills. Vayner, a self-described disabled "out lesbian" who has advocated for gay rights since the 1990s and disability rights since 2005, states, "The one way to fight bigots in all realms of society is to be out, loud and proud. If you're in the communities [*sic*] line of vision everyday eventually they have to admit you're there and when they admit that your rights must be enforced." Vayner's activism is premised on the familiar notion that visibility leads to rights. She continues to describe the event:

> There were . . . and rightfully so gay groups proudly representing every ethnicity in our wonderful borough of Queens, but not ONE disabled group. . . . Rolling around for 1 hour I saw 2 dozen wheelchairs and twice as many mobility scooters covering at least ten nationalities. So with this cross section at one small gathering in an outer borough, why is there no representation of the gay disabled community?[10]

Vayner conjures LGBTQ people of color with disabilities to argue for the need for representation of LGBTQ (non-racially-marked) people with disabilities. LGBTQ people of color with disabilities were, and presumably could be, represented via groups of LGBTQ people of color. Vayner, then, either is directing her question solely at white people with disabilities or expecting LGBTQ people of color with disabilities to come together around their disability rather than their race or nationality. In making these claims, Vayner recognizes race. Yet, she does so by relegating the significance of race—and, by extension, the potential for racism—to the past, a classic feature of post-racialism. Vayner's deployment of this variety of post-racial discourse speaks to what scholars have described as the problems with multiculturalism: the recognition and celebration of race without—indeed, so that we might avoid—challenging the systems that perpetuate differential access to resources based on this construction (Gordon and Newfield 1996).

Assumptions about the value of visibility enable Vayner's post-racial claims: In Vayner's estimation, people of color have that (visible representation) for which disabled gays must strive, a discursive move that dismisses those issues LGBTQ people of color with disabilities—or people of color who are not LGBTQ or disabled—might experience. For Vayner, visibility challenges bigotry both within and outside of LGBTQ communities. It is that which can counter ableism within LGBTQ subcultures and also "fight bigots in all realms of society," which, in Vayner's estimation, leads to political rights. Those who are visible as

(racially) different and, even more so, who organize around this difference, then, are assumedly better off than those whose problems remain
invisible or underrepresented, in either an embodied or political sense.
In calling for increased visibility of LGBTQ people with disabilities,
Vayner ignores the ongoing significance of race and reduces identity to
visibility and symbolic representation, simultaneously conflating and
hierarchizing various forms of marginality,[11] and depoliticizing the histories of those (distinct and overlapping) identities for which she seeks
representation. This is post-raciality in action.

Similar post-racial assumptions are evident on "Disaboom," a website that describes itself as the "largest online social network and information resource for people with disabilities."[12] An article posted on
the site entitled "LGBT and Living with a Disability: Where to Find
Support" begins:

> Being gay or lesbian with a disability makes you a minority times
> two. Discrimination can come from many different sources, even
> within either of those communities, the very places where you'd
> expect support. But there are locations where people exactly like
> you can find a community of comfort and inclusion. LGBTs with
> disabilities have unique challenges to face. Do you out your sexual
> orientation? How about a hidden disability?

Accompanying these assertions is an image of the faces of a Black man
and a white man, neither with visible disabilities.[13] The men are meant
to appear as "an attractive interracial gay couple," as described by the
stock image website iStock (Azndc 2008).[14] The placement of the image
next to the article's opening lines suggests that both men are equally
"minorities times two," rendering race invisible, a nonsignifier devoid
of meaning. No other "differences" or markers of experience or identification, visible or not, are as important as being gay and disabled.
The men's disabilities and sexualities make them exactly alike, and if
you are disabled and LGBTQ (regardless of your race!) "exactly like
you" too. Although the article's "minority times two" language also
disregards classism, sexism, metronormativity, xenophobia, and other
ways people experience minoritization, it does not draw from imagery that intentionally calls up these issues in order to actively eschew
their significance. Of course, the author's claims cannot possibly apply

to LGBTQ disabled people of color, LGBTQ people with visible disabilities, or anyone who experiences the world through more than two axes of marginalization. In many ways, this article epitomizes what Cho describes as the "aspirational" "retreat from race" that is central to colorblindness (2009, 1598). Here, colorblindness is deployed (we will not acknowledge race) in order to fulfill its own post-racial aspirations (talking about race is unnecessary).[15]

The colorblindness inherent in the Disaboom article depends upon assumptions regarding who is meant to be visible and in what ways. The difference visibility is meant to confer is enigmatic: Certain forms of (visible, racial) difference are literally unrecognizable whereas "coming out" and becoming visible (as disabled or gay) is framed as a move toward "comfort and inclusion." The assumption that visibility leads to individual satisfaction and (sub)cultural recognition relies on the image of the Black man—always already visible as oppressed without needing to come out—as no longer marginalized, as also a "minority times two." Any racial oppression he might face is untenable for this narrative, not only because acknowledging the potential for this form of oppression situates racism within the present, but also because LGBTQ and disability visibility politics rely on the assumption that his visibility as an oppressed person (in a prior historical period) is precisely what saved him and our society. When it comes to race, both on the Disaboom site and more broadly, the hypervisibility of the Black body actually functions as a type of social invisibility. Such "hypervisibility," Avery Gordon argues, "is a persistent alibi for the mechanisms that render one *un*-visible" ([1997] 2008, 17). Indeed, the Black man's Blackness was unrecognizable to Disaboom.

Just as the post-raciality of calls for visibility is unmistakable in both examples I consider above, so too is their post-spatiality, the iterations of which point to the assumption that visibility has "a spatial location and a social value" (Gray 2009, 9). The location is urban and the value is progress, evident in Vayner's aforementioned claim: "The one way to fight bigots in all realms of society is to be out, loud and proud. If you're in the communities line of vision everyday eventually they have to admit you're there and when they admit that your rights must be enforced." Vayner's claim rests upon imagining a homogenous "gay community" that functions everywhere in precisely the way Vayner's New

York City community does. The ubiquity of metronormative assumptions allows Vayner to ignore that her perspective has been influenced by geography—an irony, considering that, as a wheelchair user, she is, presumably, reminded frequently that marginalization transpires along the lines of space and place. The language used in the Disaboom article speaks to this very point. The promises ("comfort and inclusion") and the dangers ("discrimination" from an assumed community of support) of coming out and becoming visible are represented in inherently spatialized terms; oppression transpires in a *place*, while people "exactly like you" find comfort in a particular *location.*

Despite approaching inclusion and marginalization as spatially contingent, Disaboom does not question how inclusion or oppression manifest differently along geographic lines. In framing inclusion as predicated on finding people "exactly like you," Disaboom covertly stitches inclusion to the urban. The rural can never be the site of comfort for LGBTQ people with disabilities precisely because it is from rural places that LGBTQ people ostensibly must escape. Indeed, metronormativity traffics in the idea that the rural is where there will be no others "exactly like you" if you are LGBTQ. Here, metronormative ideologies circulate through the superficial deployment of discourses that gesture toward the spatiality of knowledge formation while simultaneously ignoring the continued role that place plays in people's lives, particularly those marginalized by metronormativity.

The ideologies implicit in such calls for LGBTQ and disability visibility are, in this contemporary moment, hegemonic in nature; they transcend movements and place and emerged in my conversations with LGBTQ women in rural South Dakota and Minnesota. In what follows, I consider how visibility discourses, with their accompanying post-raciality and post-spatiality, surfaced as my interviewees discussed their relations to (their own and others') LGBTQ sexuality and disability. As it turns out, the sociality of LGBTQ women in the rural Midwest is a particularly generative location from which to consider these problematics precisely because calls to be out, loud, and proud hold far *less* cachet in rural areas than they do elsewhere (Gray 2009). Put otherwise, that interviewees also reproduced post-racial and post-spatial logics through discourses of visibility in a locale in which this method of political organizing is already a site of contestation and negotiation points to the hegemonic allure—and depth of the problematics—of such discourses.

A Note on Methodology and Epistemology

In the remainder of this chapter, I draw from three of the fifty interviews I conducted: one with a "not-straight" woman in central Minnesota, one with a lesbian-identified woman in eastern South Dakota, and one with a lesbian-identified woman in the western part of the state. Each of the narratives I feature here are those of white women. That white women in the rural Midwest (a place erroneously imagined as homogenously white) articulate difference in post-racial terms suggests not only that white women's lives are racially structured, as Ruth Frankenberg argues (1993), but also that this racial structuring occurs through *post-racial* ideologies. I expand upon Frankenberg's classic work, in which she suggests that race, race differences, and whiteness ought to be explored through the lenses of invisibility and visibility, to suggest not only that post-raciality (like the whiteness, race, and race differences Frankenberg considers) can be examined through visibility discourses but also that visibility politics *enable* post-raciality—a concept similar to and different from Frankenberg's "whiteness": while whiteness refers to "locations, discourses, and material relations," (1993, 6) as does "post-racial," it also gestures toward an embodied way of experiencing the world in ways that "post-racial" does not.

I focus here on a few key interviews because highlighting how multiple concepts—disability, sexuality, race, visibility, space and place—converge requires analyzing various parts of interviewees' stories closely. I chose these vignettes because they illustrate the theoretical intervention I make here, not because they are (or are not) representative of my sample. Let me explain: At the time when I conducted these interviews, I saw my project as in alignment with and extending scholarship in queer theory and rural queer studies. As such, I asked questions about rural life as well as LGBTQ community, identity, and visibility. I did not ask specific questions related to disability or even embodiment. Despite this, disability came up in nearly every one of my interviews. Women expressed that they care for a partner, child, or loved one with a disability, volunteer and work for nonprofit organizations dedicated to disability justice, have an intellectual or physical disability themselves, and work as caregivers to people with disabilities. Even for those women who did not discuss disability as a structuring or quotidian part of their lives, ideas about disability still infused the interview. The significance of disability to the lives of my interviewees led me to examine various sites through which disability and LGBTQ discourses and advocacy converge. Through reflecting on interviewees' narratives, I began to consider the epistemological relations among race, space, disability, and LGBTQ visibility.

That I can draw from interviews I conducted in which I did not explicitly ask questions about race or disability to examine how disability and LGBTQ visibility discourses can further post-racial and post-spatial ideologies speaks to my point that the assumptions undergirding calls for disability and LGBTQ visibility are deeply intertwined with one another and further problematic notions of race and place. To be clear, my interviewees are not the object of my critique. In what follows, I consider the existence of post-racial and post-spatial epistemologies in interviewees' narratives in order to examine the ways in which calls for LGBTQ and disability visibility may render race and place ideologically obsolete, rather than to critique interviewees for drawing from those cultural ideologies in wide circulation.

"Better Than New"

On a cold night in late 2011, I made my way to a middle-class neighborhood in a town in eastern South Dakota to interview Kay, a middle-aged, white, lesbian who had adopted two daughters from China. Early in the interview, I asked Kay if the adoption process was difficult.

> At the time, Chinese adoption was open for women, single women, single men, married, whatever. Although, I did have to sign a statement . . . to the Chinese government that said I was straight. . . . I am a very honest person, but I had no trouble doing that. I did have to have a home study . . . where they asked about prior relationships and I sort of fudged on that, but they did not really probe much.

By the time Kay adopted a second baby from China, the regulations around international adoption had shifted. Kay explained that the

Chinese government had reduced the percentage of babies that could be adopted by single women to 8 percent, because, according to Kay, the government had become

> concerned about too many lesbians adopting these little Chinese girls. . . . And now it's a lot tighter. . . . I had decided that I wasn't going to get a second child because I didn't want to stop any other single women from being able to get one child. So I got [my second daughter] through the Waiting Child Program. . . . She had a heart murmur, heart defect. . . . She wouldn't count against the 8 percent. . . . She had surgery about six months after we got back from China. That's been corrected and she is as good as new or better than new.

Kay continued, referencing, in her next breath, a question I had asked earlier regarding any racism the girls face at their largely white school in rural South Dakota. "Oh, yeah and [my daughter] doesn't have any issues at school. Plus, their school principal is a lesbian, although, that is a secret." Kay framed her lesbian sexuality and her child's disability as both having a significant impact on how she has come to live her life. Kay expressed that she felt lucky to be a lesbian because had she been in a heterosexual relationship, she likely would have reproduced "the old-fashioned way," rather than adopting. Had Chinese adoption policies not shifted to make a distinction between impaired and healthy babies, Kay would not have adopted a second Chinese daughter.

That Kay's daughter's disability was able to be "corrected" to make her "as good as new or better than new" required a spatial move, in this case, from the non-West to the West. When I asked about the impact of the children's race on their lives, Kay dismissed the potential for racism through conflating sexuality and race, claiming that her daughter "doesn't have any issues [with racism] at school." For Kay, that the school principal is a (secret) lesbian accounts for the lack of racism her children face. Kay's narrative—her adopting of Chinese daughters and their move to South Dakota, her daughter's invisible disability, the erasure of visible racialization, and the secret lesbian principal—points to the ways that visibility discourses can be deployed to undermine the continued significance of race and place in people's lives.

"What Brought Me Here Was"

Just as Kay's child's disability and her own sexuality deeply inform her narrative of her life, Linda, a white, working-class lesbian with a disability who lives in rural western South Dakota, framed disability as a driving force in the unfolding of her life. Linda moved to South Dakota from Chicago in her late twenties for college. I asked why. She responded:

> A lot of it revolves around my learning disability. I was in special ed my whole life and my father was dyslexic but undiagnosed. So I always had somebody in my life that I could look up to. . . . He's a very good man and good role model. . . . When I was growing up I was in special ed., like I said, and I already knew what discrimination was from the get-go. . . . That helped me to form my personality. . . . One day I had a broken arm and I stayed home from school and I was watching one of my mom's soap operas and I was just praying she wouldn't walk into the room 'cause two girls were gonna kiss. And I thought, there! There really are other people like me.

For Linda, disability is foundational to her life trajectory, which she says, "revolves around [her] learning disability." She described her disability as a source of discrimination that formed her personality so that later she was more prepared to deal with homophobia. Visibility is central to Linda's narrative; for Linda, having a role model in her father and witnessing same-sex intimacy on TV was formative. She continued to describe the importance of having a gay community:

> I found a place called Gay Horizons. . . . It saved my life. . . . I used to sneak down there one day a week, and I made friends, and I went to the parade and there was a quarter of a million people. So I knew I wasn't nuts. . . . Um, but what brought me here was, you know, my life blew up as a gay person. I was out and loud.

Within a matter of minutes, Linda went from explicitly stating that her disability was at the center of her move to South Dakota to saying that her life as a gay person accounted for the move. At this point, I still did not understand what *exactly* encouraged Linda to move to South Dakota from Chicago. I reasked the question, and Linda responded that there were only "two schools with Indian studies programs [in the country]."

> I didn't know what I wanted to be but I knew I wanted to learn about Native American people, so let's go. . . . My first handful of years going through the Indian Studies Program, my college was just impeccable, incredible, the student support service—I even signed up for the student gay club at the time. . . . I decided because I did so good in Indian studies [to] . . . do the teaching thing. Maybe I could help a couple kids not go through the crap that I [went] through. And it was perfect . . . for me because Native American studies is very oral . . . it's about the stories and the humor. Well, I fit right in.

For Linda, her learning disability allowed her to "fit right in" with the culturally derived pedagogical approaches (the focus on orality and story-telling) of the Indian Studies Program. Without skipping a beat, Linda stated that her positive experience in Indian studies led her to join the gay club, and later, to teaching, through which she hoped to help students with learning disabilities avoid the troubles she had encountered. In much the same way as Linda's analogizing of her experience as a white disabled lesbian with those of Native people disregards race, so too does her articulation of her move to South Dakota as being informed first by her disability and then her sexuality. In this articulation of Linda's story, neither her disability nor her sexuality actually accounts for her move; the only thing encouraging Linda to move to South Dakota was the Indian Studies Program. Race and place—the racialization of place, the place of race—motivate Linda's life choices, and yet the significance of race and place to her trajectory disappear as she frames her life story in relation to her disability and sexuality. These are the discourses of post-raciality and post-spatiality.

Linda's life story also offers new ways to think about the relationship between disability and visibility politics. Linda's visibility as a lesbian in her rural community is intricately interwoven with her disability. Linda's dyslexia makes it arduous for her to read or write, so communicating via email, a common political organizing tool, is a significant challenge. As the sole staff person of an LGBTQ organization, Linda fundraised, planned social events, and served as the organization's spokesperson—without reading or writing extensively. In this process, she became visible as a lesbian (via her attachment to the LGBTQ center) and also as disabled (in the difficulty she experiences filling out forms or in her asking for particular types of assistance), blurring the line between invisible and visible disabilities, and highlighting, what is for Linda, the mutually constitutive nature of her disability and sexuality.

Linda tentatively described her organizing work as political—as she said, "Isn't everything political?"—but she also qualified her claim: "I think it's a lot different than the national thing. I know there are several people who come into [a community center] that are gay, and I don't think they're ashamed of it. I think they just are in their own little cliques.... Even though we're not political people, it's a political thing." She continued, "I mean if I were Black, you know, trying to get . . . a group of people that could all go into the same bar and just have a drink, is it not political?"

Ideas about visibility shape Linda's understanding of the political. Linda knows things are done differently in the rural Midwest because people are not asserting their sexuality in the ways that national gay rights groups demand; they are "in their own cliques" rather than publicly visible, an approach that Linda notes does not connote shame in the Midwest. For Linda, invisibility does not translate into apoliticality. It makes sense, then, that Linda understands the work that she does as different from that of national gay rights groups whose centering of visibility is antithetical to the goals of many rural LGBTQ women Linda knows through her organization.

To frame the quotidian experiences of LGBTQ people as inherently political, even of those Linda describes as "not political people," Linda deploys the visibility of the Black body and references approaches of the civil rights movement (e.g., getting together a "group of people" to sit in a public place). Both are interesting rhetorical moves, as they center Blackness in a state in which just 1 percent of the population is Black but 8 percent is American Indian. Such references function to situate racism in the past and ignore the ongoing racism faced by American Indians, South Dakota's largest minoritized racial group. It is, I suggest, the hypervisibility of Blackness that Linda indexes in her deployment of a racialized person, a deployment that is meant to call up the visibility of particular bodies. The visibility of the Black body, then, comes to stand in for the types of differences Linda referenced between rural and national LGBTQ organizations. Although Linda attached the rural Midwest to the political by relying on the post-spatial claim that "everything" (everywhere) is political, she ultimately displaces politicization from the rural Midwest by framing the political as what rural Midwestern people are not—even if the issues are political. Politicization, and the visibility that is understood to make it possible, exists elsewhere; it is called for through national organizations and is recognizable as the body of a Black person—things that exist outside of Linda's imagination of the here and now of the rural Midwest.

"I Have to Deal with So Much Shit Legally Already with the Disability Stuff"

Claudia, a white, disabled woman in her late twenties who lives in central Minnesota and is in an interracial relationship, arrived at her interview wearing a Human Rights Campaign "Legalize Gay" T-shirt.[16] As we discussed public displays of affection, Claudia pointed to her shirt, saying that such forms of affection are "not really political for me at all . . . In fact, this is as political as it gets. Wearing this T-shirt that I got from Pride. It's not political. I just want to hold her hand like everybody else."

Despite wearing a marriage equality T-shirt (a form of political visibility), Claudia does not view public displays of affection (another form of visibility) as political. I followed up by asking if she views her sexuality as political. She responded, "I think because of the time and place that I live in, it has to be. . . . I can't really opt out of it being political because it just is simply political right now." Like Linda, Claudia understands the political as inherently spatial and temporal; she is required to be political because of the time and place in which she lives:

> If I can opt out of being political, I might. I might pick and
> choose when I want to be political and when I don't. . . . Having
> a chronic illness . . . a disability, and dealing with insurance
> company issues and . . . financial stuff. We have one income in-

stead of two. And not being able to get partner benefits . . . it's a nightmare. Probably every day I make some sort of phone call, some sort of paperwork, or something that has to do with some sort of legal something for me with disability insurance. There's certainly . . . institutional homophobia.

For Claudia, a discussion of the political is impossible outside of her disability and the homophobia embedded in the social structures with which she must interact. As long as she remains a dependent of her parents (and, thus, unmarried) she can access her father's governmental benefits. If Claudia were to marry her partner, to whom she was engaged, Claudia would risk losing her disability benefits, even though the federal government did not recognize same-sex marriage at the time of the interview.

Claudia represents a paradox of the political: her disability both necessitates that she cannot opt out of viewing her sexuality as political and also might prevent her from acting in a political manner; it is Claudia's fight for access to disability-related resources that simultaneously constructs her sexuality as political and makes it difficult for her to participate in certain forms of political action. For Claudia, the political sits where her sexuality and disability meet; the political is the lived, the quotidian, the exhausting, the practical. Discourses of visibility buttress Claudia's articulation of the political.

So the visibility piece . . . part of it is very personal, right? About just . . . being accepted . . . for who I am in my community. . . . And then part of it for me, I think, is feeling a responsibility to give a name and a face . . . to the cause. I know the research that says that peoples' attitudes change when you know somebody who's LGBT. You know, race attitudes change. The more Black people and the closer that they are to you, then your attitudes change. More so than just simply wearing a T-shirt around public, I think [being known] might have a positive effect. But for the people who are really homophobic, it doesn't . . . change anything. . . . And so I feel that my responsibility to be visible is sort of to be known and be out to those people . . . that are close to me who aren't necessarily pro-gay.

Claudia suggested that being visible can lead to personal acceptance and political rights, but she also pointed to what she sees as the limits to this strategy: it won't change "really homophobic" people. In this articulation of the value of visibility, which both mirrors and departs from the ideologies of national gay rights groups (for whom there appears to be no limit to the value of such approaches), Claudia, like Linda, conflated ideas around race and sexuality, assuming that strategies that have supposedly worked for people of color will also have political relevance for LGBTQ people, and vice versa.

Despite this brief mention of race in relation to gay rights, that Claudia is in an interracial relationship still had not come up more than an hour into our conversation. I met Claudia and her partner at a Pride event and knew that Claudia's partner is Black. I asked if she had experienced any issues related to being in an interracial relationship. "I don't think so. I think that being a lesbian couple kinda trumps that as far as society goes. I think that they don't really care." Despite framing race as less important than her sexuality and her disability to organizing her life, Claudia went on to describe various situations that she sees as occurring due to people's responses to her partner's race, situations in which people stare at them or go out of their way to be overly nice to her partner.

> My theory is that they're not used to seeing very many Black people in the area. And so when they see Black people it's a difference that they can't help to notice. And it's the only thing they can think of and they feel guilty about the fact that they can't get the idea out of . . . their head that she's Black, and so then they feel that they need to do something to help make themselves feel better. . . . I think that they're scared that they're gonna come across like they're racist. . . . Like it's gonna be revealed that that's the only thing that they're thinking about. . . . And so then I think that they go out of their way to be nice to her to compensate for that. . . . But the people in public don't typically know that we're a couple. And then if they do, it's the lesbian thing that gets them more than the interracial.

Claudia's astute description of the etiquette of racial recognition reflects the demands of post-racialism: we must not acknowledge race because it no longer exists. The very recognition of race operates as a fissure in these beliefs; the proliferation of these ideologies requires that we view such cleavages as our own failures (evidenced in people being overly nice to Claudia's partner), rather than the failures of the ideologies themselves. Claudia's analysis of her encounters with the material manifestations of post-racialism depends upon spatial claims: people "in the area" rarely see Black people. Post-racialism circulates in Claudia's narrative in two ways: she points to her encounters with post-racial ideologies and also deploys these ideologies herself, evident in her position that sexuality trumps race "as far as society goes." Such post-raciality and post-spatiality inform one another. Claudia suggests that her lesbianism is a problem *in society*—an a-geographical claim. Meanwhile, for Claudia, people in the Midwest respond to her partner as they do because they have not seen Black people—a simultaneously post-racial and post-spatial position that suggests Blackness does not compel a response elsewhere. The post-spatial claim that sexuality trumps race everywhere enables the post-racial positioning of race in the past. By extension, those (rural) people who live in (rural) places that recognize race become anachronistic, pointing to the circular thinking that bind post-racial and post-spatial ideologies.

These ideologies are evident in each of the three interviews I discussed here. Kay's daughter's impairment was fixed through a move from China to South Dakota, Linda's desire to learn about Native people led her to South Dakota, and Claudia suggested that she and her partner experience racism because people in the Midwest rarely see Black people. Although interviewees utilize spatial and racial discourses to tell their stories of their lives, they do so in ways that suggest their lack of importance. Furthermore, the post-racial and post-spatial logics I examine here often manifest discursively via conflations of race with other marginalized subject positions. Kay believes her daughter does not experience racism at school because the principal is a lesbian, Linda views American Indian studies as perfect for her due to her learning disability, and Claudia argues that being in a lesbian relationship "trumps" any racialized discrimination she and her partner could face. Visibility discourses enable these slippages. Linda believed that she was better equipped to deal with her disability and her sexuality because she had visible role models and communities, Kay described the principal's lesbian sexuality as a "secret," and possibilities for Claudia to be political as a lesbian had been circumscribed by her disability and related need for insurance. Each woman articulated connections between sexuality and disability through discourses of visibility in ways that draw from and reproduce post-racial and post-spatial ideologies.

Such articulations are not unmoored from the visibility politics of LGBTQ (and) disability activists, whose approaches are the object of my concern. Examining post-racial and post-spatial ideologies as a symptom of visibility politics makes clear the paradoxical nature of such calls: although certain visible differences can be (and are) rendered invisible, LGBTQ and disability rights organizations remain invested in the idea that marginalized individuals becoming visible both already represent and will engender further social transformation. These visible markers of (racial) difference are, as the evidence I have presented here suggests, called up for the purposes of analogy and then ignored when and where they manifest as material markers of difference. That the marginalization of some bodies that evidence difference can be ignored while bodies that may not be read as marginalized are encouraged to verbalize an identification with that marginalization speaks to the nebulousness of visibility politics—and the ways in which they can function in the service of unbecoming things.

Critical engagement with visibility discourses and their accompanying post-raciality and post-spatiality, then, is crucial for the creation of the "transformative feminist disability theory and practice" for which Kim Hall calls (2011, 10)—a theory and practice that will be enriched by centering race, rethinking dominant assumptions regarding the place of place in LGBTQ and disability imaginaries, and, ultimately, refusing fixed understandings of visibility and the related hierarchizing of oppressions so that we can recognize those oppressions (re)produced in the name of LGBTQ and disability liberation.

[4]

Queer Labors

Visibility and Capitalism

I just never told them but I think they know because my manager
was telling me about how her son is gay and I was like "What
is she trying to get at here?" I think she was trying to *make
me say* . . . "Yeah well I am too." So I think they know but they
don't. . . . This lady I work with she has . . . two daughters that . . .
have red hair . . . and I was just like "I just don't like red hair" . . .
and she's like "Well at least I know you're not going to hit on my
daughters." And I was like "Mmm what are you trying to say?"
They do but they don't kind of know. I am [out] but I'm not.

Nissa, northern Minnesota, Native, late twenties

Coming out as LGBTQ+ can always be difficult, but it can be
even more so in the workplace. We will spend the majority of
our lives there, and we spend more time with our colleagues
than we do our own family. Which is why it's so damaging
that for some LGBTQ+ people, it's the very place they feel
they can't be open and their authentic selves.

Whitney Bacon-Evans, *Cosmopolitan* magazine, 2018

ON JUNE 25, 2018, the Human Rights Campaign released the results of
its survey on the experiences of LGBTQ people in the workplace with
an article entitled "Startling Data Reveals Half of LGBTQ Employees
in the U.S. Remain Closeted at Work."[1] Within the next few months,
CNN,[2] *The Harvard Business Review,*[3] and *The Washington Post*[4] reported on HRC's findings. Around the same time, *Cosmopolitan* ran a

story entitled "Everything to Know about Coming Out at Work: How to Assess Whether It's Safe, and Whether Your Employer Is Truly Inclusive."[5] The article calling for outness at work is written by lifestyle bloggers Whitney and Megan Bacon-Evans—or "Wegan," as they are known online—who, notably, do not have traditional jobs. The pair is, perhaps, most well known for "endur[ing] four years of long distance" throughout their ten-year relationship, as they note on the "About Us" page of their website.[6] Wegan have certainly capitalized on this framing of themselves: they were the first lesbian couple on TLC's *Say Yes to the Dress,* they were featured on *Ellen,* and they were named to *The Guardian's* Pride Power Couple List in 2018, which describes them as "the vlogging formerly long-distance couple [who] were civil partnered in 2012 and married in 2017."[7] Considering that creating a blog and living geographically separate from one's partner are not exactly noteworthy activities, we might ask how exactly Wegan attained their relative fame. In an article entitled "What Wegan Did Next: A Journey of Lesbian Love and Visibility," *AfterEllen.com,* the website attached to the *Ellen* television show, describes Wegan as "a face and a voice for femme visibility."[8] Wegan's visibility—and their framing of invisibility as both a problem in need of being fixed and something they are actively fighting through their very existence—is understood as a cause for celebration and appears to account for Wegan's (internet) fame.

Such understandings are consistent with Wegan's story of themselves. The couple states that although they created their blog in 2009 "to document [their] lives and have memories to look back on," they "also wanted to put [their] story out there due to the lack of visible lesbian role models, in particularly femme/ lipstick lesbians."[9] The couple is particularly concerned with those who "suffer from femme invisibility."[10] In a *HuffPost* article entitled "Femme Invisibility," Wegan describes their work to launch what they term a "campaign" to "help tackle the conundrum of femme invisibility." The totality of the campaign, aptly entitled "Femme Visibility," involves "inviting femme lesbians to send in their photos and together take a step toward shattering stereotypes and pulling off our invisibility cloak."[11] Never does Wegan, *The Guardian,* or *Ellen* articulate what the material benefits actually are of pulling off such figurative cloaks, of posting femmes' photos to a page within Wegan's lifestyle website, or of Wegan's being a "face and a voice for femme visibility."

This is, of course, unsurprising—not only because of the prevalence of visibility discourses and the broadly assumed social value of outness, as I've discussed throughout the rest of this book, but also because Wegan has benefited financially from being visible lesbians and from others believing that their visibility is valuable, although their visibility is unlikely to materially benefit others. What is most surprising, perhaps, is that Wegan calls for visibility *at work* in particular, but that, as lifestyle bloggers, neither woman works at a typical job or has an actual workplace at which to come out.[12] We might even say that the couple has made being visible lesbians part of their *job*. In doing so, they reproduce many of the problems I have discussed throughout this book, including positioning LGBTQ visibility as a determinant of social change, harnessing authenticity to visibility, and assuming that all strategies work transgeographically and transracially.

As it turns out, the metronormativity evident in activists' calls for outness and visibility, which I have outlined in the rest of this book, is particularly pronounced in their calls for visibility *at work*. The "So, Here's What You Should Know about Coming Out at Work" section of Wegan's *Cosmopolitan* article begins with the assertion that those looking for jobs "can seek out inclusive workplaces." They continue: "If you're worrying about a company not accepting who you are, then you have to question whether it's the kind of company you really *want* to work for. Look for one that is open and accepting, and where your career can thrive!" (emphasis added).[13] It seems obvious that many people do not get to work at jobs they actually *want*. Furthermore, in many rural places, where stable and financially secure jobs are often scarce, people might not be able to seek out workplaces based on their ostensible LGBTQ inclusivity.

Beyond this, how might one learn about whether one's potential workplace is inclusive? According to Wegan, and others calling for outness at work, a key first step is doing research. Wegan encourages people to check out "Stonewall's yearly research [which] highlights the best companies to work for." The Human Rights Campaign "Coming Out at Work" web page similarly suggests utilizing resource lists compiled by national gay rights organizations. You should, HRC suggests, ask: "Is your company ranked on the Human Rights Campaign Corporate Equality Index? If so, what rating has it earned?"[14] Not surprisingly, of the 1,038 companies included in the HRC Corporate Equality Index,

842 are headquartered in urban areas, and 845 are in geographic regions other than the Midwest. Just 43 of the 1,038 companies included are headquartered in places that are both Midwestern and nonurban—although many of these companies are in suburbs of metropolitan areas. More to the point, not a single company in HRC's list is located in South Dakota or, in the case of Minnesota, outside of the greater Minneapolis/St. Paul metropolitan area, the area of the world where my interviewees largely would be looking for work.[15]

This simple accounting highlights the ways in which activists' calls for visibility at work, and their suggestions for *how* to come out at work, ignore the material conditions of rural life. Beyond this, activist calls for visibility at work ignore that some people may not want to come out at work, that one can feel authentic (whatever that means) without being out (at work or otherwise), and that one can feel out without being out to *everyone.* Having extended transnational and rural queer studies scholars' assertions that LGBTQ visibility does not work for everyone everywhere throughout the rest of this book, my argument in this chapter is that being visible *is* work for everyone, everywhere.

This chapter considers activists' calls for LGBTQ visibility at work and interviewees' refusals of these calls through the lens of queer Marxist thought. Doing so opens up possibilities to consider outness itself as laborious. I argue here that the performative process of becoming visible as LGBTQ *is itself work* and, further, that considering how these demands inform the experiences of LGBTQ people at work, in particular, allows us to explore the work of the production of legible LGBTQ sexual subjectivities in new ways. Through conceptualizing living visibly as labored, I consider the modes of labor that visibility, as a political ideal, relies upon and is indebted to, and thus reflect on the relationship of visibility to capitalism. My discussion of the labors of becoming recognizable as LGBTQ should not suggest that I view the closet as an unlabored site. Of course, as activist discourses suggest, maintaining one's closet might be incredibly labored. This is, however, already assumed to be the case. A *Newsweek* article entitled "How Facebook Is Kicking Down the Closet Door," for example, details what it describes as the "painstaking *labor* that goes into being secretly gay" (emphasis added).[16]

My interests are different. I am concerned with how labor is compelled of us without our even recognizing it, and, as frighteningly, under the guise of authenticity. I suggest that becoming recognizable as an authentic LGBTQ subject occurs through labored processes so insidious that they are illegible as such. Calls for LGBTQ visibility, which relentlessly demand constant laboring (even as they obscure this very laboring) thus reflect and affirm capitalist relations. LGBTQ visibility is best understood, I suggest, as both labor and commodity, the fetishization of which relies on both those logics that connect outness to sexual authenticity and also an obscuring of the labor required to produce oneself as visible (which are, as I show here, deeply intertwined). These labors are at once social, political, affective, and intimate, and the commodity being fetishized is authenticity, actualized via visibility.

In what follows, I first reflect on the ways in which performing "authentic" LGBTQness (which is impossible without being understood as visibly LGBTQ) is labored. I then outline how the argument I make here builds upon the work of poststructuralists, queer Marxists, and Marxist feminists, focusing, in particular, on how this chapter extends queer Marxist discussions of visibility. I then briefly return to gay rights advocates' calls to come out at work. I close the chapter by drawing from my interviewees' negotiations of demands for visibility at work, with the goal of highlighting already existing fissures in the capitalist underpinnings of calls for LGBTQ visibility. Interviewees' positions—particularly their refusals of coworkers' invitations or, perhaps more accurately, polite demands, to come out at work—are especially worth considering in this moment marked by the predominance of such demands and the related celebration of the slew of cultural workers (professional athletes, musicians, and Hollywood stars alike) who have recently come out "publicly," that is, in their workplaces. My analyses here are informed by a question posed by the editors of a 2011 special issue of *GLQ: A Journal of Lesbian and Gay Studies* entitled "Queer Studies and the Crises of Capitalism": "How might a methodology attuned to both sexuality and the specificities of capitalist crisis orient us toward a world other than the one in which we find ourselves currently mired?" (Rosenberg and Villarejo 2012, 1). Indeed, it is the contention of this book that we cannot create a queer "world other than the one in which we find ourselves currently mired" without rethinking demands for LGBTQ visibility. Being attuned to how these demands play out at work offers unique opportunities to think through the problem of visibility politics.

The Labor of Performing Authenticity

In their introduction to the aforementioned *GLQ* special issue, Jordana Rosenberg and Amy Villarejo draw from Marx's analysis of commodity fetishism to argue that "outward appearances of commodities conceal their inner relations, but furthermore these mystifying appearances themselves also and crucially belong to the social realities they conceal" (Rosenberg and Villarejo 2012). LGBTQ visibility, itself a form of commodity fetishism, does exactly this work; it is the very paradox and mystique of visibility (simultaneously something dangerous that queers must avoid in certain "backwards" places, and that which, if we manage to achieve it, will liberate us) that conceals the many problematic social realities of visibility politics—including the ways in which the demands for visibility render us inauthentic unless we work, work, work, and then work some more. The task, then, is to "see lodged within the production of value a spectrum of human relationality and social regulation not fully captured by the identity-labels of gender, sexuality, race, and kinship or family" (Rosenberg and Villarejo 2012, 12). Examining how visibility is produced as valuable makes apparent forms of relationality that become naturalized when the mode of analysis is grounded in identity.

Here, I consider visibility politics as an extension of neoliberal ideologies, which advance the expectation that individuals should constantly labor. We do more work at work for less pay. And then when social services and programs are cut, we do even more work; when a public bus route is cut, for instance, those relying on that form of transportation must work harder just to get to work and, thus, to maintain their lives. Many of us have gotten accustomed to working incessantly, even, at times, convinced that we are not working at all (Weeks 2011, 70). This is certainly true of the work it requires to produce ourselves—and whatever subjectivities we dare to dream, to construct, to live. In the case of the production of LGBTQ subjectivities, labor is compelled of us under the guise of authenticity and liberation—discourses that obscure that becoming visibly authentic or liberated is deeply laborious and performative.

For poststructuralists, the performative enacting of ourselves vis-à-vis social demands is precisely what marks us as legible or unintelligible—we literally do not exist as such a priori. Further, the extent to which such performative and repetitive corporeal acts are naturalized allows these very acts to be viewed as a reflection of our inherent desires or identities, gendered, sexual, or otherwise (Butler [1990] 1999). This naturalization of complex social processes renders certain bodies, genders, and sexualities authentic or inauthentic. Put otherwise, it is, in part, the naturalization of visibility politics that functions to link visible LGBTQness with authentic LGBTQness and that makes it difficult to view becoming authentically LGBTQ as labored. After all, it is the authenticity of the self that LGBTQ subjects work to produce, the labored aspect of which is lost via discourses of authenticity.[17] Furthermore, who doesn't want to be their best authentic self?! And who wants to view something they have come to see as an expression of their authenticity as a reflection of the largely unquestioned political approaches of mainstream gay rights groups? Calls for LGBTQ visibility are one mode through which repetitive performances are compelled and naturalized, subsequently rendering certain (out loud and proud) LGBTQ people as authentic and others as inauthentic or unintelligible (or worse, all too intelligible in their pitiable closetedness).

To understand more clearly how becoming and being visible as LGBTQ is labored, we must look more closely at the work of poststructuralists, queer Marxists, and Marxist feminists. In the following two sections, I explicate how my argument expands upon these bodies of thought, and more specifically, queer Marxist analyses of LGBTQ visibility.

Feminist, Queer, Marxist

Feminist and queer studies rightly have been critiqued for largely ignoring class and its attendant relations, experiences, and identities. Alan Sears, for example, claims that queer theory has neglected to analyze "class relations and divisions of labor, the dynamics of state regulation, the specific impact of capitalist restructuring and the cultural logic of processes of commodification" (2005, 94). Vivyan Adair makes a similar point about feminist studies. She argues that despite a stated commitment to analyzing race, class, gender, sexuality, and other axes along which marginalization transpires, discussions of working- and poverty-class experiences are far less common than are discussions of race, gender, and sexuality in both feminist studies journals and classrooms, reflecting what Adair terms "class absences" (2005).

At the same time, Marxist feminism and queer Marxism are important veins of both fields. Marxist feminists have long critiqued classic Marxist thought for its inability to account for women's oppression under capitalism (Federici 1975, 2004; Hartmann 1979; James 1983). They are, perhaps, most well known for their calls to recognize as work those deeply gendered intimate, affective, and reproductive labors that exist outside of what typically counts as work, focusing primarily on the unpaid and underpaid labors women do.[18] Marxist feminists' insights regarding gendered labor have also informed scholarly analyses of sexual politics, experiences, and identities, what we might call queer Marxisms. This is because, as Rosemary Hennessy asserts, Marxist feminism is "the most fully articulated effort to explain two of the social arrangements through which sexuality has historically been organized: patriarchal ideologies of difference, and class relations" (Hennessy 2000, 10). However, at the same time, "most of the archive of Marxist feminist work has been more attentive to developing an analysis of gender oppression than developing a materialist approach to sexuality" (2000, 10).

We ought to ask what such a materialist approach to sexuality might look like, especially when queer and Marxist theory have been positioned as incommensurable (Floyd 2009)? In his tracing of what he describes as an impasse between queer and Marxian theories, Kevin Floyd notes that the two sets of theories approach totality and reification—two concepts that are, as Lukács famously writes, deeply intertwined (1971)—in fundamentally oppositional ways. Totality thinking refers to Marxism's tendency to prioritize sameness, rather than difference (Floyd 2009, 6). Relatedly, according to the Marxist theory of reification, social differentiation reflects a misunderstanding of capitalist social relations and "preempt[s] any critical comprehension of the social" (Floyd 2009, 17). As Floyd notes, Marxists "tend to emphasize connection rather than differentiation . . . because a social and epistemological severing of connections is precisely one of capital's most consequential objective efforts" (Floyd 2009, 6). Focusing on the differences between and among workers (in terms of their race, gender, ability, sexuality, geography, and so on) might be viewed as in contrast to Marxian thought and politics, as a focus on difference participates in the mystifying of life under capital (Floyd 2009, 17). If focusing on differences among people is understood as synonymous with thwarting a critical reading of the social, "the persistent Marxian tendency to deprioritize questions of sexuality when those questions were acknowledged at all, to subordinate these questions to other, more 'total' concerns—to represent sexuality, in other words, not only as 'merely cultural' but as always already localized and particularized" (Floyd 2009, 5), makes perfect sense.[19]

Queer theorists, by contrast, have argued that we can learn a great deal—about sexuality, sure, but also about globalization, nationalism, capitalism, development, and so on—by focusing on particularization and the differences among different people in different places in different historical moments. From a queer theoretical perspective, doing so might require questioning some largely taken-for-granted tendencies of Marxists and Marxist feminists alike. These include taking social categories (woman, worker) as axiomatic, analyzing power as if it operates in a top-down manner (so that men and the owners of the means of production are seen as having power over women and workers, respectively),[20] and approaching capitalism as omniscient and fixed, a position that makes it seem as if nothing exists outside of capitalism. For queer theorists, each of these assumptions is contestable. First, women and workers are not predetermined as such, and both come to exist through their (discursive and material) interaction with the social order, a position that obliterates the binary upon which seeing women and workers as distinct from men and management relies. Second, as Michel Foucault so famously argues, power is multidirectional and productive, rather than unidirectional and repressive ([1978] 1990). And, third, as the recent queer theoretical focus on utopia suggests, there might be epistemological and political benefits to focusing on that which *cannot* be fully explained via an examination of capitalism, and further, to *feeding* those fissures in capitalist logics that already exist, and in so doing, enacting anticapitalist practices in the here and now.

Despite these differences, which contribute to the sense that queer and Marxian thought are incommensurable, there are significant overlaps in these bodies of thought, as well. In fact, Kevin Floyd suggests that such overlaps exist even in relation to theories around which it appears that queer and Marxist theorists differ most significantly: totality and reification. Floyd argues, for example, that, like Marxists, queer theorists privilege epistemologies marked by a "refusal of sexual particularization, a refusal of sexuality's routine epistemological dissociation from other horizons of social reality, [that] has given rise here again to particularization's dialectical opposite" (2009, 7). Floyd makes this point by drawing from Michael Warner's classic *Fear of a Queer Planet: Queer Politics and Social Theory* (1993), referencing what he describes as "one of queer theory's most widely cited assertions": "the preference for [the term] 'queer' represents, among other things, an aggressive impulse of generalization; it rejects a minoritizing logic of toleration or simple political-interest representation in favor of a more thorough resistance to regimes of the normal" (Warner as quoted in Floyd 2009, 7). While I agree with Floyd's assessment of the centrality of Warner's work to queer theory, my sense is that it is Warner's arguing for resistance to normalcy, rather than his brief and questionable assertion regarding generalization, that has solidified the text's place in the queer theory canon.

In fact, many other queer theorists make arguments that challenge this framing of generalization as central to queer thought, and, in doing so, some take on Warner directly. In his work on rural queer aesthetics and subcultures, Scott Herring, for example, questions Warner's position that "the sexual culture of New York City serves people around the world, even if only as a distant reference point of queer kids growing up in North Carolina or Idaho, who know that *somewhere* things are different" (Warner quoted in Herring 2010, 3). Herring argues that such assertions write over interesting and robust rural queer subcultures, and, in effect, produce queer culture as monolithic. For Herring and others, the problem is not just that this sort of "impulse to generalization" erases certain (rural, in this case) queers—and the transgressive potential of their spaces, aesthetics, and desires—but rather that such generalizations reproduce the sorts of dominant (metronormative, in this case) narratives queer theory otherwise insists on disrupting.

In line with Herring's assertions regarding the problematics of generalization, other scholars have questioned whether totality is actually "a productive joint analytic," instead describing it as a "hurdle" for queer Marxists to overcome (Rosenberg and Villarejo 2012, 4). In fact, the editors of the aforementioned *GLQ* special issue on queer studies and capitalism suggest that queer studies offers tools to *critique* the totality thinking associated with Marxism, asking, "Is there something that just *feels wrong* about conceptualizing totality within the ambit of queer studies—itself so finely tuned to the interstices, glimmerings,

and fleeting connections that somehow miraculously seem to have es-
caped the thudding reductions and empty equivalences of capitalism
to heteronormativity?" (Rosenberg and Villarejo 2012, 7, emphasis in
original).

In addressing their question, Rosenberg and Villarejo link queer
studies and Marxism through contradiction, rather than through reification and totality: "The encounter between queer studies and Marxist and historical-material analysis, at its best, offers the possibility
for analyzing capitalist culture in its dynamic, geographically diverse,
and contradictory articulations" (Rosenberg and Villarejo 2012, 4). At
the same time, the editors, like Floyd, see queer possibilities in totality thinking. However, they differ from Floyd in this regard too; they
speak of multiple totalities, critique "the conflation of totality and uni-
versalism" (8), and suggest that totality can be—and indeed, already is
being—rehabilitated for queer purposes (7–8).[21]

While there is no simple agreement about what queer Marxism is
or could be, this brief overview of scholarly articulations of the relations between Marxist and queer thought should give pause to those
who view these two bodies of thought as incommensurable. Indeed,
scholarship that examines sexuality in relation to political economy,
capital, commodification, and class challenges this ostensible incom-
mensurability.[22] Scholars have focused, for example, on gay tourism,
travel, and leisure as a way to examine the role of consumption in
the performance of gay authenticity, the flow of capital through gay
rights activism, and gay rights movements' production of subjects who
are recognizable as good consumers and good citizens—which are, it
turns out, one and the same.[23] Others have taken a broader approach,
focusing on how gay identities and communities have been *produced*
through capitalism. Miranda Joseph, for example, suggests that a common LGBTQ identity is not the glue that binds LGBTQ individuals,
as gay rights advocates' discourses suggest, and that these discourses
obscure the capitalist processes of consumption and production that,
for Joseph, create both communal subjectivities and also communities
(2002a). And John D'Emilio argues that capitalism created the conditions for sexuality to become disconnected from procreation and for
the development of a gay identity (1983). As D'Emilio notes, "There was,
quite simply, no social space in the colonial system of production that
allowed men and women to be gay. Survival was structured around

participation in a nuclear family" (241). As individuals started to earn money through wage labor, the family moved from being a site of economic to emotional interdependence, and in this shift, the meanings of heterosexuality—and thus sexuality—changed. In short, D'Emilio argues that capitalism weakens the social necessity of the family and enables people to earn a living outside of the family structure. At the same time, he warns that capitalism has a stake in perpetuating heterosexual relations insofar as they produce the next generation of workers, and further, that the family serves as an ideological site for the creation and actualization of heterosexism and homophobia. This scholarship inspires and informs my analyses here, which I hope will add to queer Marxist discussions of LGBTQ visibility politics, to which I now turn.

Queer Marxism: On Visibility as Labor and Commodity

In the single in-depth analysis of LGBTQ visibility politics through a queer Marxist lens that has been written to date, Rosemary Hennessy argues that "the visibility of sexual identity is often a matter of commodification, a process that invariably depends on the lives and labor of invisible *others*" (2000, 11, emphasis added). Hennessy asks, "What would it mean to understand the formation of queer identities in a social logic that does not suppress [the labor of invisible others]?" I suggest that an analysis of the production and enactment of sexual identities requires an expansion of Hennessy's probe to ask: What would it mean to understand the formation of sexual identity as simultaneously a matter of commodification and a reflection of *one's own* labor? Put differently, I contend that the visibility of sexual identity depends on the labor not only of invisible others, as Hennessy suggests, but also of the selves whose labored production we are pushed to conceal—an argument that extends Hennessy's formative work on the labored politics of visibility.

It is precisely the affective, embodied, and political *work* of producing *oneself* as a recognizable commodity that feminist and queer studies scholars have explored less, and which is of primary interest to me here. This might seem a strange claim to make since I have drawn throughout this book from those poststructuralist queer theorists who have long argued that subjects are produced through performances, acts, and discourses. The little work that has examined how these processes are *labored,* however, has focused on the production of *gendered* subjectivities—one's own (Wesling 2012) or those with whom one is intimately engaged (Ward 2010). Jane Ward, for example, argues that femmes with transmasculine partners perform what she terms "gender labor" in order to support the development of their partners' desired gendered subjectivities. Although this work has considered, at times, how gendered subjectivities are constructed and made apparent via sexual acts (Ward 2010), the *labor* required to produce *sexual* subjectivities has received little attention; perhaps due to the common conflation of gender and sexuality that Gayle Rubin famously argues against (1984), we assume erroneously that it has been done.[24] And although queer studies has long critiqued the normalizing logics of lesbian and gay movements, no scholars have critically considered the ways in which such movements compel labor via calls for visibility.

Here, I bring together the work of Judith Butler and Meg Wesling to analyze the production of sexual subjectivity as both distinct from gendered subjectivity and also as labored. Judith Butler's arguments that gendered subjectivities are created via the naturalization of repetitive performances and that the speech act enables the constitution of the subject (1993, [1990] 1999) and Meg Wesling's position that gendered performativity must be considered labored (2012) buttress my analyses. As Butler argues, our bodies should be viewed "not as a ready surface awaiting signification, but as a set of boundaries, individual and social, politically signified and maintained" (Butler [1990] 1999, 44). If our bodies, genders, and sexualities are not natural, but become intelligible and meaningful through maintenance and repetitions that have been naturalized, we ought to consider, Meg Wesling argues, these processes as labored. Wesling deconstructs the representation of drag in the film *Mariposas* in order to analyze the "production of gendered bodies and desiring subjects as a repetitive form of labor," arguing that "the compulsory repetition of gender as performance might usefully be understood as a form of self-conscious labor that produces value, both material and social, even when (or precisely because) that performance is asserted to be natural" (Wesling 2012, 108). Extending Butler's analysis of gender as performative, Wesling asks "how we might articulate the labored economies of sexuality and gender more generally—how the performance of gender and sexuality constitutes a form of labor, accruing both material and affective value" (108). In the cases of both gendered and sexual subjectivity, "one comes to exist by virtue of this fundamental dependency on the address of the Other. One 'exists' not only by virtue of being recognized but, in a prior sense, by being *recognizable*" (Butler 1997, 5). For LGBTQ people in this moment, such recognizability is predicated upon being visible as such. *Becoming* and *remaining* recognizable as LGBTQ requires not only repetitive performance but also its appearance as natural, that is, as unlabored. For Wesling, such labors are "valuable precisely in the extent to which the gendered subject submits 'freely' to the imperative of this continual labor, and regards the product of that labor—gender identity—not as an imposition from the outside but as something that originates from within" (2012, 109).

That Wesling does not mark a distinction between sexual and gendered economies allows the labor of *sexuality* to fall out—an important point for my argument precisely because calls for LGBTQ visibility necessitate that one does not become recognizable as an authentic sexual subject through the performance of gender(ed labor) alone. The processes by which LGBTQ people come to be recognizable in this particular historical moment and geographic location make requisite particular types of speech acts (a "coming out," if you will) *in addition to* the naturalization of the quotidian, performative repetitions Butler and Wesling identify as central to the construction of gender. For Butler, all subjects are constituted through speech acts and, as such, subjectivities are not predetermined but are crafted (1997). At the same time, Butler notes that all gendered and sexual subjects are not compelled to speak in the same way, and, further, the speech act itself might be differentially expected based on the speaker in question. To provide an example, gender-conforming men or women are not expected to state "I am a man" or "I am a woman" in order to be understood as authentically so; normative gender is widely assumed to be able to be read by others onto one's body in ways that can render unnecessary such speech acts. Such speech acts are rarely viewed as unnecessary for LGBTQ people. Even in the case where one works to present their sexuality to the world via a nonnormative gender presentation, this is no longer enough to be viewed as "out" as LGBTQ—at the workplace or otherwise.

Coming Out at Work (as Work)

Gay rights supporters' demands to come out at work certainly did not begin with the 2018 HRC study and related press with which I opened this chapter. In a 2011 article posted on *CNN.com*, Brian McNaught, a diversity consultant for large corporations, urged employers to create environments where lesbian and gay employees can come out and encouraged employees to take advantage of opportunities to do so. McNaught suggested that coming out at work is important because studies show that "40% of closeted gay employees are less likely to trust their employer than those gay employees who are out. That lack of trust comes into play in their productivity" (2011). For McNaught, and others calling for outness at work, being closeted is the problem and leads to lack of trust; therefore, coming out would create trust, alleviate workplace tension, and increase productivity. Perhaps McNaught has it backwards; perhaps the lack of trust between companies and employees is a symptom of broader workplace dissatisfactions spurred by the acceleration of neoliberalism and late capitalism. A 2019 survey of 6,600 workers concluded that more than half of U.S. employees are unhappy in their jobs, after all. Not surprisingly, this number increases for those in low-paying jobs and for Black workers, and particularly Black women (Kelly 2019). Workplace outness will do nothing to change the conditions that lead to worker distrust and dissatisfaction—concerns that are themselves more relevant to nonrural workers. Indeed, the same survey found that workers outside of large cities—where workers' outness is imagined as especially constricted—actually experience higher job quality, "even if they are earning significantly lower incomes" (Kelly 2019). Following Hemangini Gupta, we might view McNaught's approach as an "entrepreneurial experiment," whose benefits and consequences alike manifest along geographic lines (2019, 85).

McNaught's concern with productivity and career advancement is echoed by the HRC, for whom coming out can relieve the ostensible stress associated with maintaining the closet. HRC's "Coming Out at Work" page of their website claims that doing so can "relieve the daily stress of hiding who you are," potentially resulting in increased productivity and "benefit[ing] your career because your peers will see you in a new, perhaps even courageous, light."[25] Doing so, it is assumed, benefits more than careers and corporations; in fact, social progress itself is understood to rely upon it. An article titled "Come Out at Work on National Coming Out Day" posted on the National Gay and Lesbian Task Force's website links visibility, authenticity, and political rights, and argues for the social benefits associated with coming out in one's work environment:

> Despite the remarkable progress made by the LGBT community there are still no clear protections for workers, meaning it's still risky for many to be out in the workplace. That's why the federal Employment Non-Discrimination Act (ENDA) is so important to protect people in the workplace based on sexual orientation and gender identity. . . . On this National Coming Out Day, stand up for an America where everyone can be out at work without fear of losing their job because of who they are or whom they love. . . . And, if it feels right and safe, be honest with your co-workers when having conversations in the workplace. The more people who have visible LGBT colleagues the more people will accept us as equals.[26]

For the National Gay and Lesbian Task Force and other gay rights activists, coming out is necessary because they assume that visibility acts as a precursor to acceptance and political rights—a belief I challenge explicitly in this book's Introduction. But calls for visibility at work, in particular, are especially egregious, and for precisely the reason the National Gay and Lesbian Task Force notes in the above quote: No federal workplace protections exist for LGBTQ workers—or at least that was the case until the summer of 2020, when the U.S. Supreme Court ruled that the Civil Rights Act of 1964 protects LGBTQ workers. Put more directly, HRC, the National Gay and Lesbian Task Force, Wegan, and others quoted throughout this chapter were calling for outness at work when there were no federal protections for those being encouraged to be out at work. (Incidentally, scholars and activists have noted that, much like hate crimes legislation, such protections actually do little to prevent discrimination, a point to which I return in this chapter's conclusion). For the National Gay and Lesbian Task Force, ENDA was not only that which would allow people to be visible (without being fired); it is that which visibility would enable—a position grounded in circular logics and with potentially heinous consequences for LGBTQ workers.

In short, calls for visibility function both to create an authentic (out) LGBTQ subject and to place responsibility for the state of the social on those continually called upon to maintain their authenticity via their visibility. Being the right kind of worker requires authenticity, and, by extension, inauthenticity is refusal—and employers regard it as such.

Calls to come out at work, a site where one labors in exchange for wages and other (though increasingly fewer) material benefits, imply that those marginalized by current sexual norms will (and should) labor for free, even in the very place one expects to receive wages for their work. In a labor market in which "more jobs require workers to supply not only manual effort but also emotional skills, affective capacities, and communicative competencies," training workers to become accustomed to giving of themselves for free does the work of capital (Weeks 2011, 89). It is about precisely this context that Emmanuel David writes in his ethnographic analysis of the "purple-collar labor" transgender women workers perform in their jobs at call centers in the Philippines. While their affective and feminized labors—which include tasks geared toward calming workplace tensions, creating a sense of workplace community, and boosting morale—are uncompensated, they do, David argues, produce value for the companies (2015). That workers can feel anything other than resistance to expectations that they give of themselves for free speaks to the power of what Yousef Baker calls "the affective wages of neoliberalism," which are, of course, not wages at all (2020, 48).

Being an LGBT-friendly workplace, it turns out, is a small price to pay for the increased surplus value that companies can extract from trusting, pliant employees. But increased extraction from current employees represents just one small sliver of the value to employers of appearing as a "safe-(work)space." As HRC's employer database and related campaign suggests, such an appearance is useful for recruiting a field of potential people to be employed and exploited. Beyond this, being viewed as an LGBT-friendly workplace means that people who would never or could never—including for geographic reasons—work for these companies make an active choice to support them in other ways. Corporate sponsorship of Pride parades and marketing campaigns geared specifically toward LGBTQ people suggest that companies already believe that they stand to gain a great deal by positioning themselves as LGBTQ friendly. That gay rights activists champion such companies because they ostensibly do not fire their employees for displaying their "true selves" at work should concern all of us. How low our bar has become. In order to think through what resistance to being visible as LGBTQ in the workplace, in particular, might tell us about the labored production of authentic LGBTQ sexual subjectivity, I now turn to my interviewees.

(Out?) On the Job

Nissa, a middle-class Native woman from northern Minnesota who is in her late twenties, goes to college and also works at a bank as a teller. She describes her experience as a lesbian in her workplace:

> I just never told them but I think they know because my manager was telling me about how her son is gay and I was like "What is she trying to get at here?" I think she was trying to *make me say* . . . "Yeah well I am too." So I think they know but they don't. . . . This lady I work with she has . . . two daughters that . . . have red hair . . . and I was just like "I just don't like red hair" . . . and she's like "Well at least I know you're not going to hit on my daughters." And I was like "Mmm what are you trying to say?" They do but they don't kind of know. I am [out] but I'm not (emphasis added).

Nissa does not talk about her sexuality at work and mentioned that her coworkers and bosses "do but don't kind of know." Her colleagues make comments that suggest that they are trying to connect with her via discussing her sexuality, which she is not interested in chatting about with them. In fact, she feels as if her manager was pressuring her to come out.

Yonni, a Native woman in her midforties who lives in northern Minnesota and describes her class status as "rich in the heart, low on money," similarly refuses to engage in conversations about her sexuality at work:

> I work construction. Some guys will be like, "Ugh, man I can't understand [lesbians and gays]." You know, it's not for you to understand! You're sitting around and [the guys will say], "Can

I ask you a personal question?" And you already know what it is. I'm like, "No, you can't. Can I ask you a personal question?" [The guys respond] "Oh, sure! Yeah, you can." I said, "No, I won't." And I just leave it like that. Why? That's just the way I am. . . . I don't care if you're knowing me for five years or whatever. Go buy a magazine or something, or go buy a book if you want. . . . I'm just private about that. I'm a private person, but I'm open.

Yonni has refused to allow coworkers to ask her questions about her personal life because she anticipates that those questions will be about her sexuality, which she does not want to talk about with them. Nonetheless, we might read her coworkers' requests to ask her personal questions as a reflection of their viewing her as "open," to use the word Yonni uses to describe herself; at the very least, they feel as if they know her well enough to ask if they can pose personal questions. They also had made comments about LGBTQ people—"Man, I can't understand lesbians and gays"—in ways that could open up possibilities for Yonni to come out to them if she so desired. We might also read these comments as invitations for her to do so. Despite these attempts, however, no one on Yonni's job sites had asked her about her sexuality explicitly and Yonni had never commented on her sexuality. But, still, she views herself as "open."

Like Yonni, Leila, a Native woman in her midforties who lives on a reservation in northern Minnesota and describes her class status as "rich in all sorts of ways," works construction. She mentioned that she rarely talks about her sexuality at work. For Leila, this decision has a great deal to do with the racial differences between her and her coworkers:

At the work site, I don't say nothing to anybody. Really. I don't . . . get into my life or anything like that. First of all, a lot of [my white coworkers] . . . just don't understand Native life. They don't understand how we think and how we feel about things and operate.

I followed up and asked if she talks about other parts of her life while at work. "Hmm, No. Guys would ask me, 'Where are you from?' I would tell them, 'Never mind.' They would ask me, 'Are you married?' 'Never mind.' 'Do you have children?' . . . I just tell them, 'Never mind.'"

That Nissa, Yonni, and Leila are all Native women is certainly relevant to their positions regarding coming out at work. But because the white women I interviewed articulated remarkably similar positions regarding coming out, a point evident in my analysis of coming and being out in chapter 1, race alone cannot account for Native women's disidentification with dominant LGBTQ discourses. Thinking along racial lines does, however, illuminate differences in how interviewees articulated their reasons for approaching visibility in ways that are distinct from LGBTQ organizations. White women tended to account for their disinterest in visibility through referencing their rurality while Native women rooted this difference in their experiences as Native women.

That Leila, Yonni, and Nissa do not talk about their personal lives at work did not translate into their feeling unknown or closeted. And although none of these women mentioned being discriminated against at work due to their sexuality, I thought it was certainly plausible that prior discrimination at work—or a fear of discrimination at work—informed their desires to avoid discussions about their sexuality. So, I asked each of them if they had ever faced discrimination at work in regard to their sexuality. Nissa and Yonni answered in the negative. Leila paused briefly before answering:

Maybe a little bit but nothing . . . to fight or squabble about. . . . One time . . . at work . . . I caught them . . . talking shit about . . . lesbian people. I had to walk down there and tell them to shut the fuck up. . . . "Who the hell are you to judge anybody?" . . . I was like "Well it's not up to you. . . . What if your sister or your wife's sister is gay or lesbian or whatever she wants to call herself, if she is happy?" Well, they shut up. They . . . don't talk shit to me at all over there. I've never ran into that on any job site and I've been doing construction for like twenty something years. . . . Nope it goes to show you [the] rarity. Don't hide it in the dark cause that's . . . dangerous. Definitely show it off.

Although Leila says to "show it off," in her twenty or more years as a construction worker, she has never come out to her coworkers. Yet, she does not feel as if she is closeted or hiding anything important about herself and she is not afraid to reference LGBTQ issues on the job site. On the one occasion Leila heard her coworkers making homophobic comments about lesbians—that she made clear were not directed at her—she stepped in and told them to stop. And they did. Leila, like Nissa and Yonni, sees herself as out. Each of these women said that their family members and friends know about their sexualities, and they described situations that suggest that their coworkers do, but kind of do not, know, as Nissa said. Although each woman described moments in which she refused an invitation to come out to her coworkers, she engaged in other behaviors that would make it difficult to see this refusal as symptomatic of being closeted: Nissa wears rainbow bracelets to work, Yonni describes being affectionate with her girlfriend in public after having a few drinks at a local bar in their small town (where her bosses and coworkers are likely to see her), and Leila stops her coworkers from making homophobic jokes and comments.

For other interviewees, who did not receive the types of explicit questions about their sexuality that Yonni, Leila, and Nissa got from their coworkers, deciding when and how to talk about their sexuality at work was challenging. Avery, a middle-class, white woman in her early thirties who lives in a town near a Minnesota border, for example, said that she was out at work "to an extent." Although she has introduced her fiancée to her boss, she makes a point of not discussing her partner with her "team," the staff she supervises at the national big box store where she works. At the same time, she said, "I don't deny it. It's kinda hard. I just say my fiancée [Kasen] . . . most of the time and [because of her gender neutral name] it . . . could go either way."

Like Avery, Bethany, a middle-class, white woman in her late forties who lives in southeastern South Dakota and works for a regional grocery store chain, also shared with just one coworker that she is gay:

Most of the people that I know *except for my work-related people* know that I am gay. There's one guy that I've worked with [who] was just always joking. And I joke, you know, and I think he was kind of taking [it] a little bit wrong. At one point, I sa[id], "You don't have a chance in hell cause I am gay." Plus he just isn't anything that I would, you know . . . bad teeth and heavy, just doesn't do it for me. And he goes, "Ahh, [but] you [have been] joking with me." And I sa[id], "Well you were joking with me."

And [then] I sa[id], "You know I don't tell anybody that." So he's the only one that knows out there. . . . So, work wise, I just don't. (emphasis added)

Although Bethany is out to nearly all other people in her life, she does not discuss her sexuality with coworkers—with a single exception that had the purpose of ensuring that she was not leading on a fellow coworker with whom she was friendly.

Klaudette and Pauline, two middle-class, white women in their midsixties and fifties, respectively, who have been partnered for decades and live in central Minnesota, also see themselves as out in general but view the necessity of outness at work differently from one another. Both women are retired professors; Pauline worked in the sciences and Klaudette in the humanities and athletics. When the topic of work came up in our conversation, Pauline mentioned that she was not out at work. Klaudette, by contrast, stated that she came out to "every one of [her] classes" she taught. Both women also shared anecdotes that complicate these statements: Klaudette describes coming out while teaching humanities courses as "very simple. Obviously I can't come out teaching racquetball or something . . . Oh by the way I'm queer." And Pauline noted:

It's interesting because I have some things around my office, and I don't hide who I am, but I don't . . . announce it to my classes or anything. One of my students . . . was meeting with me in my office, and I had a button [that] said "Out and proud in [the town where I live]" . . . that I had gotten from the LGBT Resource Center, and she said "Oh I like that." And then she told me that their son came out to them. She said "Oh he would really like this," and I said "Well take it. I can get plenty more."

Pauline views herself as not out at work because she does not announce it to her classes, even though her coworkers know about her partner (who worked at the same university) and she has LGBTQ swag in her office, which she has shared with her students. Klaudette, by contrast, views herself as out, despite not coming out in her athletics classes.

Kay, a middle-class, white woman in her early fifties who lives in eastern South Dakota and works at a bank, similarly stated, "I'm not out to people at work." At the same time, she noted:

I have a couple of coworkers that I'm out to, but for the most part . . . it's not something that I talk about, just like straight people don't talk about the fact that they're straight, although they might mention a husband or girlfriend or boyfriend or whatever. And I don't go there because it's . . . it's nobody's business and my philosophy is that people give you permission to tell them. And if they don't give you permission to tell them then it's just better just not to go there because you don't want them to think that [is] the main thing . . . about me. . . . There's a lot more to me than just my sexuality. So, that's not really relevant. People say, "Do the people you work with know that you're a lesbian?" And I say, "Well if I ever came out as straight there would be a lot of very surprised people." I think a lot of them have a pretty good idea and . . . they don't hassle me.

Although Kay does not see herself as out at work, she is out to some coworkers and mentioned that some people at work "suggested that I invite [my partner]" to the workplace Christmas party.

Just as Kay and Pauline are choosy about the coworkers with whom they share information about their personal lives, Maggie, a middle-class white woman in her midforties who lives in southeastern South Dakota and works at a school, suggests that it is only important to be out to her colleagues with whom she feels affectively close:

The people I work with know, if there is somebody that I am close to. I mean if a new teacher starts at my school, I may talk to him five times in the whole school year. That's not what I bring up. But after five years if I continually talk with them . . . I'll talk about the kids. If they ever asked, "Oh what's your husband do?" I go, "Oh well it's my wife, you know."

Other interviewees had less ability to control to whom they were out at work. Lou Anne, a lower-middle-class white woman in her midsixties who lives in a town near a South Dakota border, transitioned from living as a man to a woman in her midfifties. At the time of her transition, she was working as a manager for a large construction-related dealership where she had worked for nearly twenty-five years. Prior to transitioning, she had

> visited with the corporate manager and we kinda had a plan. That, when I was ready, the old person would leave . . . and [the new me] would show up as the manager at another town. And that was kind of the whole thing. Well . . . the president of the company found out about my situation, and fired me . . . with the words "Deal with your gender issues elsewhere." So I filed a discrimination suit against them. So out of that, I became somewhat um, notable, I guess you might say.

Lou Anne's description of her situation is modest; one might actually describe her as a local celebrity. The city newspaper "did a two-day feature article" on her, she became a board member for two local LGBTQ organizations, and she gave "tons of speeches . . . all over the Midwest" about transgender rights and issues. Beyond this, she was a guest on a national talk show based in California. Her approach caused some friction in her life: "Some of my family thought I was going overboard . . . too visible and too vocal." However, Lou Anne, who transitioned nine years prior to my interviewing her, noted that her approach had changed. "I don't do that anymore. I've gotten to the point where, I'm just another old, white-haired broad walkin' down the street . . . whatever. You know, and that's kinda . . . I like that." I asked what precipitated Lou Anne's decision to stop participating in LGBTQ politics:

> A lot of it career. When I was in [a larger Midwestern city], you could kinda lose yourself, you know, just in the size. Then they asked me to come up here and manage the store. Uh, so I thought, okay. I don't need those kind of issues here in this town, with me trying to be the manager. So I did drop that.

Lou Anne became the store manager at the coffee shop where I interviewed her, working "anywhere from 70 to 80 hours" per week. She noted "I lived here, this was my life." Despite this, Lou Anne never told anyone at work about her transition or gender identification:

I would guess, if they don't know—they have an idea. But they
don't acknowledge it. And that's the way I want it. I did have one
gal that worked for me here. We both were working here when
[I got kicked out of my church for living as a woman] and all of
this crap hit the fan. But . . . she left me alone. She never went
there. I just knew that she knew. Uh, I don't ever talk about it
with anybody. Past history. I'm just a grandma.

Lou Anne later quit her job as the store manager and went back to
school:

Now that I'm in school, I'm just basically everybody's grandmother out there. You know, and I go out for a job, and I don't
want all that stuff kinda hitting me and coming up. . . . At
school, I told one person. This was the head of my department,
and . . . I kind of decided that she needed to know what was
going on. I know she's made a lot of recommendations about
me to people outside [of school]. And I thought, okay, before
somebody comes back and goes, "You're recommending *that*,
this person, to us?" She needed to know. . . . She'd been my head
instructor, I'd had at least two classes from her every semester
for at least a year and a half. And she goes, "I had no idea." But
she's the only one I ever told in school.

Just as Lou Anne carefully selects those colleagues, employees, and
mentors with whom she shares information about her personal life, she
also operates with caution in public. She has asked her adult son, who
still calls her "Dad," to be careful about calling her by this name around
classmates and coworkers, in particular. "That's who I am. I am his Dad,
always will be. I have asked him, that you know, say, we're around my
classmates, or my work—people I work with, you know—if you couldn't
bring up 'Dad,' [Lou Anne] is fine. You don't have to call me Mom." Lou
Anne shared a story that speaks to just how "fine" with it she is:

I've had some interesting things [happen]. I used to own a
Harley. [My son] and I were at the Harley Davidson shop one
afternoon. And he was over looking at bikes on one end of
the showroom, and I was getting something, and all at once

[he yelled], "Hey, Dad! Come look at this!" And all the people in the Harley shop are looking around thinking, "Who's this kid talking to?" It is what it is. He's my son, I'm his father. And . . . we're both going with that.

Each of these women speak to the complexity of what it means to be "out" in general and at work, in particular: Are you out if you reference your fiancée by name, but do not state that you are LGBTQ? If you do not feel as if you "hide" your sexuality but, at the same time, have told only a few coworkers or wait five years to share with them this information? If you have LGBTQ pride buttons in your office, but do not explicitly connect this to your own sexuality? If you have shared that you are LGBTQ with your friends or family but not your coworkers? Regardless of how my interviewees or I might answer these questions, it seems obvious that they are not the "visible LGBT colleagues" that national gay rights groups envision and call for.

By way of thinking through the labor of becoming and being visible, I now return to Wesling's analysis of the labor of the production of gendered and sexual subjectivities. As I noted above, for Wesling, "this labor is valuable precisely in the extent to which the gendered subject submits 'freely' to the imperative of this continual labor, and regards the product of that labor—gender identity—not as an imposition from the outside but as something that originates from within" (2012, 109). My interviewees' insights both support and call into question Wesling's assertions here. As I've shown throughout this chapter, the women I interviewed do not "submit freely" to demands to come out at work—by their coworkers, managers, or gay rights activists more broadly. They are refusing to labor in the ways that, for Wesling, allows this labor to be viewed as a reflection of internal desire, as nonlabor. At the same time, they—like most people, including those about whom Wesling writes—do not tend to view gender identity as an imposition from the outside. In fact, many of my interviewees are strongly connected to the idea of being a woman. At the same time, they tend to be wary of strongly identifying with a sexual identity—a difference that Wesling's formulation cannot capture precisely because Wesling does not make a distinction between gender and sexual identity and the labors required to produce them.

Such a lack of interest in identifying with one's sexuality was not, however, true across the board. Nissa explained that she proudly identifies as a lesbian and Native because she sees each of these things as unique. She wears rainbow bracelets to work and claims that she would go to LGBTQ rallies if she had time (although, perhaps ironically, because of her workload, she does not). For Nissa, who felt pressured by her boss to come out and whose coworkers made comments that suggest they know about her sexuality despite her never having told them, the imposition is the expectation that she do the labor of *telling*. Of course, the distinction between viewing as an imposition the labor to produce an identity and the identity itself is blurry—precisely because if one does not labor in prescribed ways, one's authentic relationship to a claimed identity might be called into question. Nissa resisted confessing her sexuality to her coworkers, explaining that she felt as if her manager and coworker were trying to force her to come out. In resisting, Nissa, along with the other women featured in this chapter, challenge both the imperative to come out at work and the image of the authentic gay as someone who is necessarily "out," at work or otherwise.

In stark contrast to the aforementioned image of the good LGBTQ worker as necessarily "out, loud, and proud" at work perpetuated by the National Gay and Lesbian Task Force, the Human Rights Campaign, and related diversity consultants, many of my interviewees were not "out" at work in the ways that gay rights groups ask of LGBTQ people— that is, divulging one's sexuality through a particular speech act that is understood as a formal "coming out" to coworkers, bosses, clients, and so on. Interviewees overwhelmingly articulated that their sexuality was not relevant to their work. Some mentioned that they had no desire to be out at work and others, who stated they are "not out" at work, had in fact told some coworkers with whom they felt emotionally close. Perhaps more importantly, no one who expressed disinterest in workplace outness felt closeted at work or more broadly. Others who viewed themselves as "out" were not out to everyone. In short, interviewees who viewed themselves as out at work and as not out at work alike told stories that might appear to contradict their framing of themselves—a point that speaks to Steven Seidman's argument that the trope of the closet no longer captures the experiences of LGBTQ people, as I discuss at length in chapter 2.

Authentic out-, loud-, and proudness requires that subjects perform the speech act(s) of coming out, center sexuality as their primary mode of identifying in the world, and politicize this identity. Although I have focused here primarily on the labored nature of coming out, such speech acts are not the only work one might do in order to produce one's sexual subjectivity; wearing rainbow bracelets or putting a stop to coworkers' homophobic comments, as my interviewees mentioned, are also labored. But donning rainbow attire or putting an end to homophobic comments cannot produce the LGBTQ person in question as someone who is authentically so—at least not when, as I have suggested, this authenticity is sutured to the confessional performance of the coming out speech act. If one does not explicitly confess their sexuality to others so that these others might be able to acknowledge this part of the LGBTQ person, that person will never be considered "out." Calls for LGBTQ people to come out at every possible moment obscure the many labors of coming and being out by naturalizing the sexual identity that is produced through these labors and suggesting that coming out is the fulfillment of the internal desire to do so. Resisting the call, like answering the call, is labored, of course. But the former position is already assumed to be the case. Put otherwise, maintaining "the closet" is considered labored in ways that coming out—through which one produces oneself as an LGBTQ subject who is authentic, real, and honest—is not. We do not see the latter as labored because coming out (so that we might be visible) has been so naturalized, framed as both a reflection of our internal desire to speak and as that which liberates us. In short, the authenticity of the self hinges on the appearance of nonwork.

The Fruit(loop)s of Our Labors

What is perhaps most nefarious is that such nonwork compels so much work of LGBTQ people. Not only is becoming visible itself work, as I've argued here, but one is hailed to do additional work once one is properly out as LGBTQ. Wells Fargo reports on the LGBT Resource Center page of its website that it was "named the top company for LGBT employees by DiversityInc" in 2012, 2013, and 2015 and has "achieved a 100% diversity score on the Human Rights Campaign Corporate Equality Index for thirteen consecutive years." The company further notes that it offers its "LGBT team members . . . opportunities to plan and participate in LGBT community outreach and events."[27] Notably, it is

Wells Fargo's *LGBTQ employees*, not all employees, who are given "opportunities" to participate in outreach and event planning, work that often goes unpaid and takes place outside of one's typical workday. A lesbian employee of a Minnesota Wells Fargo bank branch told a friend of mine, for instance, that she was invited to be a part of a Wells Fargo committee on LGBTQ issues but that the committee work was uncompensated and took place after work hours.[28]

Scholars have termed those who get saddled with expectations to do the work of social justice "diversity workers" and their work as "diversity work" (Ahmed 2012). Diversity workers are hailed to do this work because of their embodiment or identification. Their presence makes those companies and institutions to which they are attached appear more progressive, inclusive, and diverse than they would without their presence. Assumptions about the value of diverse representation are not limited to capitalist enterprises; they are rampant in universities, as well. While I am rarely called upon by my academic institution for my expertise in queer studies or queer politics, I am often expected to represent the institution's commitment to LGBTQ inclusivity by virtue of my presence—despite the fact that my academic training means that I am typically critical of the variety of work the college is doing to appear more inclusive. I get asked, for example, to do additional service, including providing support to LGBTQ students, attending university functions, and participating on various committees, because my presence does particular work for an institution that undervalues my actual work as a queer studies scholar.

Visibility's labors produce more than (in)authentic LGBTQ subjects, who become authentic via the labored processes I've outlined here and who are hailed to do additional work once they have properly achieved their authenticity. They produce more than political identities for those people and institutions that become socially liberal or conservative through taking a position on LGBTQ rights. In the several previous chapters, I have outlined many ideas that the visibility imperative aids in producing: metronormativity, progress narratives, nationalism, post-raciality, and post-spatiality. Beyond the production of ideologies and subjectivities, visibility is itself a commodity; it can be bought and sold, both in ideological and material terms.

As the aforementioned scholars writing on LGBTQ tourism have noted, visibility is achievable, in part, through the purchasing of (other) commodities. LGBTQ tourist agencies trade in the idea that being able to be visible as LGBTQ is inherently valuable and desirable, an idea that LGBTQ people buy through the consumption of other more material items, including "gaycations" to places where people ostensibly can be "out, loud, and proud," cruises marketed toward LGBTQ families, and trips to Pride celebrations in destination cities. In short, visibility politics are both furthered via commodity culture and further commodity culture, producing the desire for commodities that assist in becoming visible. For visibility to function as a commodity, it needs buyers—subjects (loved ones, employers, states) seeking to craft themselves in relation to a visible other, but it cannot have workers (those discernibly laboring to produce it). And yet it does, along with refusers of this very work.

By way of concluding this chapter, I want to spend a moment outlining the political possibilities of my argument—or the fruits of my labors, if you will. My position that becoming visible is labor and further that calls for coming out at work, in particular, offer specific opportunities to reflect on the labored nature of the production of authentic LGBTQ sexual subjectivities is not simply meant to inform queer Marxist theory. Far from purely theoretical, this argument allows us to reflect on legislative battles for workplace protections for LGBTQ employees. In what follows, I focus primarily on the Employment Non-Discrimination Act (ENDA), a piece of legislation that, for the last twenty-five years, had been at the center of gay rights groups' work regarding workplace discrimination. In the summer of 2020, the U.S. Supreme Court ruled in *Bostock v. Clayton County, Georgia* that the Civil Rights Act of 1964 protects employees from discrimination based on their sexuality or gender, essentially making ENDA obsolete. Nonetheless, the lessons we can learn from critically considering ENDA remain useful, especially because ENDA's impulses—its beliefs in the value of LGBTQ visibility, especially at work—are likely to be amplified by the recent Supreme Court ruling.

A bit of additional context about ENDA: Although Congresspeople introduced the legislation into nearly every congressional session since 1994, it never passed both the House and the Senate, and thus, no federal workplace protections for LGBTQ workers existed until the summer of 2020. During ENDA's twenty-five-year lifespan, approaches to passing the legislation created contentious divisions among LGBTQ rights advocates. In 2007, gender identity was added to the proposed legislation so that, if passed, it would also protect transgender employees. Some advocates believed that this move might undermine chances for passing legislation that would extend antidiscrimination policies to cover sexual orientation. As a result, protections against discrimination rooted in gender identity were removed from the proposed legislation. Some trans studies scholars and LGBTQ activists responded with outrage, noting that, once again, gay rights groups made decisions that left trans people and issues behind.[29] In the end, Congress, which was controlled by the Democratic party at the time, did not sign ENDA into law anyway. Up until the summer of 2020, LGBTQ workers legally could be fired for being LGBTQ in more than half of U.S. states, including South Dakota. ENDA's advocates claimed that, if passed, the legislation would make it illegal for at least some companies (those with fifteen employees or more) to fire someone for being LGBTQ.

We might ask what we can learn by considering gay rights activists' infatuation with LGBTQ workers' outness at work when there were no federal protections in place for LGBTQ workers—particularly when the gay rights groups demanding that people come out at work are the very organizations that had prioritized marriage equality, access to the military, and hate crimes legislation. To be clear, I am not advocating that gay rights groups should have simply shifted from prioritizing protecting marriage equality to campaigning for workplace protections, particularly when activists' discussions of ENDA further precisely the visibility politics I critique throughout this book. But considering that, for most people, working is mandatory in ways that getting married or having children is not, the lack of national attention to ENDA should seem peculiar. But LGBTQ workers do not as easily produce the kinds of homonormativity that has become synonymous with the work of gay rights groups. In short, campaigns for gay marriage shore up homonormativity in ways that workplace protections do not. Nonetheless, if gay rights activists cared about people coming out at work, one might rightly assume that they would have prioritized making the conditions available for workplace outness without potential repercussions, rather than calling for outness at work and assuming that this outness would change people's minds such that workplace protections would be the inevitable outcome. Their approaches were backwards, and the result was that the risks of workplace outness fell entirely on LGBTQ workers.

As such, it seems that gay rights groups' calls for workplace outness reveal more about their unbecoming belief in the power of outness than any potential concerns with the very real problems workers (of all sexualities and genders) increasingly experience under neoliberalism and late capitalism—lower pay, more demanding workload, fewer benefits that cost more and more, and less separation between work and nonwork. Passing ENDA would do nothing to address these issues, a position informed by trans studies scholars' critiques of LGBTQ activists' work to pass antidiscrimination legislation, and particularly gender-identity-inclusive varieties of such legislation. In outlining the limitations of what he describes as "a legal rights agenda that provides little redress," Dean Spade suggests that antidiscrimination laws fail "to address the legal issues that create the greatest vulnerabilities for trans people: criminalization, immigration enforcement, lack of access to ID that reflects current gender, placement in sex-segregated facilities (bathrooms, shelters, residential treatment programs), and exclusions of gender-confirming health care for trans people from Medicaid, private insurance policies, and various health care programs for people in state custody" (2015, 14). Beyond this, such policies are rarely enforced, even in the places where they do exist. As such, Spade notes that even those antidiscrimination campaigns that have been "deemed successful . . . have not sufficiently improved the lives of trans people" (14).

Spade's positions were echoed by some of my interviewees, a few of whom mentioned that their places of employment did not have an antidiscrimination policy, although no one appeared particularly bothered by this fact. Kay, who has a JD and knowledge of how the law operates, articulated exactly what such a lack of antidiscrimination policy meant for her life:

> I could be fired for being gay. So that's a little bit scary. *I don't, in fact, think I would be likely to be for that reason.* But if uh, if they wanted to fire me for some other reason, they could fire me for that reason. And it's perfectly acceptable—perfectly legal I should say. And so . . . I think there is employment discrimination.

Kay noted that while, at the time of our interview, she legally could have been fired for being gay, she did not believe that she would have been, despite South Dakota's lack of antidiscrimination legislation, as well as her company's. But for Kay, and others who referenced such legislation, the nonexistence of protective laws and policies would not keep them from coming out at work if they wanted to anyway. Indeed, the vast majority of my interviewees were out to some degree at work, and largely without problems from coworkers or bosses. And for Kay, the fact that employment discrimination against LGBTQ people was legal was not necessarily enough reason to prioritize and invest in passing ENDA. As Kay said, passing such a law would not *prevent* employment discrimination; it would only provide individual victims with legal avenues for recourse *after* the fact, should they be able to access and utilize those avenues. Kay mentioned that similar laws exist that are meant to prevent "employment discrimination based on race, which is not legal, but it happens." Kay's positions are in line with those of queer and trans studies scholars who also note that antidiscrimination legal strategies misunderstand how power operates, view harm as something that happens to individuals by individuals (rather than by systems, which are much harder to change), and propose as a remedy the punishment of individuals by precisely the systems that have disproportionately targeted trans people (Spade 2015, 9). In short, ENDA would have done nothing to create the conditions within which homophobia or transphobia would be unimaginable. The same can be said, of course, of the recent Supreme Court ruling.

My concerns are related—but I suggest that shaking advocates' beliefs in the power of such approaches requires something others have not yet explored: taking on the logics of visibility. Put more directly, the scholars and activists who have offered trenchant critiques of antidiscrimination legislation have largely left intact LGBTQ rights activists' beliefs in the power of visibility, ignoring that what motivates the drive for such policies is a belief that being visible as LGBTQ is crucial for being authentically ourselves—at work or otherwise.

My concern is not, of course, with creating the conditions for outness, workplace or otherwise. Although neither ENDA nor the ruling in *Bostock v. Clayton County, Georgia* necessarily produce an imperative for visibility—their legal function is to protect those who "choose" to be out, after all—their being on the legislative table, so to speak, reflect and inform the cultural imperative for outness, embodied here by the good, honest LGBTQ worker who is authentically LGBTQ via their visibility. Indeed, it is difficult to imagine a context in which a boss's inability to fire an employee over their sexual preferences or identifications, the desired goal of ENDA and *Bostock,* might challenge the cultural expectation to come out and the subsequent linking of that outness to authenticity. Indeed, refusing to come out at work might be just as dangerous for LGBTQ workers, as the labored confessing that makes one recognizable as visible, it is assumed, can lead not only to individual workplace advancement, as the diversity consultants cited earlier suggest, but also to social progress. Those who are not intelligible as out will be especially inauthentic with the elimination of legal barriers that had ostensibly prevented this very outness.

This is precisely my concern. The passing of laws that enable a kind of outness that LGBTQ women in the rural Midwest do not tend to value or perform will render them even more unintelligible and inauthentic.

For supporters of this variety of antidiscrimination legislation, such critiques might seem especially odd, precisely because, these advocates might say, workplace protections could disproportionately benefit both rural LGBTQ people, who tend to live in places without the supposedly LGBTQ-friendly companies touted on diversity lists, and also Midwestern LGBTQ people, many of whom live in states without antidiscrimination protections. Still, I hope that pieces of my argument resonate with even the staunchest supporters of liberal legal rights approaches. Gay rights activists' calls for workplace outness when workers had no legal protections should make us all cringe. Furthermore, activists' beliefs that all LGBTQ workers desire to be out at work and their related stitching of authenticity to visibility, at work and otherwise, are misguided at best and, at worst, write out of LGBTQ subjectivity those for whom such assumptions do not work. More ambitiously, and informed by a long line of poststructuralist feminist and queer theorists, I am asking that we think of the production of ourselves as labored, and further, to recognize that visibility discourses are responsible for making doing so difficult. Ultimately, I am asking that we refuse to labor more and harder, and especially under the guise of authenticity. Now, let's go have a cocktail.

The More Things Change, the More They Stay the Same

Metronormativity on the Move

2010. THE YEAR I BEGAN the initial research for this book. A decade ago. For my students, who were in elementary or middle school at that time, this feels like a really long time ago. Informed at least in part by gay rights groups' "It gets better" mantra, they often ask me what has changed in the past decade. We do, indeed, live in a different cultural moment than we did in 2010. Gay marriage has been legalized; Don't Ask, Don't Tell repealed; and President Barack Obama replaced by Donald Trump who was then replaced by Joe Biden. And, perhaps most importantly for my purposes, the rural came to occupy a new place in political discourse during this same period—both within LGBTQ rights circles and more broadly.

In 2016, for instance, liberals watched with horror as Donald Trump ascended to the White House, a process through which they articulated a new-found infatuation with the rural and essentially came to blame Trump's election on rural, white, working-class voters. Headlines read: "'Deaths of Despair' in Rural America Helped Trump Win His Presidency,"[1] "Trump Is Only Popular in Rural Areas,"[2] and "How Trump Seduced the White Working Class by Preying on Their Physical Pain."[3] In their attempts to explain, "Why Rural America Voted for Trump,"[4] as one headline in the New York Times read, those who sloppily tethered Trump's political ascension to rural, white, working-class voters necessarily ignored a great deal. Exit polls show that voters with annual incomes of less than $49,999 voted *more often* for Clinton than for Trump. As income *increased,* so did the number of people in that income bracket who voted for Trump.[5] While it is true that the majority of voters in rural areas did vote for Trump, this common narrative ignores several key things: 35 percent of voters in *cities* also voted for Trump (59 percent for Clinton), while 50 percent of voters in suburbs did the same (45 percent of suburban votes went to Clinton). And, further, while 62 percent of rural votes went to Trump (and 34 percent to Clinton), the sheer number of urban voters means that the actual number of voters who live in urban areas and voted for Trump is higher than the actual number of rural voters who did the same.[6] In many ways, then, it seems that the rural working class was the most simple scapegoat. How might our narratives of the election, the state of the nation in 2021, and future political possibilities be different if, for instance, headlines read: "Why Middle-Class Suburbanites Voted for Trump?"

Just a couple of years prior to the election, once marriage equality seemed imminent, mainstream gay rights groups turned their attention to the rural and launched expensive campaigns claiming to address LGBTQ issues in the rural United States for the first time in their organization's history—and, in the process, the rural came to occupy a new place in gay politics. I view these two things, marriage equality and the turn to the rural, as related. As gay rights activists had worked successfully at both the state and federal levels to roll back restrictions on gay marriage, they were keenly aware that the issue that they had relied upon in order to galvanize broad support for gay rights was about to be resolved. Concerned about the future of their movement, activists connected to national gay rights groups and governmental bodies convened to talk about what had not been done, and they floated the idea of turning to rural America.[7] In 2014, the Human Rights Campaign launched "Project One America" and the U.S. Department of Agriculture, in collaboration with the National Center for Lesbian Rights and other gay rights groups, held their first Rural LGBT summit. When I first learned about these campaigns, I was intrigued and, admittedly, excited, although cautiously so. Even a superficial focus on rural LGBTQ issues, I thought, marked a shift in the efforts of national LGBTQ organizing, and could enable new possibilities for rural queer studies scholars. Or so I hoped.

Beyond these campaigns, bloggers and journalists increasingly have taken an interest in rural LGBTQness over the last decade. In fact, with increasing frequency over the last several years, friends, colleagues, and students have sent and continue to send me news articles and blog posts on the topic, which speaks to an increase in the circulation of these ideas among those interested in LGBTQ studies and activism. In the months prior to my writing this chapter, headlines in major news outlets proclaimed: "How 'Real America' Became Queer America," "Nearly 4 million LGBTQ People Live in Rural America and 'Everything Is Not Bias and Awful,'" and "The Last Frontier for Gay Rights: A Powerful Liberal Activist, a Rural Conservative Town and a Debate that Won't End."[8] Despite the increase in the circulation of cultural commentary surrounding rural queerness, many of these texts, which often proclaim to want to diversify representations of LGBTQ life by focusing on the rural, leave intact the very metronormativity that has rendered rural LGBTQ life illegible. In short, metronormativity continues to saturate many of these articles, as well as cultural representations and LGBTQ political campaigns focused on LGBTQ rurality more broadly.[9] Furthermore, even among these articles, cultural representations, and campaigns, very few focus on either the Midwest or on women, an absence I noted when I first began the initial research for this book in 2010 (Thomsen 2016). Indeed, many of the issues that I observed in representations of rural queer life in 2010 remain evident in what has been produced in the decade since—including painting the rural as negative and focusing on the U.S. South. To put it colloquially, the more things change, the more they stay the same.

In this chapter, I reflect on what we might learn about the relationship of metronormativity to visibility politics through a retrospective look at how representations of rural queerness have changed over the course of the last decade and how they have stayed the same, despite the appearance of change. The chapter contains two parts. In the first section, I return to the roots of this project to think about the relationship of visual representation to visibility politics. When I became infatuated with Jene Newsome's case in 2010 and tried to make sense of the differences between the discourses that gay rights supporters discussing Newsome and Newsome herself used (see chapter 1), I turned to the internet, hoping to find additional cases to reflect on alongside Newsome's. Considering the common assumption (both at the time and today) that LGBTQ people in rural places are increasingly finding community via the internet, I expected to find an array of online representations of LGBTQ women in the rural Midwest. I found remarkably few. I begin this chapter here with an analysis of the Suburban and Rural Gay Life Flickr account I conducted in 2010, arguing that the absence of visible representations of LGBTQ women within the images on the site functions as part of the story, as evidence itself of the limits of visibility politics. I then conduct a similar analysis of current rural gay Instagram accounts, demonstrating that my analysis from a decade ago remains relevant in a moment in which the rural and rural queer ostensibly have become more visible, so to speak.

At the same time, as the very existence of rural LGBTQ Instagram accounts and increased cultural commentary around rural queerness suggests, we can no longer effectively analyze rural queerness primarily through the lens of absence. In the second part of this chapter, I turn my attention to the first campaigns and events that mainstream gay rights groups launched related to rural place: the Rural LGBT Summits organized by the United States Department of Agriculture and National Center for Lesbian Rights, the Human Rights Campaign's "Project One America," and a rural LGBT event held at the White House. In so doing, I examine how the rural is produced by national gay rights groups conducting outreach *in rural areas* as well as those liberal supporters of this work. Through analyzing these campaigns and events, none of which existed when I started this project, I consider the possibilities and limits associated with gay rights groups' recent turn to the rural. Ultimately, I argue that a stated focus on rural place may do nothing to shift perceptions about place or inspire a more nuanced approach to understanding differences that manifest along spatial lines.

Absence as Evidence: Suburban and Rural Gay Life at Flickr.com

Flickr is an image-hosting and -sharing application through which participants can upload and organize photographs or videos and communicate with groups of like-minded people. Flickr notes that it is "home to tens of billions of photos and two million groups," up from approximately five billion images in 2010. One key difference between Flickr and Instagram, its even more popular cousin, is that Flickr is meant for sharing photographs within groups, including among those who have assembled as the Suburban and Rural Gay Life group. In what follows, I draw from an analysis I conducted in 2010 of this group and the images they shared.

First, an overview: The Suburban and Rural Gay Life account is not attached to a particular region or locale. It also, as its name suggests, conflates the rural and suburban, positioning both in relation to the urban and implying that nonurban-ness is a commonality around which LGBTQ people might gather. In September 2010, its 124 members had posted 388 photographs. Of these, 190 overtly evoked a sense of place: landscapes, flowers, foods, and animals suggestive of rurality dominated the photographs.[10] The prominence of such imagery speaks to the importance of place to contributors' constructions of themselves as well as their collective construction of rural gays. Such representations of rural gayness reproduce dominant conceptions of the rural as "natural or pure spaces," as a "refuge away from the oppressive spaces of the city" (Johnston and Longhurst 2010, 95)—but, importantly, they do so in the service of disrupting other dominant narratives of the rural as homophobic, backwards, and dangerous for LGBTQ people, recapitulating hegemonic ideas about the rural in the service of disrupting common assumptions about queer rurality.

Perhaps somewhat ironically, the version of queer rurality in circulation within this Flickr group—the very existence of which some might say makes visible the presence of LGBTQ people in nonurban places—relies on an erasure of overt sexuality. The group moderator directs its members: "Please avoid pornography or nudity. There are plenty of other groups available on Flickr for that. If they are posted, they will be deleted." Group members have obeyed. Images of people on the site, which are far less prominent than those of place, feature normative and intelligible same-sex relations rather than any explicit sexual content. It is through the simultaneous erasure and visibility of sexuality within the Flickr group that participants come to constitute good (homonormative) rural folks *and* good (homonormative) gays. In fact, the possibility of rural gayness depends upon constructing both gays as normal and unthreatening and the rural as idyllic and unthreatening.[11] If the rural is understood as unsafe or homophobic, gays cannot plausibly exist there happily. Likewise, images that frame gays as outside of normative constructions of the gay subject challenge representations of the rural as wholesome.

Who constitutes the normative gay subject here is clear: they might not be urban, but they are still men. The vast majority of the photographs were posted by (people who presumably wish to be read as) men, the top five contributors to the site were men, and images of men dominate the site. Of the site's 388 photographs, 124 contain men, often as the sole person in the photograph. Forty-five of these images include different configurations of two men who are presumably meant to be read as coupled based on the actions captured within the image, comments provided by the photographer or other group members, or as understood within the context of other photographs posted on the site. By contrast, only twenty images contain people recognizable as women or girls, including two of young girls, one of flag dancers, mixed-gender groups of friends, a (potential) family, and one LGBTQ political activist. Aside from the activist holding a protest sign, none of these images of women connote their sexuality or desire.

Even more striking, the site contains just *one* photograph of affectionate or coupled women.[12] In this image, two women enjoy a moment of intimacy outside in the rain, hidden from the camera by a bright blue umbrella, rain drops falling into the puddles filling their (rural or suburban) street, complete with cookie-cutter homes, a U.S. flag, and a nondescript car—a picture of normalcy that is fully in line with the group's representation of rural and suburban gay people as firmly rooted in their communities.[13] The kissing women stand in the center of a neighborhood's flooded street, taking the time to kick up their feet and share a moment of intimacy. The position of the umbrella at once shields the lovers from the photo's viewers and makes them visible to their rural or suburban community. But these women are not concerned with the neighbors. They own this street. They are not in a rush. They belong here.

In many ways, this anomalous image exists outside of the norms established by the Flickr group and challenges their stated purpose: "While suburban and rural gay life might not be quite as visible as gay life in the cities, we are out there and are living our lives. Here's your chance to show it off."[14] The women in this image, as presented by their photographer, are not interested in showing it off. They are not interested in using this site to increase the visibility of rural and suburban gays. In the *only* photograph of two women together, in which sexuality is hinted at but not made explicit, the women are veiled behind an umbrella. Viewers are, of course, meant to assume their intimacy. The genders, and thus sexualities, of the women are largely ambiguous, only made clear in a comment by Jackson H., the photographer who posted the image: "love(EXPLORE) . . . hahaha i didnt have a guy with

"Love(EXPLORE)," an image posted in Suburban and Rural Gay Life at Flickr.com.

me so is [*sic*] used 2 girls hahahah." Jackson's light-hearted comment suggests that he would have preferred to have been in the photograph with another man. Within the context of this site, the comment also suggests that Jackson H. recognized that his posting a photograph of two women, an obvious rarity, required an explanation.

The dearth of representations of women on the Flickr site, as well as the veiled or partial visibility in the site's sole image of two intimate women, was my first clue that visibility is not terribly important to rural LGBTQ women, a trend evident online more broadly. I have yet to locate a single blog or website authored by an LGBTQ-identified woman from the rural Midwest. Of course, it is possible that these women are blogging and creating websites without writing about their sexuality or that their blogs and websites are not open to public viewing. In either of these speculative cases, the women would not be utilizing this medium as a way to increase visibility or gain the rights to which increased visibility ostensibly will lead.

The lacunae of online representations of LGBTQ rural women—including but not limited to their striking absence on sites dedicated to rural gay life, here exemplified through the Flickr group—is an argument for the significance of a null set: the online invisibility of rural LGBTQ women, from the Midwest or otherwise, speaks to the limits of visibility politics and contextualizes the differences I noted between Jene Newsome's approach and those of liberal gay rights supporters discussing her case (see chapter 1), which drove me to seek additional cultural representations of rural LGBTQ women. But I conducted this analysis of media representations of rural queer life in September 2010, before any major gay rights organizations had launched campaigns in the rural United States and prior to the existence of Instagram, another image-hosting and -sharing site whose popularity has since surpassed that of Flickr. Instagram gave us not only the hashtag #Instagay but also rural gay accounts so popular they have made it onto widely circulating lists of the best LGBTQ accounts. In fact, the author of one such list states that of all online social media platforms, "It's Instagram . . . to which queer culture has moved."[15] So, let's move with it, with the goal of analyzing what an ostensible increase in rural queer visibility means for my analysis of visibility politics.

Time Travel: Instagram Ten Years Later

Instagram was launched on October 6, 2010, just a couple of weeks after I completed the analysis of Flickr's Suburban and Rural Gay Life account. On its first day in the world, 25,000 people joined Instagram. Just a decade later, more than one billion people worldwide have Instagram accounts. In 2016, Autostraddle—a website that describes itself as a "feminist online community for multiple generations of kickass lesbian, bisexual & otherwise inclined ladies (and their friends)" whose mission is to gain "equality and *visibility* for all marginalized groups and ultimately . . . to change the world" (emphasis added)[16]—posted a list of "16 Lesbian, Bisexual and Queer Instagram Accounts to Introduce You to Our Herstory."[17] That same year, Mashable posted a similar list of can't-miss LGBTQ Instagram accounts.[18] Mashable and Autostraddle are very different types of sites. Autostraddle, which gets 3.5 million hits monthly from one million unique users, is decidedly queer woman centered. The content on Mashable, by contrast, is not necessarily LGBTQ, progressive, or even political. The site, which gets a whopping 45 million unique hits monthly, describes itself as "a global, multi-platform media and entertainment company," after all.[19]

Despite these differences, there is remarkable overlap in the Instagram accounts included on both lists. Of the fourteen and sixteen individual Instagram accounts that make up the Mashable and Autostraddle lists, respectively, five accounts appear on both lists. It is not terribly surprising that one of the overlapping accounts is the single account connected to rural queerness on either list: @queerappalachia.[20] One might assume that this overlap reflects either progress among gay activists, who are expanding their representations of queer life to include rural LGBTQ people in ways that would have been unimaginable a decade ago, or, alternatively, the dearth of representations of rural queerness on Instagram.

Before providing an overview of the rural queer Instagram landscape, I first reflect on the Mashable and Autostraddle authors' commentaries on the @queerappalachia account, as described within their lists. The author of the Autostraddle list notes, for example, that the @queerappalachia account "is absolutely essential viewing, whether you're *a rural queer looking for community* or an urban queer looking to be a better ally to queer folks who don't live in your trendy city" (emphasis added). For this author, community-less rural queers are necessarily looking for community, something urban queers have found and, thus, the latter are in a position to actively seek out ways to support their less well-off rural brethren. While Autostraddle describes rural queers as always already searching (for that which they could not possibly have), Mashable describes the @queerappalachia Instagram account as the best place to find "queer rural Appalachian memes (and social services)." Notably, this is the only time the author mentions social services in the article, a move that functions to imply that LGBTQ people in other places do not need services, and, further, that those in Appalachia do, of course. But do not get too excited about "Instagram's best account for rural queer Appalachianism," because, as the author notes, the "competition is, uh, limited." The author's playful use of "uh" in their assertion speaks to that which we think we know: that there would not be other rural queer accounts, of course, and the thought that there might be is quite funny.

We ought to pause here to ask: What if rural queers are not using the internet to find LGBTQ community in the ways in which the New York City–based author of the Autostraddle list imagines? What if they aren't actually looking for that community or, by gosh, feel as if they already have community?! We also ought to ask what the competition, to use Mashable's term, looks like and, more importantly, what the landscape of rural LGBTQ Instagram accounts suggests about visibility politics?

My research assistants, who are far more adept at using social media than I am, and I set out to answer these questions, searching Instagram using every possible combination of rural, Midwest(ern), and gay(s), queer(s), lesbian(s). What we found suggests that all of queer culture actually has *not* moved to Instagram, despite Mashable's assertion. This point should not be taken as a suggestion that there is a lack of representation of rural queerness on Instagram; to the contrary—although no other accounts have created anywhere near the 2,825 posts or have nearly the 172,000 followers that @queerappalachia has, perhaps, in part, because this account has made it onto the very lists I discuss here.[21] @countryqueers is the next most robust account dedicated to rural queerness I could find; the account has posted 645 images and has 6,786 followers. Like @queerappalachia, the account is connected to the South, although it does not make this clear in its bio, describing itself as "a multimedia oral history project gathering rural & small town LGBTQ+ stories since 2013."[22] The account's connection to the South is evident in its inaugural post, which includes an image of a cell phone resting on top of a paper map of West Virginia. And clicking on the link in the account's bio takes one to the website of the Highlander Research and Education Center, which is based in Tennessee. As such, it is not terribly surprising that very few of @countryqueers' posts include tags that link the images to the Midwest. Other rural queer accounts, such as @ruralqueers, @ruralqueer, @queerrural, exist and are public, but none of the administrators of these accounts have posted a single picture.

Furthermore, none of these accounts are specific to women or to the Midwest, of course. @midwest_queers, which is specific to the Midwest, as its name suggests, has posted just fifteen pictures, all of which are selfies of sultry gay men. @mwqueercollective (where "mw" is short for Midwest) exists but has not posted a single photo and has no followers.

@countrylesbians, which is not specific to the Midwest but does center women, has posted seven photos, none of which suggests any particular connection to the Midwest. @midwest_lesbian_moms, the only account specific to Midwestern LGBTQ women has no posts or followers, and is not necessarily connected to the rural Midwest. Personal accounts such as @midwest_gay, @midwest_gays, @gaymidwest, @midwest_lesbian, @midwest_lesbians, and @lesbian_midwest appear to exist, but they are not public.

As it turns out, if you are looking for rural, Midwestern, LGBTQ women, Instagram will not help you much more than Flickr would have a decade ago. In fact, we did not find a single public account by and for this demographic—or at least not an account in which its owner marks that she is an LGBTQ woman in the rural Midwest. In many ways, the arguments I made in 2010 become more pronounced when considering cultural representations of queer rurality that did not exist a decade ago—including those associated with the three aforementioned rural LGBTQ campaigns and events, to which I now turn.

The Elusive Lesbian Farmer: A Discussion of the Rural LGBT Summit

In the summer of 2016, lesbian farmers got conservative radio show host Rush Limbaugh all hot and bothered. Reflecting on the group in his unmistakable voice, Limbaugh shrieked, "Have you heard the latest Democrat scam? Have you heard about the Agriculture Department's financial grants to lesbian farmers? . . . I never before in my life knew that lesbians wanted to be farmers." The "scam" to which Limbaugh was referring was the LGBT Rural summit, which was held on August 18 in Des Moines, Iowa, and organized by the United States Department of Agriculture (USDA) in collaboration with the National Center for Lesbian Rights (NCLR) and the True Colors Fund (an organization for homeless LGBT youth founded by musician Cyndi Lauper). Although the USDA and company had organized fourteen similar summits since its inaugural event on June 6, 2014, in Greensboro, North Carolina, the summit in Iowa was the first to garner national attention.

Limbaugh, along with his fellow conservative bloggers and pundits, consistently described the event as one for lesbian farmers—to celebrate them, recruit them, or use them to "replace conservative farmers."[23] According to Limbaugh, the summit was part of a broader "disinformation campaign":

> What the point of this is, folks, it's not about lesbian farmers. What they're trying to do is convince lesbians to become farmers. . . . They are trying to bust up one of the last geographic conservative regions in the country, and that's rural America. Rural America happens to be largely conservative. Rural America is made up of self-reliant, rugged individual types. They happen to be big believers in the Second Amendment. So here comes the Obama regime with a bunch of federal money and they're waving it around, and all you gotta do to get it is be a lesbian and want to be a farmer and they'll set you up. . . . I'm like you; I never before in my life knew that lesbians wanted to be farmers. I never knew that lesbians wanted to get behind the horse and the plow and start burrowing. I never knew it. But apparently enough money can make it happen, and the objective here is to attack—they're already attacking suburbs . . . and they're going after every geographic region that is known to be largely conservative. They never stop, folks. They are constantly on the march.[24]

What a feminist- or queer-inclined reader likely finds fantastical here is the tethering of lesbian farmers to a conspiracy by the Obama administration, to imagined threats to the Second Amendment, and to attacks on (families in) the suburbs, in addition to the suggestion that federal funding is easily accessible. (Ha! All you need is a pitchfork and a vagina, folks!) What a feminist- or queer-inclined reader is perhaps less likely to find fantastical is the suturing of homophobic conservatism to rural place, the need for a rural LGBT summit (because of rural homophobia), and the possibility that such an event might center lesbian farmers—all of which, I learned through participating in this event, also turn out to be fantasies.

On the evening prior to the summit, while en route to dinner with the summit organizers, I learned about Rush Limbaugh's comments. One of the event organizers read aloud Limbaugh's framing of the event and, together, we laughed. At the same time, we were keenly aware that such commentary could lead to backlash and also might inspire additional press to attend the event. Amid our joking, we collectively brainstormed how we might address any potential fallout. In the end, there was none. Limbaugh's commentary had very little effect on the summit. While a few members of the local press covered the event, reporters or activists overtly associated with any political camp never appeared. Neither did the lesbian farmers, for that matter.

The summit began as many of the other summits had, with a welcome by the mayor as well as Tiana Banks and Ashlee Davis, two employees of the USDA and the primary event organizers. Banks and Davis gave an overview of what was to come and highlighted the work of Donna Red Wing, executive director of One Iowa, the USDA's local collaborative partner for the summit. I then gave a synopsis of the field of rural queer studies and outlined its relationships to feminist and queer studies and LGBTQ activism before highlighting some key findings from my research that I anticipated would be interesting to summit attendees.[25] Following an open-floor conversation I facilitated as part of the event's opening discussion, the morning panel, moderated by Julie Gonen from the National Center for Lesbian Rights, focused on economic security and health care for LGBTQ people in rural places. During lunch, Tom Vilsack, former governor of Iowa and the then USDA secretary, gave a keynote address. The afternoon sessions included four breakout panels: LGBT Youth, LGBT Seniors, Family Law, and LGBT Farmers/Agriculture. *One* of the four breakout panels, then, addressed issues related to LGBTQ farmers; this panel was composed of five men and one woman, who began her introduction by stating that she is *not* a farmer. Further, men composed the vast majority of conference attendees. We might ask how a day-long conference at which *one* of four breakout panels focused on agriculture and LGBT life—which included one woman who is not a farmer—at a summit attended primarily by men came to be described as an event for lesbian farmers?

Considering the fact that there were essentially no lesbian farmers at an event ostensibly for lesbian farmers, it seems likely that the goal of the conservative commentary surrounding the summit was not to provide an accurate description of the event. Some scholars responded to Limbaugh's commentary, claiming that its function was to trivialize and mock the summit. In an article on NBC's website, entitled "Why Is Rush Limbaugh So Afraid of Lesbian Farmers?," Julie Moreau, a feminist political scientist, draws from the reflections of Colin Johnson, a rural queer studies scholar, to discuss the ways in which the mockery of the summit relies on both sexist and metronormative assumptions:

> It's the lesbian part of lesbian farmer—the woman part of farmer—that makes it the definitive joke on the right. From the position of somebody who imagines rural people to be these "independent" [men], women farmers strike [Limbaugh] as absurd. . . . People who come from farm families know women have been directly involved in farming. The sexism of that statement is profoundly disturbing and an insult to everyone who comes from a farming family.[26]

Limbaugh's commentary is as informed by metronormativity as it is sexism. As Johnson argues, "Limbaugh is also relying on the stereotype of rural America as homophobic and 'backwards.' . . . It strikes people as inherently funny" that LGBTQ people might (want to) live in rural places. Moreau suggests that this is "because of the equation of rurality with religiosity and conservatism by *people like Limbaugh*" (emphasis added). People like Limbaugh, sure, *but also* those self-identified liberals who responded to Limbaugh. Put otherwise, it is too easy to blame the illegibility of the (literally nonexistent, in this case) lesbian farmer on right-wing ideologues. It is also fundamentally inaccurate. In what follows, I outline liberals' responses to Rush Limbaugh's discussion of lesbian farmers, suggesting that such responses rely on stereotypical portrayals of rurality not terribly distinct from Limbaugh's. When it comes to imagining and representing rurality, conservatives and liberals are, it turns out, on the same page: the rural is made up of conservative, gun-toting farmers and is devoid of happy, safe, and liberated LGBTQ people.

Celebrating Lesbian Farmers: Liberals' Responses to Limbaugh

Thom Hartmann, host of the Washington D.C.–based "number one progressive talk show" *The Thom Hartmann Program*, responded to Limbaugh's critiques of the summit through caricaturing the rural in ways that overtly yoke the rural to homophobia and hate:

What part of the United States is the most intolerant of diversity? I think that you could say history shows that it is the rural
parts of this country. It was in rural Texas where . . . the young
man—I'm very sorry I'm forgetting his name 'cause this was just
a horrific crime that led to all kinds of outcomes. . . . The young
gay man who was dragged to his death behind a truck . . . a
decade or so ago. . . . Crimes against gay people in rural communities are . . . legendary is not quite the right word . . . and
of course against people of color as well. But this specifically
was an attempt by the United States Department of Agriculture and the National Center for Lesbian Rights to reach out
to gay people in rural communities and say we're going to help
you feel safe. You have a right to be here too. . . . Don't LGBT
people have a right to be part of America without fear, without
harassment?[27]

Hartmann subsequently played the aforementioned and widely circulating clip of Limbaugh shrieking, "I never before in my life knew
that lesbians wanted to be farmers. Nobody's ever heard of a clamoring
among lesbians to be farmers. Lesbians are claiming that they're discriminated against in a lot of ways but you've never heard them say that
farming is unfair to them." Hartmann responded:

Right, going off on this and trying to make it funny. And it's
not. Giving more purchase, giving more power, giving more
legitimacy to people who would ridicule, trash, harm, ultimately
kill—Matthew Shepard was his name, the young man who was
dragged behind the truck—who would kill people like Matthew Shepard. Doing that is not only bad programming . . . it is
un-American.[28]

Despite Hartmann's confident assertion to the contrary, Matthew Shepard was not dragged behind a truck; the person Hartmann presumably meant to reference here was James Byrd Jr., a Black man killed by
white supremacists who beat him, urinated on him, and dragged him
behind a truck by his ankles until he died. Byrd died in Jasper, Texas.
Matthew Shepard, on the other hand, was a white gay man remembered
for his death at the hands of homophobes, who—the story goes (see

chapter 1)—tied him to a fence, tortured him, and left him to die over several days.[29] Shepard died in Laramie, Wyoming. Approximately a decade after their deaths, these two men—remembered as victims of two different types of hate—were joined together through the passage of the Matthew Shepard and James Byrd Jr. Hate Crimes Prevention Act.

Beyond this, the circumstances of their deaths are very different, not only because of the motivations of the killers, but also because of the locations of the murders. Laramie is the third largest city in Wyoming, a state with a total population of just five hundred thousand. Jasper is a town of 7,500 people in a state with twenty-seven million people. Rather than a simple mistake, this conflation of the deaths of two men—by a progressive radio show host attempting to show his support for the LGBT Rural Summit—reflects precisely the metronormativity among liberals to which I am pointing here: all rural places are so "intolerant of diversity" that we need not distinguish between rural places or the people who live (and, in this case, die) there. Rural place, and its lives and deaths, matter so little that we conflate them to argue for the dangerousness of rural place. It is so dangerous—a place where people would "ridicule, trash, harm, and kill" LGBTQ people— that it is "un-American." This variety of commentary simultaneously displaces the rural from the United States and from LGBTQ life.

Such representations of rural LGBTQ life are not, of course, limited to Hartmann. Samantha Schacher, a host of *PopTrigger*, an "unfiltered talk show"[30] based in Los Angeles, California, and hosted on the Young Turks Network, laughed as she introduced the episode entitled "Lesbian Farmers Invading Rural USA." For Schacher and other liberal supporters of the event, Limbaugh is not meant to be taken seriously. His comments are, for them, despite Hartmann's claims to the contrary, quite funny. In the episode, which has a distinct light-heartedness to it, Schacher says, "There are farmers and there are people in rural areas who are same-sex couples and *they need outreach* and *they need help.* And the reason they have this initiative is to reach these people" (emphasis added). She continues:

> There are so many statistics—I don't have them in front of
> me—that talk about the discrimination . . . against the LGBTQ
> community but even more so in these rural areas. So you can
> imagine that because they're discriminated against or they're

not offered certain jobs—and it said specifically transgender
men and women of color—if they're not offered jobs, they need
help. Again, this is *an assistance program* to help people that
aren't getting a fair shot like some privileged people out there.
So, it's important to make sure there is outreach especially in
these rural communities (emphasis added).[31]

The problem here is not just this framing of the rural—always in need
of help and outreach, always a site of discrimination, intolerance, and
related joblessness—but also that these self-identified liberal commentators reproduce the very framing of the event crafted by Limbaugh
as one *for lesbian farmers.* Although Hartmann didn't believe that the
summit was about lesbian farmers, calling this framing "not real," other
liberal commentators, including those on *Pop Trigger,* reproduced the
idea that the summit is "an assistance program" with particular relevance for lesbian farmers. Grace Baldridge, another cohost of *Pop Trigger,* laughed as she described Limbaugh's comments as "a little bit true"
because "lesbians love farming!" Baldridge's evidence for her position
included a Facebook post from her girlfriend on the topic and the accompanying comments by her Facebook friends, some of whom apparently were excited by the possibility of starting a (lesbian) farm. In
response to Baldridge's story, Hasan Piker, the third cohost, exclaimed,
"Oh my god, maybe [Limbaugh] is right!" To be clear, the summit series
is in no way an assistance program and, frankly, the events would not
help a lesbian (become a) farmer in any material manner. The rural
LGBTQ person has so little cultural resonance that it is difficult for
urban LGBTQ people and supporters of LGBTQ issues to imagine the
rural outside of a farming framework and to imagine that there might
be issues particular to rural LGBTQ life—outside of discrimination,
intolerance, or farming—that such a summit could address.

This very cultural illegibility is particularly overt in the reporting
on the event by Cenk Uygur, host of *The Young Turks,* a liberal news
outlet that claims it is the largest online news show in the world. In
response to the conservative claim that the summit "will teach lesbian
and transgender hillbillies how to get subsidies from the government
like rural housing loans and 'community facility grants,'"[32] Uygur
laughed as he joked, "Now, I didn't know that there were lesbian farmers, because I put no thought into it. . . . I don't know that there is [such]

a thing as transgender hillbillies. I don't think that is a thing." Uygur, in his attempt to mock conservative responses to the summit, laughed at the thought of the very existence of LGBTQ people in rural places, saying "I didn't know that there was much bullying on the farm. I didn't know that farmers ran into each other that often. But OK, [the summit] seems like a perfectly normal, in fact, quite boring get-together, if you will."[33] For Uygur, LGBTQ people in rural places are people he didn't know existed, people who are not "a thing." In making such comments, Uygur, along with Tom Hartmann and the *Pop Trigger* hosts, reveals the degree to which rural LGBTQ people and issues remain unintelligible, even for those supporters of LGBTQ rights.

It is striking that none of those (conservatives or liberals) who discussed this case addressed what actually transpired at the summit; none reached out to the series organizers, summit attendees, or activists in these locales. Perhaps even more surprisingly, the summit organizers did not make clear what transpired at the summit series. According to a press release put out by Drake University, where the Des Moines summit was held, the event "aims to elevate the voices of the rural LGBT community, highlight the important federal policy efforts to protect this community, and identify next steps to ensure all rural communities have access to the resources they need."[34] What is missing from this description as well as the related conservative and liberal commentary is what actually was discussed at the summit. As such, we lose out on a great deal—understanding the materiality of rural LGBTQ people's lives, tensions that emerge between the approaches of national LGBTQ organizers and the people in the places where they drop in, issues that are particular to rural LGBTQ people, and how events like the Rural LGBT Summit (and the discourses surrounding it) both challenge and reproduce broader cultural assumptions about queer rurality. Even in discourses surrounding a series that ostensibly focuses on rural LGBTQness, the material realities of queer rurality are displaced through gross and unsubstantiated stereotypes that have been naturalized through the ubiquity of metronormativity. In none of the conversations about the summits that made it into broad circulation do we hear from anyone with knowledge about either the content of the summit or rural LGBTQ issues more broadly; these voices are overwritten by political commentary of urban LGBTQ people and supporters of LGBTQ issues—a form of epistemological, social, and political displacement also evident in Project One America, a second campaign a major gay rights group launched in 2014 in the rural United States.

Dispatches from Washington D.C., Part I: Project One America

Just six weeks prior to the first Rural LGBT Summit, the Human Rights Campaign unveiled Project One America, a campaign that seeks to "dramatically expand LGBT equality" in Alabama, Arkansas, and Mississippi. An HRC report accompanying the April 26, 2014, press release for the campaign launch states:

> Project One America is necessary because, after last year's historic U.S. Supreme Court rulings, this country is divided into two Americas when it comes to equality. In one America, *mostly on the coasts,* LGBT people enjoy nearly complete legal equality. But in the other America, *in the Midwest, the Great Plains, the Mountain West, and particularly in the South,* even the most basic protections of the law are nonexistent. (emphasis added)[35]

HRC's Project One America focuses on "the other America," the defining feature of which, for HRC, is its lack of LGBTQ equality. By contrast, in One America, a progressive coastal America, all is, apparently, well—an assertion that requires ignoring ongoing oppressions that transpire in urban and coastal places along the lines of race, class, gender, ability, nation, age, religion, and, yes, despite HRC's suggestion to the contrary, even sexuality. Such a place is imagined in binary relation to the noncoastal and homophobic "other" that the HRC has set out to fix. Although the HRC explicitly names that which is the other— "the Midwest, the Great Plains, the Mountain West, and particularly . . . the South"—they also leave out other important markers of place. In the five-page document explaining the Project One America campaign, never once does HRC deploy the words "urban" or "rural." We know, however, that the "one America" of the coasts is imagined as urban (the country's two largest cities are coastal, after all) while the "other America" is not. HRC makes this clear with the event they sponsored to launch the Project One America campaign: a screening of *deepsouth,* a documentary film that, as HRC says, "shines a light on a *region* in crisis and the often-ignored issues concerning LGBT communities of color in *rural America*" (emphasis added). Here, the South—one of the regions that makes up this "other America"—is necessarily rural.

Armed with a budget of $8.5 million and a three-year timeline, HRC identified nine goals it hoped Project One America would reach in each of the three Southern states it targeted. These included the oft-heard calls to "create safer environments for LGBT young people," "create more inclusive workplace[s] for LGBT people," "empower LGBT people (and straight allies) to come out," and "raise the visibility of LGBT people and issues with the general public." What is notable in the list of goals specific to HRC Mississippi, Alabama, and Arkansas is their very lack of specificity; the goals of this campaign simply mirror those of the national organization. This includes their prioritization of visibility and outness, both of which lack cultural traction in many rural places. HRC's geographically neutral, one-size-fits-all approach does not allow for a recognition of place-based complexity and manifests in their description of rural and noncoastal areas as part of the "other America." In a campaign titled Project One America, which assumes that the ways in which the "other America" does things are inherently less advanced than those of the "one America," this oversight may come as little surprise. Through Project One America, HRC displaces LGBTQ people from rural place and from an imagined rights-possessing gay subjectivity and also, ironically, displaces the place-based specificity of LGBTQ life from these campaigns. It does so through framing the United States as two distinct countries, one of which must be obliterated for the existence of the other.

Three months prior to the launch of the campaign, HRC cosponsored a panel discussion entitled "Bringing Equality Home: LGBT in Rural America" along with the National Center for Transgender Equality, the National Center for Lesbian Rights, and the National Gay and Lesbian Task Force. According to the HRC website, this event held on January 28, 2014, was "the first" on the topic and sought to address "current issues facing the LGBT community and individuals living with HIV/AIDS in rural America":

> It's critical that as a community we acknowledge and support
> the lived experience of LGBT communities across the country—

including those *struggling to thrive in rural areas.* According
to recent studies, LGBT people make up a significant portion
of the overall population in predominantly rural states, including Vermont, South Dakota, and Kentucky. Same-sex couples
living in the South are also more likely to be raising children
than couples living on either coast. Although the LGBT community has experienced a series of significant victories over the
past two years, many *LGBT people living in rural areas still face
systemic inequality.* Discrimination in health care, housing, and
employment often leads to an increased risk for poverty and
social isolation for LGBT families, and also creates an additional
barrier to accessing critical state and federal social services. We
hope yesterday's discussion will be the *first of many* highlighting
the needs of members of our community all across the country,
including in rural areas. (emphasis added)[36]

In this landmark event on rural LGBTQ issues, the rural is a caricature
of itself; it is a place where LGBTQ people face discrimination, poverty,
and social isolation and struggle to thrive. The other America, of course,
is the site of the "series of significant victories" for LGBTQ people. At
this point in this book, such a framing of rural place by LGBTQ rights
supporters and activists is likely unsurprising. What is surprising is that
nowhere in the 416-word description of the event posted on the HRC
website was the *location* of the event mentioned—and this is in a description of *the first* conversation in which HRC engaged in discussions
about issues related to (rural) place. HRC might have more accurately
framed their event as *HRC's* first conversation on rural LGBTQ issues,
as others had been engaging in similar conversations for quite some
time. By 2014, rural queer studies was already a vibrant (and growing!) subfield of LGBTQ studies; scholars had been publishing work on
LGBTQ rurality for decades, and four years earlier, in 2010, scholars
at Indiana University had organized an entire academic conference on
rural queer studies. Through a phone call to HRC and brief conversation with Robin Maril, senior legislative counsel at HRC and author of
the website post, I learned that the "first" conversation on rural LGBT
issues was, unsurprisingly, held at the HRC headquarters in Washington, D.C.[37]—where, approximately two years later, I found myself at a
meeting on rural LGBT issues held at the White House.

Dispatches from Washington D.C., Part II:
The White House Meeting

Friday, December 2, 2016, was a day of at least two firsts: the White House's first time convening a meeting on rural LGBTQ issues, and my first time attending a meeting at the White House. As I put on my white blazer and red lipstick in my hotel room, walked briskly toward 1600 Pennsylvania Avenue, braved the intense White House security, and, finally, wandered the stately corridors of the White House en route to the meeting room, I felt a strange mix of things. I was honored to be invited, excited to be a part of what I thought was a watershed moment, and anxious because I had no idea what to expect from the event—although I realized later that I did, indeed, have expectations. I also did not know exactly how I ended up on the invite list. I suspected it had to do either with my scholarship or my involvement with the Rural LGBT Summit series, in which I participated in Iowa earlier that year. When I first saw my colleagues who had spearheaded the summit series, I hugged them excitedly and asked if they knew how in the world I, an assistant professor in her first year of a tenure-track job, ended up at the White House?! All three of them informed me that they put me on their list of suggested invitees. In other words, my being there had less to do with my scholarship on its own and more to do with a network I had created through sharing my scholarship with activists—a realization that has informed my research, teaching, and activist engagements since, and upon which I reflect further in chapter 6.

Once the event started, it did not take long for my critical feminist and queer training to unravel the positive affects I had attached to the event. In short, I was surprised by the organizers' choice of panelists. Very few actually were working in rural areas, and, further, nearly all of the panelists—including those few living and working in the rural United States—were deploying discourses and strategies that rural queer studies scholars have critiqued for being steeped in and reproducing metronormativity. There was no discussion whatsoever about the specificity of rural queer life, and panelists' presentations largely started from the position that being an LGBTQ person in a rural place must be terrible. In sharing this reflection with one of my colleagues who had suggested that I be invited to the event, I noted my surprise that none of my fellow rural queer studies colleagues had been invited and, further, that the event would have looked much different if rural queer studies scholars had been involved with its conceptualization or actualization. My colleague, who organizes the aforementioned summits but was not involved with putting on the White House meeting, was receptive to these critiques, sharing with me that she had suggested that the event organizers invite me to speak on one of the day's panels, a suggestion that the D.C.-based organizers ignored.

Instead, the first speakers of the day included JoDee Winterhof, senior vice president of policy and political affairs at the Washington, D.C.–based Human Rights Campaign, and Dave Isay, a radio producer and founder of the award-winning StoryCorps, a New York City–based oral history project. Isay discussed his 2014 launching of Outloud, which the StoryCorps website describes as "an initiative to collect the stories of LGBT people in America."[38] I found this an odd way to start the day, particularly as neither speaker commented on the specificity of rural LGBTQ life. Instead, they discussed a project to which largely urban-based LGBTQ people had contributed and that reflects precisely the kinds of commitments to visibility politics that other rural queer studies scholars and I have critiqued for their metronormativity. Apparently, some of my fellow attendees found this opening panel curious too. In the brief Q&A session following the panel, an audience member asked "if the person from StoryCorps knew of any rural communities conducting oral history projects."[39] This question, as well as the inclusion of it in reflections on the event written by HB Lozito, the executive director of Green Mountain Crossroads in Brattleboro, Vermont, speaks to attendees' desire to think about the specificity of rural LGBTQ life.

This erasure of the rural at an event on rural LGBTQ issues also is evident in the discussion of the White House meeting posted on the HRC website: "Winterhof sat down with StoryCorps founder Dave Isay to talk about how LGBTQ Americans have used storytelling to create change. When people know someone who is LGBTQ, they are far more likely to support equality under the law. Beyond that, our stories can be powerful to each other." Notably, in their discussion of the value of storytelling, HRC says nothing at all about LGBTQ people who live in rural places. Instead, HRC champions precisely those strategies that scholars have argued do not resonate with LGBTQ people in rural places, approaches that I have suggested do not result in the kinds of social progress it is claimed they do (see Introduction), and further, that place the burden of eradicating homophobia on those marginalized by homophobia (see chapter 4).

HRC was not the only participating organization to reflect on the White House meeting afterward. In an article on the California Rural Legal Assistance Fund's (CRLA) website, Lisa Cisneros, the organization's program director, described her fellow panelists in the following manner: "Chris Wood from LGBT Technology Partnership and Institute in *rural Virginia*, Chris Hartman from the Fairness Campaign in *Kentucky*, and Erin Rook from Saving Grace in *rural Oregon*" (emphasis added).[40] Let's pause here: Chris Wood's LinkedIn page says he is based in the Washington, D.C., metro area; Chris Hartman and the Fairness Campaign are in Louisville, Kentucky, a city with approximately 800,000 residents; Erin Rook and Saving Grace are in Bend, Oregon, a city with a population of approximately 100,000. Cisneros's description of the day provides some context for her deployment of "rural" to describe fellow panelists' work:

> We discussed rural LGBTQ youth issues, the *challenges* facing LGBT people seeking employment in rural communities, the *prevalence of* anti-transgender *violence*, and the *lack* of quality data collection and cultural competency in our law enforcement agencies. (emphasis added)

For Cisneros, the rural is a place of challenges, violence, and a lack of cultural competency, a framing echoed by the organizations for which other panelists work. HRC described the event as one for "discuss[ing] the *problems* that LGBTQ Americans are facing in rural America" (emphasis added).[41] Cultivating Change, a group whose mission is to "valu[e] and elevat[e] LGBT agriculturists through advocacy, education, and community,"[42] stated, "The meeting will focus on strategies to *improve quality of life, increase opportunity*, and *enhance connectivity* for rural LGBT Americans." They continued, "Please join fellow rural LGBT leaders, organizations and Federal officials in this important event that will focus on *driving progress* through leadership, organizing and innovation" (emphasis added).[43]

Compare these framings of the Rural LGBT meeting at the White

House to that of a 2014 (nonrural) Pride White House event, posted by Obama staffers to the White House's website:

> Yesterday, for the sixth time since taking office, President Obama joined national, state, and local community leaders, business leaders, grassroots activists, elected officials, and others for an event *celebrating* Lesbian, Gay, Bisexual, and Transgender (LGBT) Pride Month at the White House. With the First Lady by his side, the President spoke about the tremendous *progress we have made* during the course of his Administration. (emphasis added)[44]

Pride month at the White House is for "celebrating" and recognizing the "tremendous progress" that has been made. When "rural" is added to the LGBTQ equation, such framings become unimaginable. The rural, by contrast, is a place of problems, where life needs to be improved, where progress needs to be stimulated. The metronormative stereotypes evident both at the event and in discussions of it made impossible a conversation about the issues that rural LGBTQ people actually do and do not experience. Put simply, the White House event, much like HRC's Project One America and the discussions of the Rural LGBT Summit, became another avenue for advancing and disseminating the very metronormativity evident across the work of gay rights groups. Under the guise of addressing rural place and the LGBTQ people who live there, LGBTQ rights activists and supporters further entrenched dominant ideas about rurality, reaffirmed their willful ignorance of place, and displaced LGBTQ people in rural places from both the rural and from LGBTQ life. Of course, the effacing, homogenizing, and writing over of the rural within LGBTQ movements and studies is nothing new—although the degree to which the relevance (and power!) of place is displaced in campaigns and events ostensibly meant to address LGBTQ rurality is, nonetheless, especially egregious.

What is new, however, is that national gay rights organizations and the federal government have begun to express concern over LGBTQ issues in the rural United States—something that we might read as enabling (thus far unactualized) possibilities. When I first learned about the campaigns I discuss here, I felt hopeful that they might offer possibilities both for complicating common ideas about LGBTQness and also for rural queer studies scholars. Up until this point, scholars have made arguments about how LGBTQ people in rural places relate to gay rights movements and vice versa by considering the ideologies *implicit* in movement discourses, strategies, and actions (or lack thereof). This is for a simple reason: until the launch of these campaigns, national gay rights groups had largely ignored rural areas, and as such, rurality was not something they discussed, making analyzing gay rights groups' discourses of rurality essentially impossible. The discourses surrounding the rural LGBT campaigns and events that I analyze here, then, represent new possibilities for both rural queer studies and also gay rights activists. They also speak to the difficulty of discussing and understanding rural LGBTQ life outside of the logics of metronormativity, even when the stated focus is on the rural.

{ 6 }

What's the Use?

Queer Critique in Motion

BY WAY OF CLOSING THIS BOOK, I want to reflect on the political and epistemological possibilities of unbecoming through considering it in relation to use, including the travel and affects that enable use and the use that enables travel and affective attachment. My desire to make these connections is inspired by Sara Ahmed who, in her book on the uses of use, notes that "What's the use?" is a question that is meant to gesture toward the pointlessness of something (2019). Drawing on Ahmed, we might ask: What's the use of the arguments I advance here? Of unbecoming as conceptual shorthand? Of feminist and queer theory more broadly? Gloria Steinem, who is likely the most well known activist in the history of U.S. feminism, might answer quite simply: nothing. There is no use. In fact, it is precisely academic feminism's valuing of education "in inverse ratio to its *usefulness* . . . its understandability" to which Steinem objects (emphasis added).[1] On the one hand, we might feel compelled to respond to such characterizations by articulating how and why feminist and queer theoretical ideas are, in fact, useful. On the other hand, we might want to resist the pull toward utilitarianism and usefulness, toward knowledge that has been deemed useful (Ahmed 2019). Indeed, feminist and queer theory are precisely the forms of knowledge that get called useless—by the right wing, by scientists, and even by feminist activists. Ahmed would likely tell us that we should resist the terms of this debate altogether, and, further, that doing so will allow us to actualize queer use—that is, using use, as Ahmed says, for queer purposes. Queer use may even involve "inhabit[ing] use all the more . . . [and] calling for knowledge that is useful to others, with this 'to' being an opening, an invitation, a connection" (222). Queer use includes inhabitation, allure, and travel. It strives to "releas[e] a potentiality that already resides in things given how they have taken shape. Queer use could be what we are doing when we release that potential" (200). The queer potential of use, the potential of queer use is precisely what I take up here: What potential, what use, resides in the shape of this book? Could another shape release its queer potentiality differently? What might releasing it look like?

In my case, answering the latter two questions looked like making a documentary film, through which I worked to translate the ideas of this book into an alternative shape and for an audience beyond those who might typically engage academic texts. The result: a 34-minute documentary short entitled *In Plain Sight* and a related educational website. Producing and directing this film stretched me because—well, perhaps it is time for me to come out, after all—I am a technophobe and luddite. Like my dad, who has never been on the internet or sent a text message, I hate technology. Gadgets are not my thing. And I knew *nothing* about film making going into this project. Throughout the process, I thought about quitting the entire endeavor many times, often expressing something akin to an expletive-laden "What's the use?" But my belief in the value of what Ahmed calls "queer doors"— "openings intended for some things to pass through [which] can end up providing an access point for others"—prevailed (2019, 203). My commitment to finishing the film is rooted in an unshakeable belief in feminist and queer theory's ability to inform thinking and action within and beyond the academy—their usefulness, if you will. But having encountered many Gloria Steinem-esque arguments from theory skeptics, I have come to believe that we need to invite people in otherwise. Perhaps we need to paint our queer door a brighter color.

In Plain Sight is my attempt to paint the door fuchsia. I rightly predicted that the film would allow me to converse about the intellectual ideas explicated throughout this book with new people and in new ways. I did not anticipate that the process of doing so would also raise new intellectual questions for me. When I told a colleague who was familiar with my critiques of visibility politics about my plan to make a film, she asked me, for example, if my making a film actually undermines the argument of my book. Why, she asked, would LGBTQ women in the upper Midwest who do not prioritize or value visibility agree to participate in a film—itself a form of visual representation? Toward the end of this chapter, I answer this question directly in order to consider the relationship between visibility politics and visual representation.

En route to getting there, I discuss interviewees' descriptions of their lives in relation to their thoughts on how others elsewhere imagine their lives. Ultimately, this conclusion outlines what I learned about the queer potential of this book's arguments regarding visibility politics—and particularly about unbecomingness through its relation to use—vis-à-vis *In Plain Sight*.

In Plain Sight: The Interviews

In summer 2016—five years after I conducted the interviews from which I draw in this book—I returned home to reconnect with some of my interviewees and to reinterview them for *In Plain Sight*. I returned again in the summers of 2017 and 2018 to conduct additional interviews, collect B-roll footage, and get feedback from some interviewees on drafts of the film-in-progress. When I conducted interviews as part of my initial research for this book, my goal was to get a sense of the lives of LGBTQ women in the rural upper Midwest. I asked many questions about where people are from, where they live now, and their relationship to place. It immediately became clear that the vast majority of the women with whom I spoke feel deeply connected to their place in the world, generally feel accepted in those places, and live full and rich lives that they would not choose to leave simply for some imagined gay community in some larger city.

Interviewees' desires to stay in the rural Midwest, as I argue throughout this book, are informed by their possessing radically different relationships to ideas about gay identity, community, and—above all—visibility than those that motivate the efforts of gay rights organizations and that they imagine are true for LGBTQ people in more metropolitan areas. As I discuss in chapter 2, my interviewees do not identify strongly with being a sexual minority and do not organize their lives around what they feel is a single aspect of their lives that is not any more important than other characteristics. They also identify strongly with being from or living in a rural place. Most express serious disdain for expectations that LGBTQ people be "out, loud, and proud" in a prescribed way, which gay rights groups link to social progress (rather unconvincingly, I might add, as I detail in the introduction). Further, their understandings of LGBTQ community are nuanced in ways I had not previously encountered. I asked interviewees about their relationship to gay communities, including if they feel like they have one and if they desire some iteration of gay community other than the one they have. One of my favorite interview moments occurred in response to this question: an interviewee quickly and casually responded that, yes, indeed, she had a gay community, but they were just all straight—an anecdote I also shared in the introduction. This understanding of community as people who support you, rather than people with similar social and political identifications, was reiterated by many of the women with whom I spoke.

When I returned home five and six years later to conduct interviews for my film, I asked some of the same questions I had asked previously as well as new questions informed by my reflections on themes that cut across the original set of interviews. New questions included: How do you think urban LGBTQ people would imagine your life? How would you describe your life? If you were to boil your previous answer down to three adjectives, what would they be? Women's responses to the latter two questions were overwhelmingly positive. Almost all interviewees responded to the question regarding how urban LGBTQ people imagine them with laughter and by lightheartedly referencing negative tropes commonly associated with rural life. Others responded with something akin to playful confusion, noting that they actually never had considered how they are imagined by people elsewhere.

In asking these questions in this way, I hoped to see if interviewees' distilled responses might confirm or complicate my reading of their lives, namely, (1) that they generally feel accepted, welcome, and supported in their rural communities and disconnected from or misunderstood by an imagined broader gay community, and (2) that such a disconnect is rooted in different conceptualizations of what visibility means and assumptions regarding its social value. With their answers on the table, and with five years of reflection behind me, I then shared with them the arguments I make in this book and that, I imagined, might also drive my film. This was, I thought, a risky move. What would I do if interviewees pushed back against my readings? Would I scrap the argument of my book if it did not line up with what a subset of my original interviewees said five years after I conducted the initial interviews? Would interviewees pull their participation in the film or book if they did not like my argument?

As it turns out, I wildly miscalculated the potential for risk. Most of my interviewees found my argument mundane, boring, and obvious. One interviewee stared at me blankly and then leaned forward slightly, as if to suggest she was waiting for more. Another joked, "They gave you a PhD for arguing that?!" We all laughed heartily at her mocking of me, but internally, I was beaming. Her reading of my argument as banal confirmed my analysis and gave me an opportunity to spell out exactly why this argument was intellectually innovative and politically important, something I began to do in my conversations with all interviewees from that point forward. Doing so not only reaffirmed my commitment to taking seriously interviewees' articulations of their lives, it also folded them into the intellectual work of the book and film. Through these conversations, I found that I often preferred talking with my interviewees—almost none of whom are academics nor engaged with LGBTQ studies—about my interventions to speaking with urban-based LGBTQ-identified academics and activists. Interviewees' easygoing engagement with the ideas presented in this book—alongside their largely positive framings of their lives and their lighthearted takes on how they imagine they are imagined (in less-than-glowing ways)—points to the degree to which the material realities of LGBTQ women in rural places have been displaced from common conceptualizations of LGBTQ life and provide opportunities for challenging metronormativity. Let's hear from these women one last time.

The Last Word

Georgie,[2] a middle-class white woman in her early sixties who was born and raised in rural South Dakota and now lives in a lake community of 140 people in the eastern part of the state, appeared to find my question regarding how others imagine rural LGBTQ people both charming and utterly ridiculous:

> I have to honestly say, when I think of lesbian couples in another part of the country [*laughs*], I don't. I don't. It's . . . a different world. I can't fathom, first of all, what it's like to live in such a huge city, where one thing in your life is so important. I can't, I can't imagine being that . . . tunnel visioned, I guess. Because that's not my world. My world is bigger than that. Granted, my world is [a community in rural South Dakota]. That's my

world. . . . In the grand sense, it's not that big. It is not big. Honestly, I've never considered how other people feel lesbian women are in South Dakota. I can't imagine that it's important to them. It just seems like they're so focused . . . on the issue that is theirs. You know, they're owning it . . . and that's working for them. So, them being concerned about a lesbian grandma in rural South Dakota? It's probably never . . . crossed their minds.

Georgie's world is both "not big" and bigger than that of metropolitan lesbians who are, as she describes, "tunnel visioned," and as such, unlikely to have ever thought about someone like her. Like Georgie, Angie, a working-class white woman in her midsixties who was born and raised in South Dakota and lives in western South Dakota, never before had considered the circulation of stereotypes of rural LGBTQ women. She found the idea both laughable and interesting:

I don't know how people in a big city would identify us. [My partner] could answer that, she's from Los Angeles, and she's been out here since like 1985. But they must just think we're a bunch of hillbilly dykes or something. I don't know [*laughs*], I don't know! But that would be an interesting thing to see.

While Angie notes that it would be interesting to learn how people in a big city think about rural lesbians, she is not willing to stray too far from home to find out the answer. In fact, neither Angie nor Mari, her Latina partner from Los Angeles, want to leave their home in South Dakota, which Angie describes as a "hidden paradise."

Other interviewees responded to my question by referencing stereotypes associated with rural place—ideas they found quite funny. Daryl and Joan, two middle-class white women in their early forties who live in southeastern South Dakota with their three children, stated that people likely assume:

D: That we probably all wear hats and live on a farm, pluck corn. We're not trendy. [Laughs] And you know, I have a friend out in San Diego that moved [there] from [South Dakota], and I think they kind of asked her, "Where's your cowboy hat?"

J: I think just in general people don't really understand the Midwest at all, whether you're gay or not gay, it doesn't matter. . . . They just think it's . . . fields everywhere.

D: You farm. You eat steak for every meal. And potatoes. . . . They probably look at us as not very culturally diverse, [not] appreciating music, arts, that we can dress cool.

J: [*laughs*] Well maybe not us, but there are people [who do]!

When I followed up to ask, "How would you describe the Midwest?" Daryl responded:

It's very laid back, but obviously it's not as progressive with some movements as like your East and West coasts. But I like that it's very friendly, that we've been to places where, you know, a "Hi," you don't . . . get that if you go to some of your bigger cities. . . . But I like that . . . you can be driving down a road and somebody's going to wave to you even though you don't know them. And you can always ask somebody for help and they're gonna help you. So I think it's very good values, especially when you're raising kids.

Just as Daryl and Joan find laughable the questions regarding how city people imagine rural lesbians, so too did Max, a Native genderqueer person in their midtwenties who lives in a small town in western South Dakota. Max grew up in a town of 1,000 people in South Dakota in which approximately half of the population is Native and the other half is white. They responded to my question about what people assume about rural LGBTQ life:

I think . . . the people who live in more big cities and more liberal areas who are part of the LGBTQ community think that we live in a bleak black hole. [Laughs] That's been my experience especially since my friend moved out to Seattle. And it's really not like that. I mean, yeah, there are some areas that . . . you kind of don't go there and you don't talk about it, but there is a lot more acceptance and a lot more safe space than most people think. And you have to find your own.

I then asked Max, "If you could dispel any myths, if you could tell [people] anything about what life is like [here, for you], what would it be?

> Probably in a lot of ways it's not that different. It's probably just a lot fewer of us here than there are in more populated areas. We still have our own get-togethers, we still have our own culture, we still fit in, and don't, in a lot of the same ways, because no matter where you go, people are people.

Just as Max highlights what they presume are similarities in life for rural and urban gays, so too does Karrie, a middle-class white woman in her late forties who was raised in a small town in South Dakota and now lives in the southeastern part of the state with her two daughters:

> I think that gays and lesbians in other parts of the country think that we're oppressed here, and we're really not terribly oppressed. There are isolated incidents of discrimination . . . but by and large, you learn to avoid situations that are negative, and sort of gravitate toward the positive. It's, it's like anywhere. I mean, if you have a certain religious belief that's maybe not considered mainstream where you live you probably would move out . . . unless you find other like-minded people—and I've been able to do that.

I then asked Karrie to boil down what she had said into three adjectives that she imagines LGBTQ people in urban spaces would use to describe her life:

> **K:** Oh dear. . . . One would be oppressed. Two would be . . . backwards. . . . Three would be . . . disadvantaged?
> **CT:** And if you had three words to describe your life here, what would they be?
> **K:** Um, peaceful, comfortable, and . . . not quite happy but close, pretty close to happiness.

Peaceful is a term that Toni, a white woman in her late forties who grew up in rural New York, also used to describe her life. Toni has lived and worked as a professor for nearly two decades in central Minnesota.

She responded to my question regarding how she imagines LGBTQ people in rural Minnesota are imagined:

> You'll probably get . . . the stereotypes about flannel. Maybe closeted, conservative, racist. Not very positive things, I don't think.

I followed up to ask Toni what three adjectives she would use to describe her life.

> Um, I think it's pretty peaceful. Pretty . . . affirming. I don't know how to put it any other way. I feel supported. So it's a supportive community. And again, it's not the queer community [I feel supported by], necessarily, but I feel that this community is supportive of all the different parts of who I am.

Kate, a white woman in her early forties, and her partner Jax, a white woman in her early fifties, were both born and raised in rural South Dakota. They dated for five years before getting married in 2016, and they live in rural southeastern South Dakota with their two teenage children. Kate responded to my question regarding how they imagine they are imagined by urban-based LGBTQ people, stating:

> Well, they still think we shit in outhouses [*laughs*], so . . . I think that they would be surprised. [A friend moved] here [from Arkansas]. As a gay woman, I think she was scared to come up here, and was surprised at how she was treated. . . . People tend to stay out of your business up here. But I feel like you ask someone out in California what it's like here, and they're gonna think it's oppressive and that we can't be out. I mean, I work at a Catholic hospital and I'm out and they don't have a problem with that.

I then asked Kate and Jax to list three adjectives that they thought people in California would associate with their lives.

> J: Oppressed.
> K: They probably think there's no hot lesbians here.
> J: They all look like a farmwife.

K: That is our running joke. When we see someone at the bar, it's like, are they a lesbian or are they a South Dakota farmwife, cause sometimes you can't quite tell the difference!

J: That line is fine, very fine. . . . Let's see . . . what would they think of us?

K: I would say oppressed.

J: They'd probably feel sorry for us, that we're stuck here.

I then asked the couple what words best describe their lives.

K: Comfortable.

J: Safe. Normal.

K: Easy.

J: Happy

Happy, easy, safe, normal, peaceful, comfortable, affirming, supported. These adjectives differ sharply from the stereotypes of rural LGBTQ life that my interviewees named and that circulate through the work of journalists and activists: oppressed, feel sorry for us, not hot, farmers, backwards, disadvantaged, closeted, conservative, racist, bleak black hole, hillbilly dykes.

Ultimately, my interviewees' assumptions regarding how those in urban areas view them are pretty accurate. In summer 2018, members of my research team attended the New York City Pride Parade to conduct short interviews with attendees in which they asked what they think life is like for lesbians in South Dakota. Their answers were largely in line with my interviewees' assumptions: heartbreaking, closeted, difficult, lonely, scary, sad, quiet, challenging, hard, secretive, does not exist, needs more safe spaces, needs more visibility, less access to knowledge. Other answers were less overtly negative: strong, powerful, brave, courageous, inspiring, at the forefront—but it probably doesn't seem that way, up-and-coming, improving. While each of the latter answers appears on the surface to be positive, all are rooted in the idea that it would be difficult to be an LGBTQ person in a rural place (and hence someone who is must be strong, powerful, brave) or that these places are behind (and thus have the capacity to be up-and-coming and to improve). Few outliers bucked this trend; of those that did—valid, hopeful, loving, exciting, and prideful—none were words used by my interviewees when they described their own lives.

How do we make sense of the descriptions of life for LGBTQ people in rural places offered by my interviewees alongside the assumptions that circulate about life for LGBTQ people in rural places, including, for instance, at the New York City Pride Parade? What skills and tools are required for undoing the metronormativity that renders illegible the happy rural queer? What epistemological and political possibilities might emerge if we resist the very metronormative frames that enable such assumptions? These are the questions that *Visibility Interrupted* has answered. Throughout this book, I have offered many reasons for resisting metronormativity and provided analyses that work in the service of doing so. Let me now share the reasons why my interviewees—whose concerns, I have argued, do not include becoming visible—participated in *In Plain Sight,* itself a form of visual representation.

The "Why" Question: Affective Attachments and the Performance of Normalcy

Inspired by my aforementioned interlocutor's question regarding why those interviewees whose insights generated my critiques of visibility politics would agree to be in a film, I asked interviewees this question directly. Their answers tended to fall into two categories: they know me and care about me, or they want to show that their lives are quite normal.

Jane is one interviewee whose answer was rooted entirely in the fact that we are close friends. We lived together for the majority of college, including while studying abroad in Thailand. For this book, I interviewed just one person I knew well prior to the interview and that person was Jane. For the film, I did not restrict my interviewee pool to those to whom I was not already affectively close, in part because the medium extirpates any guise of objectivity that academic scholarship often requires and also because reinterviewing people with whom I had developed connections through our initial interviews meant that this guise was already cracked. Many of my fondest memories of college, and indeed of my life, involve Jane. I knew that Jane was not enamored with the idea of being interviewed, and further, that our deep affective bond might have encouraged her to do something she otherwise would not have. I gestured toward this context when I asked: "You can pull out a bat and hit me if you want, but why did you agree to do this interview?" Jane responded, "Because I love you. . . . I laughed a lot and cried. I'm gonna have a headache." At the time of conducting this interview, I had not seen Jane for a few years. I found myself surprised by how much our interview moved me. Like Jane, I, too, laughed and cried a lot. Since we had last seen one another, Jane's mom had died and her dad had moved to an assisted living home, and we had not discussed these things in depth prior to the interview. In some ways, our on-camera exchange facilitated conversations that might not have happened otherwise. Beyond this, the interview gave me an excuse to visit Jane in her hometown in southeastern Minnesota, where I had not been since we took a road trip to see her parents while we were in college more than fifteen years earlier. Put succinctly, the interview and the film allowed us to reconnect.

Just as I was moved by Jane citing her love for me as the sole reason she agreed to the interview, I too found myself emotional listening to Gertie's response to the same question. Gertie began by discussing our original interview.

> I'm gonna have to go back a few years. Alright. When I agreed to do the original interview with you, first of all, I was surprised, touched that you [wanted to interview me]. And um, I was thinking, "Really, okay, this kid, you know, wants to do this," . . . [and] "That's really neat that somebody from Huron, South Dakota, is gonna be doing something this cool." Secondly, it was because I had come to a point in my life where I had finally accepted me . . . where I can be who I am, I can be with whoever I want to be, and it's okay. I don't need to hide anything, I don't need to discuss anything. It just, it's just me. It was never a conversation piece with anybody in this much smaller town that I was living with. I was just being me . . . and I didn't feel like I was having to hide anything or defend anything or, you know, just not engage in that part of my life. So anyway . . . we had the interview. And . . . it was just nice having the conversation. I had thought all those things and it was really, truly enlightening

for me just to have that conversation with you because I never had such an in-depth conversation about my life. And that, you know, aspect of it with anybody ever. So it was really, really a cool thing for me to have that conversation with you.

I was delighted to hear Gertie's affectively laced reflections on our original interview from more than five years earlier. Prior to that interview, I had known who Gertie was because she taught my fifth grade Drug Abuse Resistance Education (DARE) class in her role as a police officer. In high school, I took classes with her son, who was a year older than me. But I certainly did not *know* Gertie, other than knowing that she was a lesbian police officer I should try to avoid when drinking beer underage.

Like Gertie, I found our original interview, which I conducted in a police station a two hours' drive from my parents' home, immensely pleasurable. But Gertie made clear that the connection we made through our original interview and the fun we had during it did not necessarily motivate her participation in the film:

> When I was approached to be a part of [the film], it was more, I wanted to see something come to fruition. And it wasn't even for me. It was for you. It wasn't, um, something that I needed to do for me. But as something more I wanted to do for you. And it's not, it's not the big picture I'm looking at because wherever this ends and however it's perceived by whomever, is really irrelevant to me. Because if this is seen by, you know, many people, you know, in whatever venues it is, it's not gonna have an impact on my life here because this is my life. My life is here, my life is at [this lake community], my life is my family and my friends here. . . . This is where my energies need to be. You know, other people have bigger ideals or bigger challenges that they want to take on. They can take on the L . . . G . . . BTQ whatever it is. You know, go for it on the national level. I want a sewer system at [the lake where I live]. And that's how my world is.

In the years that followed our initial interview for this book and that preceded our second interview for the film, Gertie retired and moved closer to the town in which I grew up and in which she raised her son.

Now, when I return home for holidays, I always connect with Gertie. We drink wine on her patio and chat and laugh. Developing a friendship with Gertie has been one of the greatest pleasures of this project. Still, I was surprised when Gertie answered my question about her participation in the film by saying that she was doing it for me, not for her, and that, even though she thinks the project is "really cool," it is largely irrelevant to her life. Indeed, neither this book nor the film are going to get Gertie her sewer system!

The earnestness and humor present throughout my conversation with Gertie were also evident in Jax's and Katie's responses to my question regarding why they agreed to do the interview on film. Jax joked, "You're cute [and] funny." She then turned more serious, "For me, it's just because you asked. I don't really feel like our story is anything unique." Katie added, "I wanted to show a good . . . I wanted to give people a good idea of a South Dakota lesbian couple. . . . We're some normal South Dakota lesbians." I asked the couple if the reason they did this interview was different from the reason why they did the interview five years earlier. Katie joked, "Was there free beer last time?" Despite their jokes that connected their participation directly to me and to beer, Katie also noted broader reasons for giving their time to this project, including representing South Dakota lesbians well. To do so, she used the word "normal," a term that several other interviewees also used.

Like Katie, Karrie articulated her reasons for participating by gesturing toward desires for influencing broader ideas about rural LGBTQ people:

> I think it was important to do the interview because I think that there are a lot of people both in this part of the country and other parts of the country that think that we're sort of invisible and that the people in this part of the country don't think that they know anyone who's gay or lesbian, and of course they do. Um, and people in other parts of the country probably think that we live these, uh, sort of, well, either subversive or substandard lives because of where we live and we really have pretty comfortable lives.

When I asked Karrie explicitly if her reason for doing this interview was different from her reason for doing the original interview five years earlier, she laughed: "Well, I think I agreed to do it on film because I like you guys. . . . I hate to be filmed, I hate to have photos of myself taken, so you're interesting people and I thought, 'Okay, if you think I have something interesting to say, I'll just be a good sport.'" Karrie's response makes clear she never would have agreed to do an interview on film without having been interviewed five years earlier, as the initial interview is what allowed us to meet and to recognize that, well, we like one another. Furthermore, her belief that the project is important because of its potential to change how people think of LGBTQ people in the rural upper Midwest was not enough on its own to encourage her participation. She was just being a good sport because, as she noted, she felt positively toward me.

Daryl and Joan also rooted their motivation for participating in the project in something bigger than themselves and in a belief in the power of alternative representations. Daryl said that she agreed to do the interview on film "just to get the story out. Like [Joan] said, it's important to let people know who we are, that . . . we are normal, we are raising a family. Our kids are normal. I think. [*laughs*]" Joan shared her thoughts, commenting:

[When Daryl asked me] "Should I do it? Should I not do it?" Um, I said, "Why wouldn't you?" . . . We're a part of something. This is a big deal, you know. [Things are] changing. And I'm glad we're a part of that and I'm proud to be a part of it. We're proud of who we are. . . . Just 'cause we're not the type that shouts it from the rooftop, but we definitely have support and we know what's important and we have three children that I want to know that it is okay to have gay moms. . . . When we were talking about it before you guys got here, my daughter said, "What if they ask me, you know, what it's like to have two moms?" And I said, "Well, what would you say?" And she said, "It's not any different." You know, and I was like, "That's exactly why we're doing this interview." Because we want people to know that our life is no different than anybody's straight life. We all do the exact same things. Same arguments, same fun, same everything. [*laughs*] . . . We're all the same.

We're all the same. Not any different. This focus on similarity and normalcy cut across interviews. Angie commented that part of her reason for agreeing to be interviewed on film was to show that "we're all just people and, you know, no different than anybody else. And that would be my main reason, I guess, to do an interview." Angie's friend Corwin similarly commented: "To help people, but to show them that we're just like them. Common, ordinary, everyday people, you know? Your kids, your brother, your sister." Interviewees answered my question regarding why they would be willing to be interviewed for a film about LGBTQ women in the rural upper Midwest by situating themselves as *similar to* the non-LGBTQ people in their rural communities. This finding aligns with Mary Gray's aforementioned argument that rural LGBTQ folks value the familiar and similar over public articulations of the ways in which they are different from those with whom they are in close proximity (2009).

Such priorities mark a significant departure from national lesbian and gay rights groups' expectations that their constituents come out and be visible, which requires articulating oneself as *different from* those around them, a point that explains why such strategies may not be desirable or tenable for rural LGBTQ people. According to the logics of lesbian and gay rights groups, it is through this articulation of difference that we will become known to those who are unlike us, convincing them that we too are deserving of rights. This tension between sameness and difference represents a paradox of homonormative rights seeking approaches: we are compelled to express like-ness through centralizing our difference, a difference so crucial that it is impossible to be authentic or known without an articulation of this difference. We are compelled to articulate our sexual difference so that others may cast it aside as unimportant, simultaneously rendering us similar to them and producing themselves as the type of flexible subjects who are tolerant of such difference (McRuer 2006, 17–18). In short, for gay rights groups, becoming recognizable as similar requires an articulation of sexual difference, which functions to make one knowable. Visibility is both a goal and effect of the expression of such difference. Interviewees' desire for similarity without prerequisite difference, by contrast, is one significant reason that gay rights activists' calls for visibility do not resonate among my interviewees.

In response to my articulating precisely this argument, the scholar who asked why interviewees would participate in a film if they did not care about visibility made her question more pointed: How does interviewees' willingness to be on camera—which, my interlocutor noted, might reflect a desire for visibility, or in the least, requires people to be "visible," so to speak—actually *undermine* my very argument, and particularly in regard to my point that what visibility means is context specific and even, in some contexts, undesirable?

This question serves as a generative point of departure for reiterating claims I have made throughout this book and also for reflecting on the relationship between visual representation and visibility politics. Far from undermining my arguments, I see interviewees' willingness to be on camera as an opportunity to extend this book's claims. As a subset of interviewees make clear, some did, indeed, participate in the film because they wanted to offer positive representations of their lives not otherwise in circulation, although their ideas about what a positive representation of LGBTQ life looks like necessarily push back against broader cultural assumptions regarding the centrality of visibility to authentic LGBTQness. This is especially evident among those interviewees who noted on camera that although they never quite exactly came out—that is, they had not told explicitly many people about their sexuality—they *are* out. They live as out, as visible, as themselves, a point that extends my analysis of the relationships among coming out, being out, and being visible in chapter 2. Put more directly, witnessing a lesbian who is visible as such say on screen that she did not ever really come out or that the language of outness is too constricting for understanding her life—but that she is out! She is happy!—makes reading her as invisible or as closeted far more difficult than is the case when reading a nameless, faceless, and disembodied quote. As such, in some ways, the film actually makes *more* apparent the complicated nature of what visibility and outness mean—a point that is, after all, key to the epistemological goal of this book, which is to articulate both the limits of visibility politics and also how these politics operate in the service of quite unbecoming things.

The danger, of course, is that viewers of *In Plain Sight* who have not had the opportunity to recognize or dismantle the metronormative frames through which they likely see the world will miss these nuances of interviewees' lives, particularly if they are thinking about rural queer life for the first time via a medium that is far less well suited to make clear the nuances of an argument than is, say, an academic book. Or, perhaps even more frighteningly, that viewers will see the first visual representation of LGBTQ women in the rural upper Midwest as either an avenue through which interviewees achieve self-actualization via visibility or as a political victory itself. Just as this book hopes to disrupt these ways of thinking and the political approaches that emerge out of them, the film does too. It just does so in ways that differ radically from those of this book. As *In Plain Sight* grew and shifted—as it went through its own process of *unbecoming*—I began to think of it on its own terms, as informed by but separate from this book. The film highlights the pervasiveness of metronormativity in cultural representations in ways that this book does not, for example, and, while the lack of complicated or positive cultural representations of queer rurality makes possible this very metronormativity, the goal of the film was never to make rural LGBTQ life more *visible.* Visibility is a paradoxical byproduct of a project that seeks to encourage thinking critically about terms and approaches that have been produced as uncomplicated and uncontestable. My hope is that doing so will allow us to create new political horizons. Indeed, as the editors of *Trap Door* write, "if we do not attend to representation and work collectively to bring new visual grammars into existence (while remembering and unearthing suppressed ones), then we will remain caught in the traps of the past" (Gossett, Stanley, and Burton 2017, xviii).

These positions—that new thinking can enable new politics and that new visual grammars can be enabled via representation, even as visible representation ought not be a goal—rely on viewing scholarship and activism as necessarily mutually constitutive. Rather than reproducing the tired and bankrupt (but still circulating) divisions between theory and practice and activism and the academy, I see my book and film as adding to the critical work that has attempted to dismantle these simplistic dichotomies. In her examination of the relations among intellectual and activist work, Laura Briggs suggests that the scholarly "account of activism has been at once too much and not enough. That is, we give activists or oppressed people too much credit for always having a good analysis of their situation and always resisting it, something that often gets expressed through the term *agency,* on the one hand, and too little credit for their intellectual work, on the other hand" (2008, 81). Robin Kelley, in a related vein, considers the deeply intertwined nature of Black activism and intellectual thought, focusing on the importance of dreaming and surrealist art for Black freedom movements. Drawing from Kelley, I view social movements—even those of which I am deeply suspicious—as "incubators of new knowledge" (2002, 8) that might allow us to imagine the social as well as ourselves otherwise.

Actualizing this potential requires critically engaging the discourses and strategies upon which these movements rely. Ubiquitous calls to be "out, loud, and proud" now constitute a life-organizing mechanism for many LGBTQ people, communities, and movements so hegemonic it is rarely questioned, its damages unnoted and proliferating. To be clear, I am not necessarily arguing that LGBTQ people should not be visible (whatever that might mean), but rather that what visibility looks like is context specific, that it is valued differently along geographic and gendered lines, and that its political utility is far less capacious than gay rights groups have suggested. Beyond this, I am concerned with the ways in which contemporary demands for visibility operate in the service of metronormativity, post-raciality, and capitalism and make visibility itself into the political project, thwarting possibilities for collective queer political action. Inspired by Avery Gordon's position that the "devastations and afflictions to which we are too routinely subjected require from us 'something more powerful than skepticism'" (2004, 187), I find hope in the generative power of queer critique not only for articulating the contours of these devastations and afflictions but for dismantling them. I find hope in what might *become* of queer politics when we do so. "Sometimes we need to disrupt usage," Sara Ahmed says, "to bring attention to a cause. At other times, that you disrupt usage teaches us about a cause" (2019, 210). Disrupting usage can look a lot like queer usage. Making windows into doors. Inviting people in.

When I began the process of filming the documentary, I imagined it as a second invitation, but to the same party. To throw this party, I worked almost entirely with undergraduate students, whom I encouraged to put their own stamp on the project. Together we crafted an original animation of the concept of metronormativity as well as a campy song and music video, all of which comprise part of the "messy" archive of this decidedly queer film (Manalansan 2014). We created something weirder and wackier than I ever could have conceptualized on my own. In true queer form, this eccentricity functioned as an invitation. Although some students joined the project team after taking my Introduction to Queer Critique class, most had little knowledge of LGBTQ studies; they became involved because they have film editing, website building, animation, music making, or GIS mapping skills. Creating *In Plain Sight* was an exercise in teaching and learning beyond the classroom. Inviting people in. In the end, we threw two parties. Some people, ideas, and affects moved from one to the other. Others made it to just one of the parties. Turns out that some interventions are better suited to a visual medium than others.

Don't get me wrong. The process of creating *In Plain Sight* was not all roses and hay bales. The final product is raw, rustic, and in some moments, even aesthetically displeasing. Let's just say this film isn't going to Sundance. So, what's the use of this queer film? The hard-working, earnest Midwesterner in me feels compelled to point out that the film does the work I intended for it to do: It invites viewers to queer thinking and it disrupts assumptions about both rural place and the value of visibility politics. The queer theorist in me feels like we should read the film through the lens of queer use, which does not take use too seriously after all. Queer use asks us to reconfigure what we want from use.

And reconfigure I did. Throughout the process of making the film, I believed that its completion would enable the actualization of its queer use. I could not always see the queer use in front of me. Day after day, I talked with students on the project team who were new to queer theory about the intellectual underpinnings of the film. They talked with those in their networks. I wrote to funders, explaining the theoretical impulse of the film and the research out of which it initially emerged. I watched drafts of the film with some interviewees, who offered feedback. I engaged with audience members in Q&A sessions at film festivals and at screenings on college campuses. These moments were invitations. Doors. Fuchsia doors. In the end, I found that the affective connections I created or extended through working on the film were more important to me than the final product. This is queer use. Queer use enables. Queer use creates. Queer use affects and effects. Queer use requires that we consider for whom and for what we desire to be useful.

Ultimately, the process of making the film demonstrated this book's contention that interrogating that which we find unbecoming—the rural? the closet? the past? politics? women?—can enable possibilities for becoming otherwise in our thinking, engaging, and relating. Doing so is, in short, useful. While I developed this insight through examining the relations between the celebratory affects tethered to visibility politics and the disgust or confusion circling around queer rurality, there is no reason at all it should reside there. In fact, I hope it doesn't. Inspired by Maryam Griffin's work on "the *mobility* and circulation of Palestinian political thought," I view unbecoming as containing the "conceptual flexibility," to use Griffin's words, required to travel—something I view as crucial to the project of dismantling visibility politics precisely because calls for visibility have not stayed put (2020, emphasis added). Article headlines such as "Why I Came Out as Being Poor," "Coming Out as Biracial," "Coming Out as . . . Disabled," and "Coming Out on Abortion" show that discourses of "outness" permeate movements far beyond those concerned with LGBTQ issues.[3] Feminists call for people to tell their abortion stories, disability justice activists call for those with "invisible" disabilities to come out, and racial justice activists suggest that those people of color who are light-skinned or "pass" assert their race over and over. Increasing visibility—via calling for individuals to reveal something ostensibly unapparent about themselves—has become the political project in these movements, too. Beyond this, as I detail in chapters 3 and 4, analyses of visibility have particular relevance for our understandings of gender, disability, class, and race because these markers of experience, like sexuality, can be both obvious and hidden, prompting us to reflect on, as I have here, what it actually means to be (in)visible.

Taking on the cult of visibility will require that we examine its many iterations and mutations, including what precisely those advocating for visibility in relation to different causes find unbecoming. Throughout this book, I have suggested that the widespread belief in the value of visibility has deadened our ability to recognize its harms. The belief that visibility itself constitutes political work has reduced our capacity to conceptualize freedom and to develop place-based actions that will lead to justice. We might, then, approach visibility politics as an example of what Lauren Berlant terms "cruel optimism," the relations of which exist "when something you desire is actually an obstacle to your flourishing" (2011, 1). Avery Gordon, too, is concerned with developing "the capacity to let go of the ties that bind you to an identification with that which is killing you" (2004, 204). Unwinding our cruel attachments—the ties that bind us—requires unbecoming, a willingness to be undone and redone. Central to this unraveling is a belief that we could better understand both that which we despise (rurality) and desire (visibility) by considering the relations between the two. Such approaches could help us better articulate that which we are fighting for, rather than just simply what we are fighting against—a crucial epistemological move because "challenging invisibility" (Bolaki 2012) will not necessarily challenge anything else, just as achieving visibility will not necessarily achieve anything else. To challenge and achieve anything at all, we need far more than individual neoliberal visibility politics. We need to be able to deconstruct and reconstruct our assumptions, affects, and desires so that we can imagine alternative ways of being in alternative worlds. Ultimately, we need to develop a practice of freedom. For Avery Gordon, this freedom is shareable, it is usable, and it requires practice. That is, it "improves upon use" (Gordon 2004, 200). Perhaps the same is true of unbecoming. And of creating films. It is my hope that practicing how to take more seriously that which we find unbecoming will allow our thinking, our politics, and our desires to become otherwise. That it will allow us to paint more doors fuchsia.

Acknowledgments

A FEW YEARS AGO, I came across the last edition of my high school newspaper. I chuckled upon reading my response to the prompt that asked graduating seniors to predict what our lives would look like in ten years: "I will live anywhere but here," I proclaimed boldly. I was technically right. I haven't lived in South Dakota for more than a few months at a time since I graduated from high school. But the irony in my choosing a research topic that keeps taking me home—both literally and figuratively—does not escape me. Many people have been a part of bringing me home, supporting me while I am at home, and helping me create new homes all over the place.

First and foremost, thanks go to the women I interviewed. I am endlessly grateful for their time, wisdom, and stories. I enjoyed every conversation, every alpaca feeding, and every porch wine and dingy bar whiskey. Thanks, too, to those friends, family members, and strangers who utilized their networks to connect me with interviewees, and to those who fed me and housed me throughout the interview collecting process (especially Amy Hemmer, Jane Olsen, and my parents, Kent and Rita Thomsen). I appreciate my parents' willingness to loan me their car for months on end so that I could tool around South Dakota and Minnesota to collect interviews. Many people went out of their way to assist in the completion of this phase of the research process. I see their Midwestern sensibilities and generosity all over this project.

This book began as a dissertation, which I completed in the Feminist Studies Department at the University of California, Santa Barbara. What an amazing place to be a graduate student! Leila Rupp, my dissertation chair, has had a profound impact not only on my scholarship, teaching, and mentorship of students, but also on my life. She guided me through grad school and, even in the years since, her support has been seemingly inexhaustible. I have learned more from her than I could possibly capture here. Eileen Boris and Avery Gordon, two incredibly supportive members of my dissertation committee, have also influenced my scholarship (and me) beyond measure. Leila, Eileen, and Avery model what it means to think boldly, write with precision, and act in accordance with one's principles. I am grateful for learning under them. Thanks also to Paul Amar, Mireille Miller-Young, and Laury Oaks for their many forms of mentorship and support throughout graduate school. For being co-conspirators in the practice of making my graduate school experience and time in California into a mind-bending and pleasurable adventure, I thank Eddy Alvarez, Yousef Baker, Heather Berg, Lindy Chavez, Jonathan Chavez, Alise Cogger, Kristin Conover, Christine Schock Contreras, Leigh Dodson, Jody Jahn, Karis Gant, Egidio Garay, Julian Gottlieb, CJ Jones, Jasmín Llamas, Sarah Jane Pinkerton, Elizabeth Rahilly, Elizabeth Riccio, and Annika Speer. The members of End Fake Clinics, a queer reproductive justice collective, reminded me time and time again of the power of bringing feminist and queer theory to activism. Special thanks to Annie Alexandrian, Dana Bass, Shantal Ben-Aderet, Kaitlin Gerds, Brooke Hofhenke, Riese Lin, Ollie Miller, Jessica Moore, Grace Morrison, Nic Nesbit, Kensey Smart, Shane Stringfellow, Sanaz Toosi, Sweets Underwood, and Diana Vargas. I have learned a great deal about living a feminist life from Debbie Rogow, who has brought so many forms of joy and inspiration to mine. Maryam Griffin had a more profound impact on my thinking and my life while at UCSB than any other person. Since then, she has continued to exceed all reasonable expectations regarding what friendship can look and feel like.

I owe the existence of my academic life to faculty and staff at St. Cloud State University, who urged me to go to graduate school in the first place. Thanks to Beth Berila, Michael Connaughton, Catherine Fox, Jane Olsen, and Tracy Ore. Their mentorship changed the course of my life. Thanks especially to Jane Olsen for her friendship, generosity, and endless championing of me. I started to develop the tools I would need to become a scholar while a MA student in the Gender and Women's Studies program at the University of Arizona. Thanks to Laura Briggs, Miranda Joseph, and Elizabeth Lapovsky Kennedy for their patient guidance. Through my research assistantship at the Southwest Institute for Research on Women, I learned a great deal about conducting ethical feminist research from Claudia Powell and Sally Stevens. Since this time, Ayisha Ashley Al-Sayyad, Erin Durban,

Heather Fukunaga, and Alyson Patsavas have remained dear friends and important parts of my life, academic and otherwise.

I was fortunate to land a postdoctoral fellowship at Rice University's Center for the Study of Women, Gender, and Sexuality, where I met new mentors, colleagues, and friends. Rosemary Hennessy quickly went from being a stranger whose brilliant work I admired to being a generous mentor and friend (whose brilliance I still admire). I learned a great deal about navigating institutions in feminist ways from Krista Comer, whose academic and political work inspire me. Conversations with and support from José Aranda, Susan Lurie, and Brian Riedel shaped my fellowship experience in wonderful ways. How lucky I was to share an office and endless discussions with fellow postdoc Myrna Perez Sheldon. This book started to take new shape during my time at Rice.

My colleagues in Gender, Sexuality, and Feminist Studies at Middlebury College have worked to create an environment that is at once intellectually robust, politically astute, and committed to engaged feminist learning. I could not be luckier. Laurie Essig, Hemangini Gupta, Karin Hanta, Sujata Moorti, and Catherine Wright are exceptional feminist colleagues, whose support and friendship have been endless. Thanks to my many additional Middlebury College colleagues for improving my thinking and enriching my life: Jim Berg, Kristin Bright, Susan Burch, Nikolina Dobreva, William Poulin-Deltour, Erin Eggleston, J Finley, Jason Grant, Daniel Houghton, Mark Lewis, Tamar Mayer, Jamie McCallum, Dave Munro, Caitlin Myers, Daniel Rodriguez-Navas, Natasha Ngaiza, Patricia Saldarriaga, Matthew Taylor, Rebecca Tiger, Eddie Vasquez, Marion Wells, and Linda White. I would not have finished this book without the crew of fellow writers meeting at 8 a.m. daily: Sayaka Abe, Dave Allen, Niwaeli Kimambo, Sarah Laursen, Jenn Ortegren, and Moyukh Chatterjee. My life in small-town Vermont is richer than I ever could have imagined, in significant part due to my friendships beyond the college. For contributing to that richness, thanks to Aaron Brown, Peter Bruno, Andy Dosmann, Georgia Heise, Mark Jensen, Zoe Kaslow, Martha Mack, Rita Munro, Nial Rele, and Sas Stewart. Thanks, especially, to those who experience life with me in a daily way, those who are there for the mundane, ecstatic, and everything in between, those who have most supported and celebrated me while I have finished this book: Moyukh Chatterjee, Maryam Griffin,

Hemangini Gupta, David Miranda-Hardy, Matt Lawrence, Jenn Orte-gren, Laura Thomas, and Ajay Verghese.

The richness of my academic life is due to affective connections that circulate beyond those prompted within or in relation to these institutions. Abe Weil and Kelly Sharron are brilliant interlocutors and fierce friends. My introduction to the vibrancy of rural queer think-ing occurred at the Queering the Countryside conference at Indiana University in fall 2010. This conference, which took place during the second year of my doctoral program, shaped my interests and desires in profound ways. I am eternally grateful to Colin Johnson and Mary Gray for the field-forming work they did to put on this event and for their mentorship in the years that have followed. I enjoy every chance I get to reconnect with my rural queer studies crew at conferences—especially Jae Basiliere, Katie Schweighofer, and Stina Soderling. Thanks to Ashlee Davis (the U.S. Department of Agriculture) and Julie Gonen (National Center for Lesbian Rights) for including me in the Rural LGBT Summit and the related rural LGBT meeting at the White House. Participating in these events led to the reflections I share in chapter 5 and reaffirmed my commitment to moving queer studies beyond the academy.

When it came to writing, I also had incredible support. As a gradu-ate student, I benefited from workshopping an early draft of chapter 3 with Alison Kafer, Matt Richardson, and Siobhan Somerville. I later workshopped more developed drafts of this same chapter with Robert McRuer and with Kim Hall. Their insights and encouragement pushed me to keep going. I will not rename here each person already men-tioned who offered feedback on my writing, but we both know who you are and I am grateful. I will make one exception: Jenn Ortegren deserves a special shout out. She is the most generous colleague I have encountered anywhere. She has read every single word of this book, given multiple rounds of feedback, and talked through the ideas here more times than I'm sure she cared to. She is also an exceptional friend.

I am also deeply grateful for the material support I received for this research: Woodrow Wilson Dissertation Fellowship; Interdisciplinary Humanities Center Pre-Doctoral Fellowship; the Steve and Barbara Mendell Fellowship in Cultural Literacy from the Walter H. Capps Center for the Study of Ethics, Religion, and Public Life; and grants and fellowships from the Graduate Division at the University of Cali-fornia, Santa Barbara. More recently, I benefited from support from

Middlebury College's Faculty Research Assistant Fund, Undergraduate Collaborative Research Fund, and the Digital Liberal Arts. Thank you to these funders for believing in and supporting my work.

At every stage of this project, I have benefited from the research support of undergraduate students. At UCSB, I led a research team of undergraduate students who helped me to transcribe my interviews. At Rice University, Zoe Matranga and Catherine Chantre were terrific research assistants. And, most recently, at Middlebury College, I compiled a team of students with whom I created a documentary film to translate some of the arguments in this book into an alternative medium and for a broader audience. (I reflect on the film in the concluding chapter.) These student collaborators include Hannah Blake, Charlotte Cahillane, Kaitlynd Collins, Caroline Harrison, Reed Martin, Nell Sather, Lily Shale, Connor Sloan, Liza Tarr, Rebecca Wishnie, and Elizabeth Zhao. Tate Serletti has gone above and beyond in her capacity as a research assistant, on this project and others. I had a blast working with and getting to know these wonderful students. The film is a testament to its collaborative nature; it is weird and wacky—it includes an original metronormativity animation and campy music video!—and better than anything I could have conceptualized on my own. My students' excitement about the film and interest in metronormativity reminded me week after week of the value of this project. Ellie Vainker and Sinead Keirans were also instrumental to the film's completion. Thanks to CK Schartle, Sarah Keppen, and others connected to the Black Hills Center for Equality for their support of the film and to those film festival goers who have offered encouragement following screenings.

Thanks also to those colleagues who organized and attended talks I gave related to this book, including those at Castleton University, Grand Valley State University, Haverford College, Illinois State University, Middlebury College, St. Cloud State University, University of Florida, University of Houston, and University of Kansas. I benefited tremendously from the insights that emerged through our conversations.

Many thanks to my editor, Kristian Tvedten, and the University of Minnesota Press team, who have been terrific to work with. Thanks, also, to the reviewers whose careful and insightful feedback was a joy to work through. Their ideas substantially improved the book.

Anahi Russo-Garrido came into my life much later than the others thanked here, but every day I'm grateful for her ability to make the perfect cup of coffee, her excitement about ideas and willingness to deeply engage mine, and her big heart. My sister, Danielle Thomsen, is an incredible scholar and I have learned an enormous amount from watching her deftly navigate the academy. She can make me laugh like no one else, and her boldness inspires me. That Danielle is my sister is one of my greatest blessings. I owe my parents, Kent and Rita Thomsen, a great deal. They ended up with two daughters who moved far away from home, followed our dreams, and earned our PhDs. It is no coincidence that my sister and I are both inquisitive, adventurous, and hard working. Thanks to my parents for everything they have done to encourage these characteristics in us, and for their love and support along the way.

I have so much to be grateful for.

Notes

Introduction

1. I engage with a great deal of the scholarship on rural queer sexualities in the pages that follow. The body of work on sexuality or gender and place/space is so vast that it would be impossible to do it justice in a footnote. For work published in just the past decade, see, for example, Miriam Abelson (2019), Jae Basiliere (2019), Kath Browne (2011), Japonica Brown-Saracino (2017), Christina Hanhardt (2013), and Rosemary Hennessy (2013). The growth in the transdisciplinary work on sexuality and space is quite remarkable considering that just twenty-five years ago, the vast majority of scholarship on space and sexuality was, as Johnston and Longhurst note in their 2010 collection, "contained within one volume—David Bell and Gill Valentine's *Mapping Desire*" (1995). For scholarship on the racialization of sexuality, much of which also offers terrific insights into place-making, see chapter 3 footnote 9. In the pages that follow, I also engage scholarship on the racialization of sexuality, much of which offers terrific insights into place-making. See chapters 1 and 3 in particular.

2. The field has primarily focused on the U.S. South, as will become clear in the pages that follow. *GLQ*'s 2014 special issue *Queering the Middle: Race, Region, and a Queer Midwest* might appear to be an obvious exception to my claim. The volume's editors and contributors offer important analyses of the Midwest, but their laudable commitment to debunking stereotypes of the region as rural and their desire to discuss place outside of rural/urban binaries result in an undertheorization of queerness in the *rural* Midwest (Manalansan et al. 2014). *Reclaiming the Heartland: Lesbian and Gay Voices from the Midwest*, a multigenre anthology composed of various artistic and literary pieces (Osborne and Spurlin 1996), and *Farm Boys*, a collection of stories about the lives of gay men who grew up on farms in the Midwest but migrated elsewhere (Fellows 1996), both tell stories of LGBTQ people in the Midwest. Neither of these texts is academic in nature, perhaps in part because both were published before rural queer studies existed as a recognizable subfield, and neither focuses primarily on women. For an exception to my claim, see Emily Kazyak (2012).

3. Scholars, including Jack Halberstam (2005), Leila Rupp (2009a), and Elizabeth Lapovsky Kennedy and Madeline Davis ([1993] 2014, xiv) have commented on the lack of analysis of gender—and particularly women—in LGBTQ

studies and queer theory, a point particularly relevant in regard to the literature on LGBTQ rural sexualities. For exceptions, see Kazyak (2012), Colin Johnson's chapter "Hard Women: Rural Women and Female Masculinity" in his *Just Queer Folks: Gender and Sexuality in Rural America* (2013), Johnston and Valentine (1995), and Valentine (1997). Each of these texts are book chapters or journal articles (rather than full monographs) and none engage with the question of visibility. E. Patrick Johnson's *Black. Queer. Southern. Women: An Oral History* is a beautiful collection of oral histories of Black queer women in the U.S. South, but it does not focus specifically on rural places (2018).

4. Scholarly discussions regarding the relationship between feminist and queer studies are robust. See, for example: Weed and Schor 1997; Jagose 2009; Rubin 1984; Rubin 1975; Marinucci 2010. More specifically, scholars have discussed reproductive justice through the lens of queer theory, addressing what the lack of queer theoretical work on abortion reveals more broadly (Doyle 2009; Thomsen and Morrison 2020). For a journalist's take on the increasing support for gay marriage but stagnant support for abortion justice, see the work of Katha Pollitt (2015a, 2015b).

5. "Celebrate National Coming Out Day with HRC!" *Human Rights Campaign*, http://www.hrc.org.

6. "Growing Support for Gay Marriage: Changed Minds and Changing Demographics," *Pew Research Center for the People and the Press*, https://www.pewresearch.org/politics/2013/03/20/growing-support-for-gay-marriage-changed-minds-and-changing-demographics/.

7. Scholars and activists alike use "trans" to gesture to the wide range of gender nonconforming behaviors, identities, and experiences that might not be captured by "transgender," including, for example, transmasculine, transsexual, transfeminine, nonbinary, and genderqueer.

8. For provocative discussions of the limits of analyzing space through the concept of "regions," see Krista Comer (2010) and Martin Manalansan et al. (2014).

9. *Human Rights Campaign*, "HRC Story," http://www.hrc.org.

10. *Human Rights Campaign*, "The HRC Story," https://web.archive.org/web/20111022210938/https://www.hrc.org/the-hrc-story/boards.

11. The states are California, Louisiana, Massachusetts, New York, Ohio, Pennsylvania, and Texas. https://web.archive.org/web/20181220155135/https://www.hrc.org/hrc-story/boards.

12. I expand upon scholars' discussions of the racialization of sexuality and its relationship to place in chapters 1 and 3.

13. For a sampling of feminist and LGBTQ studies books that include "visibility" in their title but spend little time considering the problematics of the term, see *Becoming Visible: An Illustrated History of Lesbian and Gay Life in Twentieth-Century America* (McGarry, Wasserman, and Bowling 1998); *Circuits*

of Visibility: Gender and Transnational Media Cultures (Hegde 2011); *Invisible Lives: The Erasure of Transsexual and Transgendered People* (Namaste 2000); *Missing Bodies: The Politics of Visibility* (Casper and Moore 2009). Although the authors of the latter note that they attempt to examine visibility as it relates to invisibility, their focus on the "recuperation of missing bodies" (14) functions to reproduce the notion that invisibility is negative and ought to be extinguished. This point is evidenced in the authors' connecting invisibility to abject and marginalized bodies (those of Iraqi civilians, dead babies, and the victims of HIV/AIDS) and connecting visibility to what they view as more privileged bodies (those of celebrities, white U.S. soldiers, and politicians).

14. I do not mean to set up a dichotomy in which gay politics necessarily support same-sex marriage and queer politics necessarily contest marriage equality—although, as many queer studies scholars have argued, a key aspect of queerness is resistance to what Michael Warner calls "regimes of the normal," of which marriage is a central pillar (1999). For a nuanced alternative perspective on the queer potential of marriage equality, see Taylor and Rupp (2014).

15. Jillian A. Bogater, "Price: Visibility Key to Repealing Gay Marriage Ban," *Pride Source*, https://pridesource.com/article/20484/.

16. "Queer Organizing at UCSB," *UCSB*, http://ucsblhp.blogspot.com/2012/03/as-ucsb-queer-commission-presents.html.

17. This history of the UCSB "queer bomb" also speaks to my aforementioned point that visibility discourses rely on celebratory ideas about gay "community" and "identity." Visibility is needed "for our community" and to "celebrate our Queer identity."

18. "About Janet Mock," *Janet Mock*, http://janetmock.com.

19. Kip McClement, "Transgender Day of Visibility Celebrates the Trans Community," *GLAAD*, https://www.glaad.org/blog/transgender-day-visibility-celebrates-trans-community.

20. The "flyover zone" refers to the area that one "flies over" in traveling between Los Angeles and New York City.

21. These programs are maintained by a network of faculty who cross-list courses they teach in their home departments, rather than faculty or staff housed in a gender studies department.

22. At the time, I wanted to avoid going through LGBTQ organizations because I assumed that the goals, approaches, and ideologies of those LGBTQ people connected to such groups would be in line with the discourses evident on these groups' websites and would reflect the discourses of national LGBTQ rights groups. In some ways, I was right and in other ways I was wrong. I discuss how the approaches of Equality South Dakota are similar to and different from those of dominant gay rights groups in my chapter "In Plain(s) Sight: Rural LGBTQ Women and the Politics of Visibility" in *Queering the Countryside: New Frontiers in Rural Queer Studies* (2016).

1. Metronormativity as Legacy

1. A quick search in Google Scholar speaks to this point. Some of the thousands of texts that discuss Shepard's case include Cramer et al. (2013), Ott and Aoki (2002), and Petersen (2011). Recently, Helis Sikk and Leisa Meyer published an edited volume that reflects on Shepard's ongoing legacy (2019). Very little comprising this enormous body of work critically analyzes discourses around Shepard's death or considers the place of rurality in the case. When scholars do mention rural place, they often do so in a way that reproduces metronormativity. Ironically, this pattern is evident even in scholarship that claims to adopt a "critical queer studies approach," as does Casey Charles (2006). For an exception, see Cram (2016). It is worth noting that while there is an enormous amount of academic work on Shepard, I am the only scholar who has published on Newsome's case (Thomsen 2016).

2. While a few scholars have referenced *The Book of Matt* in their discussions of Shepard, there has been little deep and critical engagement with the text or reflection on the political possibilities it enables. Instead, scholars tend to either simply dismiss (Schattenkirk 2014) or accept (Tyburski 2015) Jimenez's arguments.

3. Matthew Shepard Foundation Facebook page, https://www.facebook .com/pg/MatthewShepardFoundation/posts/.

4. G_j, "Tonight's 20/20 Report on Matthew Shepard," *Democratic Underground,* https://www.democraticunderground.com/discuss/duboard.php?az =view_all&address=104x2754007.

5. "Turning a Gay Teen Straight Teen . . . on 'Good Morning America,'" *Broadway World,* https://www.broadwayworld.com/board/readmessage.php ?thread=861059&boardid=2&page=1.

6. Seth Hemmelgarn, "Shepard Book Stirs Controversy," *Bay Area Reporter,* October 23, 2013, https://www.ebar.com/news///243965.

7. Neal Broverman, "Op-Ed: Why I'm Not Reading the 'Trutherism' about Matt Shepard," *Advocate,* September 24, 2013, https://www.advocate.com/ commentary/2013/09/24/op-ed-why-im-not-reading-trutherism-about-matt -shepard.

8. "SRLP on Hate Crime Laws," *Sylvia Rivera Law Project,* https://srlp.org/ action/hate-crimes/.

9. "Matthew's Story," *Matthew Shepard Foundation,* https://www.matthew shepard.org/about-us/our-story/.

10. Alyssa Rosenberg, "'The Book of Matt' Doesn't Prove Anything, Other Than the Size of Stephen Jimenez's Ego," *Think Progress,* October 18, 2013, https://archive.thinkprogress.org/the-book-of-matt-doesn-t-prove-anything -other-than-the-size-of-stephen-jimenez-s-ego-c7ba5dobecee/.

11. "About Us," *Media Matters,* https://www.mediamatters.org/about-us.

12. Carlos Maza, "*The Guardian* Promotes Discredited, Debunked Book about Matthew Shepard's Murder," *Media Matters*, October 10, 2014, https://www.mediamatters.org/legacy/guardian-promotes-discredited-debunked -book-about-matthew-shepards-murder; Luke Brinker, "Debunking Stephen Jimenez's Efforts to De-Gay Matthew Shepard's Murder, *Media Matters*, October 2, 2014, https://www.mediamatters.org/legacy/debunking-stephen -jimenezs-effort-de-gay-matthew-shepards-murder.

13. Julie Bindel, "The Truth Behind America's Most Famous Gay-Hate Murder," *The Guardian*, October 26, 2014, https://www.theguardian.com/world/2014/oct/26/the-truth-behind-americas-most-famous-gay-hate-murder -matthew-shepard.

14. Broverman, "Op-Ed: Why I'm Not Reading the 'Trutherism' about Matt Shepard."

15. Hemmelgarn, "Shepard Book Stirs Controversy."

16. Andrew Gumbel, "Matthew Shepard's Murder: 'What It Came Down to Is Drugs and Money,'" *The Guardian*, October 14, 2013, https://www.theguardian.com/world/2013/oct/14/matthew-shepard-murder-wyoming-book.

17. Richard Risemberg, "10 Biggest Cities in Wyoming: How Well Do You Know the Cowboy State?" *Newsmax*, May 8, 2015, https://www.newsmax.com/FastFeatures/biggest-cities-wyoming-cowboy-state/2015/05/08/id/643207/.

18. The case I consider here obviously took place prior to the repeal of Don't Ask, Don't Tell in 2011.

19. Newsome's quote, given to the Associated Press over the telephone, circulated in many news stories about the case. See for example Timberly Ross, "Jene Newsome Discharged: Rapid City Police Told Air Force that Sergeant Was Lesbian," *Huffington Post*, March 13, 2010, http://web.archive.org/web/20160131053322/http://www.huffingtonpost.com/2010/03/13/jene-newsome -discharged-r_n_498134.html.

20. Steve Benen, "Meet Jene Newsome," *Washington Monthly*, March 14, 2010, https://washingtonmonthly.com/2010/03/14/meet-jene-newsome/.

21. "Editorial: Police Policy Change Makes Sense," *Rapid City Journal*, https://rapidcityjournal.com/news/opinion/editiorial-police-policy-change -makes-sense/article_1f1d892c-4966-11df-b6e3-001cc4c03286.html.

22. Timberly Ross, "Military Discharges Sergeant After Cops Out Her," *San Francisco Chronicle*, April 16, 2010, https://www.sfgate.com/news/article/Military-discharges-sergeant-after-cops-out-her-3195842.php.

23. While the creator of the site was anonymous, the content of the posts suggests that the creator lived in South Dakota, or, at the very least, was extremely familiar with local politics.

24. Frank Pizzoli, "Lesbian Air Force Sgt. Jene Newsome in DADT Grinder," *Central Voice*, March 20, 2010, https://centralvoice.wordpress.com/2010/03/20/lesbian-air-force-sgt-jene-newsome-in-dadt-grinder.

25. For a discussion of how Cecilia Fire Thunder, the first woman president of the Oglala Sioux tribe, influenced the local and national debates over South Dakota's 2006 and 2008 abortion bans in ways that challenge assumptions that the Midwest is inherently conservative, see Thomsen (2013, 2015b). For more information on Karen refugees in South Dakota, see: "South Dakota Town Embraces New Immigrants Vital to Meat Industry," *PBS NewsHour,* July 2, 2016, https://www.pbs.org/newshour/show/south -dakota-town-embraces-new-immigrants-vital-to-meat-industry.

26. Other than my chapter in *Queering the Countryside* (2016), in which I analyze Newsome's case, I have found just two other academic texts that reference Jene Newsome. Both scholars briefly describe her situation to argue for the necessity of abolishing Don't Ask, Don't Tell (Frank 2010; Barrett 2011).

2. (Be)coming Out, Be(com)ing Visible

1. *Bustle Digital Group,* https://www.bdg.com/.

2. J. R. Thorpe, "What Is National Coming Out Day?: Celebrating Visibility in the LGBTQ Community Is More Crucial Than Ever," *Bustle Digital Group,* October 10, 2017, https://www.bustle.com/p/what-is-national-coming -out-day-celebrating-visibility-in-the-lgbtq-community-is-more-crucial-than -ever-2801912.

3. *The Odyssey Online,* "About Us," https://www.theodysseyonline.com/st/ about.

4. Tess Christmas, "On 'Coming Out' and Gay Visibility," *The Odyssey Online,* October 19, 2015, https://www.theodysseyonline.com/coming-out-and -gay-visibility.

5. *Human Rights Campaign,* "Transgender Visibility Guide," http://web .archive.org/web/20141215194759if_/http://www.hrc.org/resources/entry/ transgender-visibility-guide.

6. Such understandings of coming out remain common today in psychology, public health, higher education, and student affairs. See, for example, the work by psychologist Vivienne Cass, who is well-known for describing the coming out "process" in exactly this manner (1979; 1996). While more recent work in psychology has attempted to complicate what has come to be termed the "Cass identity model," this work largely reproduces Cass's position that sexual identity development occurs in "stages." For examples of the latter, see: Carrion and Lock (1997) and Halpin and Allen (2004).

7. I share additional stories that speak to the complicated nature of what it means to be out for my interviewees in chapter 4, in which I consider how people negotiate visibility politics in the workplace.

8. Prior to our recorded conversation, interviewees filled out a demographic form that asked questions about their race, gender, sexual orientation,

and class (including current income, class identity, and family's class back-ground). In this chapter, I describe interviewees by drawing from their de-scriptions of themselves on this form. I do so because I believe that our social locations matter. At the same time, I did not notice substantive differences among interviewees—especially in terms of the questions I asked about sexu-ality and place—that might be explained by individuals' race or class.

9. *Two-spirit* refers to a way of viewing gender and sexuality that has been documented in more than 150 North American tribal communities over the past 130 years. Two-spirit people sometimes identify as both women and men and often possess characteristics that are typically seen in both women and men (Roscoe 1991). While some scholars have termed two-spiritedness a "third gender" (Herdt 1996), others have critiqued this framing (Towle and Morgan 2002).

3. Post-Race, Post-Space

1. *Movement Advancement Project,* "Our Work and Mission," https://www
.lgbtmap.org/our-work-and-mission.

2. *Movement Advancement Project,* "LGBT People with Disabilities," https://
www.lgbtmap.org/file/LGBT-People-With-Disabilities.pdf.

3. *UCLA Lesbian, Gay, Bisexual, Transgender Campus Resource Center,*
"Disability Resources," https://web.archive.org/web/20160323060035/http://
www.lgbt.ucla.edu/disabled.html. The exact same sentence describing "Queer-ability" appears on the web pages of other LGBTQ campus centers. See, for ex-ample, the websites of LGBTQ centers at California State University, Northridge, https://www.csun.edu/pride/resources, and SUNY Albany, https://www.albany
.edu/lgbt/38085.php.

4. Rachel Cohen-Rottenberg, "Passing and Disability: Why Coming Out as Disabled Can Be So Difficult," *The Body Is Not an Apology,* 2014, https://
thebodyisnotanapology.com/magazine/passing-and-disability-why-coming
-out-as-disabled-can-be-so-difficult/.

5. Anita Cameron, "We Should Be Natural Allies: The LGBTQ and Disabil-ity Communities," *The Mobility Resource,* November 10, 2013, https://www
.themobilityresource.com/blog/post/we-need-to-come-together-the-lgbtq-and
-disability-communities/.

6. Jessica Marshall, "I'm Here. I'm Queer. I'm Disabled," *The Mighty,* Oc-tober 19, 2018, https://themighty.com/2018/10/coming-out-queer-disabled/.

7. For disability studies scholarship that positions visibility as necessarily progressive, see Solis (2007) or Corbett (1994). Jenny Corbett, for example, frames coming out as both enabling societal progress (via creating possibilities for co-alitions) and also reflecting individual progress (through which people move from "self-oppression to self-respect" (1994, 349). In analyzing what disability

means for women with chronic illnesses, Karen Jung unsettles disability as a category, but, in doing so, leaves visibility relatively intact. The unintended result is a framing of invisible and visible disabilities as largely binary, and visibility as that which is both simple and already understood (Jung 2011).

8. This lack of analysis of disability in rural queer studies is symptomatic of broader trends in queer theory and LGBTQ studies. For a discussion of the lack of examination of disability in LGBTQ studies and the lack of analysis of sexuality in disability studies, see Robert McRuer and Anna Mollow's *Sex and Disability* (2012).

9. The scholarship on the racialization of queerness and transness is robust. See, for example: Marlon Bailey, *Butch Queens Up in Pumps: Gender, Performance and Ballroom Culture in Detroit* (2013); Erin Durban-Albrecht, "The Legacy of Assotto Saint: Tracing Transnational History from the Gay Haitian Diaspora" (2013) and "Postcolonial Disablement and/as Transition: Trans* Haitian Narratives of Breaking Open and Stitching Together" (2017); LaToya Eaves, "Outside Forces: Black Southern Sexuality" (2016); Roderick Ferguson, *Aberrations in Black: Toward a Queer of Color Critique* (2003); Gayatri Gopinath, *Impossible Desires: Queer Diasporas and South Asian Public Cultures* (2005); E. Patrick Johnson and Mae Henderson, *Black Queer Studies: A Critical Anthology* (2005); José Muñoz, *Cruising Utopia: The Then and There of Queer Futurity* (2009) and *Disidentifications: Queers of Color and the Performance of Politics* (1999); E. Patrick Johnson, *No Tea, No Shade: New Writings in Black Queer Studies* (2016) and *Sweet Tea: Black Gay Men of the South* (2008); Kara Keeling, *Queer Times, Black Futures* (2019); Martin Manalansan, *Global Divas: Filipino Gay Men in the Diaspora* (2003); Amber Jamilla Musser, *Sensual Excess: Queer Femininity and Brown Jouissance* (2018); Tavia Nyong'o, *Afro-Fabulations: The Queer Drama of Black Life* (2018); Jasbir Puar, *Terrorist Assemblages: Homonationalism in Queer Times* (2007); Chandan Reddy, *Freedom with Violence. Race, Sexuality, and the US State* (2011); Nayan Shah, *Stranger Intimacy: Contesting Race, Sexuality, and the Law in the North American West* (2011); Siobhan Somerville, *Queering the Color Line: Race and the Invention of Homosexuality in American Culture* (2000); Jane Ward and Amy Stone, "From 'Black People Are Not Homosexual' to 'Gay Is the New Black': Mapping White Uses of Blackness in Modern Gay Rights Campaigns in the United States" (2011); Abraham Weil, "Trans*versal Animacies and the Mattering of Black Trans* Political Life" (2017b).

10. Mia Vayner, "Hey New York Gay Community You Can Ignore Us, but We the Gay and Disabled Do Exist." *Disabled Access Denied?*, 2012, https://disabled accessdenied.wordpress.com/2012/06/04/hey-new-york-gay-community-you -can-ignore-us-but-we-the-gay-and-disabled-do-exist/.

11. For critical discussions of analogizing categories of difference, see Samuels (2003) and Reddy (2008).

12. *Disaboom,* https://vcelkaj.wixsite.com/disaboom/.

13. Disaboom shut down its original website, on which this article was posted, and relaunched as a new site. In this process, this article was removed. An archived version is available at http://web.archive.org/web/20100301074028/ http://www.disaboom.com/disability-dating-and-relationships-general/lgbt-and -living-with-a-disability-where-to-find-support.

14. Azndc, Couple Stock Photo 5155514, http://www.istockphoto.com/photo/ couple-5155514?st=19b74aa.

15. Cho suggests that post-racialism and colorblindness are overlapping but distinct ideologies: post-racialism "signals a racially transcendent event that authorizes the retreat from race. Colorblindness, in comparison, offers a largely normative claim for a retreat from race that is aspirational in nature" (2009, 1597–1598).

16. For a critique of this campaign, see Yasmin Nair (2010).

4. Queer Labors

1. Elliot Kozuch, "HRC Report: Startling Data Reveals Half of LGBTQ Employees in US Remain Closeted at Work," *Human Rights Campaign,* June 25, 2018, https://www.hrc.org/news/hrc-report-startling-data-reveals-half-of -lgbtq-employees-in-us-remain-clos.

2. Julia Carpenter, "Nearly Half of LGBTQ Americans Haven't Come Out at Work," *CNN Money,* July 25, 2018, https://money.cnn.com/2018/07/25/pf/ coming-out-at-work/index.html.

3. Raymond Trau, Jane O'Leary and Cathy Brown, "7 Myths About Coming Out at Work," *Harvard Business Review,* October 19, 2018, https://hbr .org/2018/10/7-myths-about-coming-out-at-work.

4. Rachel Siegel, "Half of LGBTQ Workers Are Still Not Out at the Office, a Report Says," June 28, 2018, https://www.washingtonpost.com/news/ business/wp/2018/06/28/half-of-lgbtq-workers-are-still-not-out-at-the-office-a -report-says/.

5. Whitney Bacon-Evans and Megan Bacon-Evans, "Everything to Know about Coming Out at Work," August 9, 2018, *https://www.cosmopolitan.com/ uk/love-sex/relationships/a22683403/coming-out-at-work/.*

6. *What Wegan Did Next,* http://www.whatwegandidnext.com.

7. Whitney Bacon-Evans and Megan Bacon-Evans, "We Are on the *Guardian's* Pride Power Couple List!" *What Wegan Did Next,* https://www.what wegandidnext.com/2018/07/we-are-on-guardians-pride-power-couple.html.

8. Memoree Joelle, "What Wegan Did Next: A Journey of Lesbian Love and Visibility," *After Ellen,* April 26, 2018, http://web.archive.org/web/ 20200722125428/http://www.afterellen.com/people/545579-wegan-next-journey -lesbian-love-visibility.

9. Whitney Bacon-Evans and Megan Bacon-Evans, "About Wegan," *What Wegan Did Next,* https://www.whatwegandidnext.com/p/about-wegan.html.

10. James Michael Nichols, "Are You A Femme Queer Woman? Looking for Love? There's an App for That," *Queer Voices,* August 9, 2015, https://www .huffpost.com/entry/femme-lesbian-looking-for-love-theres-an-app-for-that_n_ 55c4c68ce4bof1cbf1e4a7ff.

11. Megan Evans, "Femme Visibility," *The Huffington Post,* January 28, 2012, https://www.huffpost.com/entry/femme-lesbians_b_1237648.

12. In articles they've written for the popular press, as well as for their own blog, they describe their conventional jobs in the past tense. See, for example: Whitney Bacon-Evans and Megan Bacon-Evans, "Everything to Know about Coming Out at Work," *Cosmopolitan,* https://www.cosmopolitan.com/uk/love -sex/relationships/a22683403/coming-out-at-work/.

13. Bacon-Evans and Bacon-Evans, "Everything to Know about Coming Out at Work."

14. Human Rights Campaign, "Coming Out at Work," https://www.hrc.org/ resources/coming-out-at-work.

15. Here, I drew from the definitions used by the U.S. government and coded places as "urban" if they had populations of 50,000 or higher and "non-urban" if they had fewer than 50,000 inhabitants. Such a simple and binary approach has its limits, of course. Do towns with a population of 10,000, for example, count as "nonurban" if they are essentially a suburb of Minneapolis, one of the largest cities in the United States? Despite my reservations regarding this approach—which are informed by Scott Herring's critical analysis of using numbers to define place, which I discuss in the introduction—all towns were coded by their population alone, rather than their population along with other factors, such as their proximity to urban centers.

16. Joshua Alston, "How Facebook Is Kicking Down the Closet Door," *Newsweek,* June 1, 2010, https://www.newsweek.com/how-facebook-kicking-down -closet-door-73503.

17. Queer studies scholars have long critiqued the notion of an authentic subject, challenging the assumed relationship between actions and identities and pointing out the ways in which sexual desires and identities are historically and geographically contextual as well as discursively constructed and situated.

18. Scholarship that uses Marxist and feminist ideas to analyze gendered and classed processes and relations is vast. For examples that focus on affective, intimate, and reproductive labor, see, for example: Boris 1994; Boris and Klein, 2012; Boris and Parreñas 2010; James 1983.

19. I do not mean to suggest that Marxist thinking is homogenous or that this description applies to all scholarship that frames itself as Marxist. Indeed, there are plenty of examples to the contrary. Here, I provide a quick gloss of

what others have said regarding the similarities and distinctions among fields that have often been viewed as incommensurate in order to set up how my analysis of visibility politics draws from and adds to these discussions.

20. Of course, Marxists and Marxist feminists might also view workers and women as possessing power and agency. Nonetheless, in much Marxist scholarship, workers are produced as such through their proximate relation to management, who are not-workers, or, at the very least a different kind of—and less exploited—worker. Such approaches position those on one side of the binary as necessarily more privileged and powerful (Sedgwick [1990] 2008). As such, the implication is that management and men have power over workers and women, even though such assertions do not necessarily deny that workers and women simultaneously retain some agency and power.

21. I do not mean to suggest that different understandings of totality and reification are the only points of contention between these fields or that a focus on contradiction is their only point of overlap. Again, here, I am simply articulating what others have said regarding the relations between queer and Marxist thought.

22. For examples of scholarship that examines the relations between sexuality and political economy, capital, commodification, and class (and is differentially oriented toward queer and Marxist thought), see Bassi 2006; Berg 2014a, 2014b; Chasin 2001; Clark 1991; D'Emilio 1983; Gluckman and Reed 1997; Hennessy 2000; Jackson 2009; Joseph 2002a, 2002b; Pellegrini 2002; Salton-Cox 2013; Sears 2005; Soderling 2016.

23. See, for example, Boyd 2008; Clift, Luongo, and Callister 2002; Hughes 2003; Luongo 2002; Puar 2002a, 2002b; Skeggs 1999; Visser 2003.

24. Although scholars have analyzed the processes through which certain sexual subjects come to exist as such, this scholarship does not examine these processes as necessarily labored or utilize a queer Marxist approach. Nonetheless, for insightful analyses of the production of gendered and sexual subjects that might be read as labored, see Kulick (1998) and Rupp and Taylor (2003).

25. Human Rights Campaign, "Coming Out at Work," https://www.hrc.org/resources/coming-out-at-work.

26. The Taskforce, "Come Out at Work on National Coming Out Day," https://www.thetaskforce.org/come-out-at-work-on-national-coming-out-day/.

27. Wells Fargo, "LGBT Resource Center: Our Culture," https://www.wellsfargo.com/lgbtq/index.

28. Thanks to Heather Berg for sharing this anecdote with me and for deep engagement with the ideas in this chapter, which emerged, in part, out of a since-abandoned attempt to write an article together.

29. For academic discussions of this case, see Currah (2008) and Vitulli (2010).

5. The More Things Change, the More They Stay the Same

1. Emma Newberger, "'Deaths of Despair' in Rural America Helped Trump Win His Presidency," *CNBC*, September 4, 2018, https://www.cnbc.com/2018/09/04/deaths-of-despair-in-rural-america-helped-trump-win-study-finds.html.

2. Nathaniel Rakich, and Dhrumil Mehta, "Trump Is Only Popular in Rural Areas," *FiveThirtyEight*, December 7, 2018, https://fivethirtyeight.com/features/trump-is-really-popular-in-rural-areas-other-places-not-so-much/.

3. Vinnie Rotondaro, "How Trump Seduced the White Working Class by Preying on Their Physical Pain," *Narratively*, December 21, 2016, https://narratively.com/how-trump-seduced-the-white-working-class-by-preying-on-their-physical-pain/.

4. Robert Leonard, "Opinion: Why Rural America Voted for Trump," *The New York Times*, January 5, 2017, https://www.nytimes.com/2017/01/05/opinion/why-rural-america-voted-for-trump.html.

5. Among voters who earn under $30,000 annually, 53 percent voted for Clinton and 41 percent for Trump. Among those who earn $30,000–$49,999, 51 percent voted for Clinton and 42 percent for Trump. It is at and above the $50,000–$99,999 income bracket that a majority of votes begin to go to Trump: $50,000–$99,999: 46 percent to Clinton, 50 percent to Trump; $100,000–$199,999: 47 percent to Clinton, 48 percent to Trump; $200,000–$249,000: 48 percent to Clinton, 49 percent to Trump; more than $250,000: 46 percent to Clinton and 48 percent to Trump.

6. Skye Gould and Rebecca Harrington, "7 Charts Show Who Propelled Trump to Victory," *Business Insider*, https://www.businessinsider.com/exit-polls-who-voted-for-trump-clinton-2016-11#clinton-edged-out-trump-with-52-of-moderate-voters-more-people-identified-as-conservative-leaning-than-liberal-though-a-stark-divide-between-the-left-and-the-right-is-evident-here-5.

7. This information was shared with me by an interviewee who was at this meeting.

8. Samantha Allen, "How 'Real America' Became Queer America," *New York Times*, March 13, 2019, https://www.nytimes.com/2019/03/13/opinion/lgbt-trump-red-states.html; Susan Miller, "Nearly 4 Million LGBTQ People Live in Rural America, and 'Everything Is Not Bias and Awful,'" *USA Today*, April 3, 2019, https://www.usatoday.com/story/news/nation/2019/04/03/lgbtq-lesbian-gay-transgender-rural-america/3282217002/; Tiffany Stanley, "The Last Frontier for Gay Rights: A Powerful Liberal Activist, a Rural Conservative Town and a Debate that Won't End," *Washington Post*, April 2, 2018, https://www.washingtonpost.com/news/style/wp/2018/04/02/feature/the-last-frontier-for-gay-rights/.

9. For an example of a cultural representation of rural lesbians that positions the rural as inherently more anachronistic and dangerous than the city,

see *L Word Mississippi: Hate the Sin*. In a discussion of the film on AfterEllen. com, Ilene Chaiken, *The L Word* creator who also oversaw the production of *L Word Mississippi*, said that "the original premise was to find different parts of the country where being an out lesbian was less friendly than it is in metropolitan areas like Los Angeles" (Bendix 2014). Put more directly, metronormativity drove the very production of *L Word Mississippi*.

10. These numbers are from an analysis I conducted on September 22, 2010. The images posted on Flickr can change daily, so while the numbers I cite here would likely differ on another day, they reflect the importance of rural place to the group, a trend I recognized after following the site for several months.

11. For a historical account of the production of the rural idyll, see Gabriel Rosenberg's discussion of 4-H and the gender and sexual politics that drove the program's development (2015).

12. If you do the math, my breakdown does not total 388 photos. I classified eight photographs as gender-ambiguous because they include people with genders that appear meant to be read as ambiguous. I have no desire to impose classification upon images that appear to desire to defy classification, and as such, I did not include these images in my analysis. Clearly, my approach here is not a methodologically robust one or quantitative in nature; in providing these numbers, I simply aim to highlight that the site is dominated by people who appear to be men.

13. While this photo does not connote any particular rural aesthetics, it is posted on a site dedicated to "suburban and rural gay life"—a site that, again, does not make a distinction between the rural and suburban. Further, to assume the photo is not of a rural space (especially when posted on this particular site) reiterates the privileged space of the (sub)urban in our imaginaries. For a discussion of queer suburbia, see Karen Tongson's *Relocations: Queer Suburban Imaginaries* (2011).

14. "Suburban and Rural Gay Life," *Flickr.com*, https://www.flickr.com/ groups/suburbangay/.

15. Heather Dockray, "The Best Places to Find Queer Joy on Instagram," *Mashable*, https://mashable.com/article/best-queer-instagram-resources/.

16. *Autostraddle*, "What Is Autostraddle?" https://www.autostraddle.com/ about.

17. "16 Lesbian, Bisexual, and Queer Instagram Accounts to Introduce You to Our Herstory," *Autostraddle*, https://www.autostraddle.com/16-lesbian -bisexual-and-queer-instagram-accounts-to-introduce-you-to-our-herstory -433341/.

18. Dockray, "The Best Places to Find Queer Joy on Instagram."

19. *Mashable*, About, https://mashable.com/about/.

20. Queer Appalachia, *Instagram*, https://www.instagram.com/queer appalachia/.

21. Numbers taken from an analysis conducted in April 2019.

22. Country Queers, *Instagram,* https://www.instagram.com/country queers/.

23. For examples of such framings of the event, see: Eric Owens, "Department of Agriculture Celebrates Lesbian Farmers at Third-Rate Iowa Law School," *Daily Caller,* August 19, 2016, https://dailycaller.com/2016/08/19/department-of -agriculture-celebrates-lesbian-farmers-at-third-rate-iowa-law-school/; Matt Lamb, "USDA Teams Up with Iowa Law School and Cyndi Lauper to Celebrate Lesbian Farmers," *The College Fix,* August 16, 2016, https://www.thecollegefix .com/usda-teams-iowa-law-school-cyndi-lauper-celebrate-lesbian-farmers/.

24. Rachel Perclay, "Right-Wing Media: 'Lesbian and Transgender Hillbillies' Are the Latest Threat to Conservatism," *Media Matters,* August 19, 2016, https://www.mediamatters.org/rush-limbaugh/right-wing-media-lesbian-and -transgender-hillbillies-are-latest-threat-conservatism.

25. My involvement with the summit series transpired after I contacted the National Center for Lesbian Rights in July 2016 to see if I could interview conference organizers for my documentary film. After multiple conversations, conference organizers invited me to participate in the event. I thus became the first academic associated with the summit series, and I am deeply grateful to the conference organizers for connecting me to the series in thoughtful and meaningful ways. Special thanks to Julie Gonen and Ashlee Davis.

26. Julie Moreau, "Why Is Rush Limbaugh So Afraid of Lesbian Farmers?" *NBC News,* August 27, 2016, https://www.nbcnews.com/feature/nbc-out/why -rush-limbaugh-so-afraid-lesbian-farmers-n638736.

27. Thom Hartmann Program, "Why Is Rush Limbaugh So Afraid of Lesbian Farmers?" https://www.youtube.com/watch?v=tW7YIEetkJo.

28. Thom Hartmann Program, "Why Is Rush Limbaugh So Afraid of Lesbian Farmers?"

29. As I discuss in chapter 1, scholars and journalists have critiqued this version of the story of Shepard's death, claiming that it is not, in fact, accurate, and further, that the inaccuracies in wide circulation operate in the service of metronormativity. For related discussions, see Cram (2016), Jimenez (2013), and Thomsen (2019).

30. Pop Trigger, "About," https://www.youtube.com/c/poptrigger/about.

31. Pop Trigger, "Are Lesbian Farmers Invading America?" https://www .youtube.com/watch?v=gOWZ2ttCag8.

32. Elizabeth Harrington, "Feds Holding Summit for Lesbian Farmers: USDA Wants to Change the Image of Farmers from 'White, Rich Male,'" *Freebeacon,* https://freebeacon.com/issues/feds-holding-summits-lesbian-farmers/.

33. The Young Turks, "Obama's Lesbian Farmer Invasion Thwarted by Rush Limbaugh," https://www.youtube.com/watch?v=3MoJS_HMMnI.

34. Drake Law School, "Drake Law School to Co-sponsor Iowa LGBT Rural

Summit," August 5, 2016, https://news.drake.edu/2016/08/05/drake-law-school
-to-co-sponsor-iowa-lgbt-rural-summit/.

35. Human Rights Campaign, "Project One America Fact Sheet," https://
assets2.hrc.org/files/assets/resources/Project_One_America_More_Info.pdf.

36. Robin Maril, "Bringing Equality Home: LGBT People in Rural America," *Human Rights Campaign,* http://web.archive.org/web/201809111355
49if_/https://www.hrc.org/blog/bringing-equality-home-lgbt-people-in-rural
-america.

37. Maril, "Bringing Equality Home."

38. *StoryCorps,* "About StoryCorps," https://storycorps.org/about.

39. "Advancing the Progress of Rural LGBT America," *Out in the Open
Blog,* December 9, 2016, https://www.weareoutintheopen.org/blog/advancing
-the-progress-of-rural-lgbt-america.

40. Lisa Cisneros, "A Letter From Washington," *California Rural Legal Assistance, Inc.,* http://www.crla.org/letter-washington.

41. Hayley Miller, "HRC Joins White House for 'Advancing LGBT Progress in Rural America," *Human Rights Campaign,* https://www.hrc.org/blog/
hrc-joins-white-house-for-advancing-lgbt-progress-in-rural-america.

42. *Cultivating Change Foundation,* "Impact, Mission, Strategy," https://www
.cultivatingchangefoundation.org/impact-mission-strategy.

43. *Cultivating Change Foundation,* "The White House Convening on Advancing LGBT Progress in Rural America," https://www.cultivatingchange
foundation.org/events/2016/12/28/the-white-house-convening-on-advancing-
lgbt-progress-in-rural-america.

44. Gautam Raaghavan, "In Case You Missed It: LGBT Pride at the White
House," *The White House: President Barack Obama.* https://obamawhitehouse
.archives.gov/blog/2014/07/01/case-you-missed-it-lgbt-pride-white-house.

6. What's the Use?

1. Cynthia Gorney, "Gloria," *Mother Jones,* https://www.motherjones.com/
politics/1995/11/gloria/. Steinem made similar comments regarding academic
feminism a decade later in an article in *The Guardian:* Melissa Denes, "'Feminism? It's Hardly Begun,'" *The Guardian,* January 16, 2005, https://www.the
guardian.com/world/2005/jan/17/gender.melissadenes.

2. Some of the conversations I share here appear in the film *In Plain Sight*
and some do not. Despite interviewees' comfort with having their names and
faces in a film, several also mentioned that they did not want to be searchable
online. As such, the names here are pseudonyms and are different pseudonyms
than those I used for these same women in other chapters of this book.

3. Stephanie Georgopulos, "Coming Out as Biracial," *Medium,* April 17,
2019, https://humanparts.medium.com/coming-out-as-biracial-c25d6ae8f2af;

Victoria A. Brownsworth, "Coming Out as . . . Disabled," *The Advocate*, October 11, 2013, http://www.advocate.com/commentary/coming-out/2013/10/11/coming-out-asdisabled; "Coming Out on Abortion," *The New York Times*, https://www.nytimes.com/roomfordebate/2013/06/30/coming-out-on-abortion; Stephanie Land, "Why I Came Out as Being Poor," *The Guardian*, August 27, 2018, https://www.theguardian.com/lifeandstyle/2018/aug/27/why-i-came-out-as-being-poor.

Bibliography

Abelson, Miriam J. 2019. *Men in Place: Trans Masculinity, Race, and Sexuality in America*. Minneapolis: University of Minnesota Press.

Adair, Vivyan. 2005. "Class Absences: Cutting Class in Feminist Studies." *Feminist Studies* 31 (3): 575–603.

Ahmed, Sara. 2012. *On Being Included: Racism and Diversity in Institutional Life*. Durham, N.C.: Duke University Press.

Ahmed, Sara. 2019. *What's the Use? On the Uses of Use*. Durham, N.C.: Duke University Press.

Althusser, Louis. 1971. "Ideology and Ideological State Apparatuses (Notes Towards an Investigation)." In *Lenin and Philosophy and Other Essays*, translated by Ben Brewster. New York: Monthly Review.

Bailey, Marlon. 2013. *Butch Queens Up in Pumps: Gender, Performance, and Ballroom Culture in Detroit*. Ann Arbor: University of Michigan Press.

Baker, Yousef. 2020. "Killing 'Hajis' in 'Indian Country': Neoliberal Crisis, the Iraq War and the Affective Wages of Anti-Muslim Racism." *Arab Studies Quarterly* 42 (1–2): 46–65.

Barrett, John E. 2011. "Beyond the Soldier: The Hidden Costs of 'Don't Ask, Don't Tell.'" *Law School Student Scholarship* 30.

Basiliere, Jae. 2019. "Staging Dissents: Drag Kings, Resistance, and Feminist Masculinities." *Signs: Journal of Women in Culture and Society* 44 (4): 979–1001.

Bassi, Camila. 2006. "Riding the Dialectical Waves of Gay Political Economy: A Story from Birmingham's Commercial Gay Scene." *Antipode* 38 (2): 213–34.

Bell, Vicki. 1999. "On Speech, Race, and Melancholia: An Interview with Judith Butler." *Theory, Culture and Society* 16 (2): 163–74.

Bell, Christopher. 2012. *Blackness and Disability: Critical Examinations and Cultural Interventions*. East Lansing: Michigan State University Press.

Bell, David, and Gill Valentine, eds. 1995. *Mapping Desire: Geographies of Sexualities*. London: Routledge.

Bendix, Trish. 2014. "'L Word Mississippi: Hate the Sin' Highlights the Hardships of Being a Lesbian in the South." *AfterEllen*. http://www.afterellen .com/tv/224065-l-word-mississippi-hate-the-sin-highlights-the-hardships -of-being-a-lesbian-in-the-south#UC6Cwc3ppuARHpvp.99.

Berg, Heather. 2014a. "An Honest Day's Wage for a Dishonest Day's Work: (Re)Productivism and Refusal." *WSQ* 42 (1–2): 161–77.

Berg, Heather. 2014b. "Sex, Work, Queerly: Identity, Authenticity, and Labored Performance." In *Queer Sex Work*, edited by Mary Lang, Katy Pilcher, and Nicola Smith. London: Taylor & Francis.

Berlant, Lauren. 2000. *Intimacy*. Chicago: University of Chicago Press.

Berlant, Lauren. 2008. *The Female Complaint: The Unfinished Business of Sentimentality in American Culture*. Durham, N.C.: Duke University Press.

Berlant, Lauren. 2011. *Cruel Optimism*. Durham, N.C.: Duke University Press.

Bernstein, Mary, and Verta Taylor. 2013. *The Marrying Kind? Debating Same-Sex Marriage within the Lesbian and Gay Movement*. Minneapolis: University of Minnesota Press.

Boellstorff, Tom. 2005. *The Gay Archipelago: Sexuality and Nation in Indonesia*. Princeton, N.J.: Princeton University Press.

Bolaki, Stella. 2012. "Challenging Invisibility, Making Connections: Illness, Survival, and Black Struggles in Audre Lorde's Work." In *Blackness and Disability: Critical Examinations and Cultural Interventions*, edited by Christopher Bell. East Lansing: Michigan State University Press.

Boris, Eileen. 1994. *Home to Work: Motherhood and the Politics of Industrial Homework in the United States*. Cambridge: Cambridge University Press.

Boris, Eileen, and Jennifer Klein. 2012. *Caring for America: Home Health Workers in the Shadow of the Welfare State*. New York: Oxford University Press.

Boris, Eileen, and Rachel Salazar Parreñas, eds. 2010. *Intimate Labors: Cultures, Technologies, and the Politics of Care*. Stanford, Calif.: Stanford Social Sciences.

Bornstein, Kate. 2010. "Open Letter to LGBT Leaders Who Are Pushing Marriage Equality." In *Against Equality: Queer Critiques of Gay Marriage*, edited by Ryan Conrad. Lewiston, Maine: Equality Publishing Collective.

Boyd, Nan. 2008. "Sex and Tourism: The Economic Implications of Gay Marriage Movement." *Radical History Review* 100: 223–35.

Briggs, Laura. 2008. "Activism and Epistemologies: Problems for Transnationalisms." *Social Text* 26 (497): 79–95.

Brown, Wendy. 1995. *States of Injury: Power and Freedom in Late Modernity*. Princeton, N.J.: Princeton University Press.

Browne, Kath. 2011. "Lesbian Separatist Feminism at Michigan Womyn's Music Festival." *Feminism & Psychology* 21 (2): 248–56.

Browne, Kath, Jason Lim, and Gavin Brown, eds. 2007. *Geographies of Sexualities: Theory, Practices and Politics*. Aldershot, U.K.: Ashgate.

Brown-Saracino, Japonica. 2017. *How Places Make Us: Novel LBQ Identities in Four Small Cities*. Chicago: University of Chicago Press.

Butler, Judith. (1990) 1999. *Gender Trouble: Feminism and the Subversion of Identity*. New York: Routledge.

Butler, Judith. 1993. *Bodies That Matter: On the Discursive Limits of Sex*. New York: Routledge.

Butler, Judith. 1997. *Excitable Speech: A Politics of the Performative*. New York: Routledge.

Carrion, Victor, and James Lock. 1997. "The Coming Out Process: Developmental Stages for Sexual Minority Youth." *Clinical Child Psychology and Psychiatry* 2 (3): 369–77.

Casper, Monica J., and Lisa Jean Moore. 2009. *Missing Bodies: The Politics of Visibility*. New York: New York University Press.

Cass, Vivienne. 1979. "Homosexual Identity Formation." *Journal of Homosexuality* 4 (3): 219–35.

Cass, Vivienne. 1996. "Sexual Orientation Identity Formation: A Western Phenomenon." In *Textbook of Homosexuality and Mental Health*, edited by R. P. Cabaj and T. S. Stein. Washington, D.C.: American Psychiatric Association.

Charles, Casey. 2006. "Panic in the Project: Critical Queer Studies and The Matthew Shepard Murder." *Law and Literature* 18 (2): 225–52.

Chasin, Alexandra. 2001. *Selling Out: The Gay and Lesbian Movement Goes to Market*. New York: Palgrave.

Chatterjee, Moyukh. 2017. "The Impunity Effect: Majoritarian Rule, Everyday Legality, and State Formation in India." *American Ethnologist* 44 (1): 118–30.

Chauncey, George. 1994. *Gay New York: Gender, Urban Culture, and the Makings of the Gay Male World, 1890–1940*. New York: Basic Books.

Cho, Sumi. July 2009. "Post-Racialism." *Iowa Law Review* 94 (5): 1589–649.

Clark, Danae. 1991. "Commodity Lesbianism." *Camera Obscura: Feminism, Culture, and Media Studies* 9 (1–2): 181–201.

Clift, Stephan, Michael Luongo, and Carry Callister. 2002. *Gay Tourism: Culture, Identity and Sex*. New York: Continuum.

Cohen, Cathy. 1997. "Punks, Bulldaggers, and Welfare Queens: The Radical Potential of Queer Politics?" *GLQ: A Journal of Lesbian and Gay Studies* 3: 437–65.

Comer, Krista. 2010. "Exceptionalism, Other Wests, Critical Regionalism." *American Literary History* 23 (1): 159–73.

Conrad, Ryan, ed. 2010. *Against Equality: Queer Critiques of Gay Marriage*. Lewiston, Maine: Against Equality Publishing Collective.

Corbett, Jenny. 1994. "A Proud Label: Exploring the Relationship between Disability Politics and Gay Pride." *Disability and Society* 9 (3): 343–57.

Corker, Marian. 2001. "Sensing Disability." In "Feminism and Disability," special issue, *Hypatia* 16 (4): 34–52.

Cram, E. 2016. "(Dis)Locating Queer Citizenship: Imaging Rurality in Matthew Shepard's Memory." *Queering the Countryside: New Frontiers in Rural Queer Studies,* edited by Mary L. Gray, Colin R. Johnson, and Brian Joseph Gilley, 267–89. New York: New York University Press.

Cramer, R. J., A. Kehn, C. R. Pennington, H. J. Wechsler, J. W. Clark, and J. Nagle. 2013. "An Examination of Sexual Orientation and Transgender-Based Hate Crimes in the Post-Matthew Shepard Era." *Psychology, Public Policy, and Law* 19 (3): 355–68.

Currah, Paisley. 2008. "Expecting Bodies: The Pregnant Man and Transgender Exclusion from the Employment Non-Discrimination Act." *Women's Studies Quarterly* 36 (3–4).

Currier, Ashley. 2012. *Out in Africa: LGBT Organizing in Namibia and South Africa.* Minneapolis: University of Minnesota Press.

David, Emmanuel. 2015. "Purple-Collar Labor: Transgender Workers and Queer Value at Global Call Centers in the Philippines." *Gender and Society* 29 (2): 169–94.

De Beauvoir, Simone. 1949. *The Second Sex.* New York: Vintage.

D'Emilio, John. 1983. "Capitalism and Gay Identity." In *Powers of Desire: The Politics of Sexuality,* edited by Ann Snitow, Christine Stansell, and Sharon Thompson. New York: Monthly Review Press.

Dolmage, Jay T. 2018. *Disabled Upon Arrival: Eugenics, Immigration, and the Construction of Race and Disability.* Columbus: Ohio State University Press.

Doyle, Jennifer. 2009. "Blind Spots and Failed Performance: Abortion, Feminism, and Queer Theory." *Qui Parle* 18 (1): 25–52.

Duggan, Lisa. 2004. *The Twilight of Equality: Neoliberalism, Cultural Politics and the Attack on Democracy.* Boston: Beacon.

Durban-Albrecht, Erin. 2013. "The Legacy of Assotto Saint: Tracing Transnational History from the Gay Haitian Diaspora." *Journal of Haitian Studies* 19 (1).

Durban-Albrecht, Erin. 2017. "Postcolonial Disablement and/as Transition: Trans* Haitian Narratives of Breaking Open and Stitching Together." *Transgender Studies Quarterly* 4 (2): 195–207.

Eaves, LaToya E. 2016. "Outside Forces: Black Southern Sexuality." In *Queering the Countryside: New Frontiers in Rural Queer Studies,* edited by Mary L. Gray, Colin R. Johnson, and Brian Joseph Gilley. New York: New York University Press.

Edelman, Lee. 2004. *No Future: Queer Theory and the Death Drive.* Durham, N.C.: Duke University Press.

Essig, Laurie. 1999. *Queer in Russia: A Story of Sex, Self, and the Other.* Durham. N.C.: Duke University Press.

Esterberg, Kristin. 1997. *Lesbian and Bisexual Identities.* Philadelphia: Temple University Press.

Farrow, Kenyon. 2010. "Is Gay Marriage Anti-Black???" In *Against Equality: Queer Critiques of Gay Marriage,* edited by Ryan Conrad. Lewiston, Maine: Against Equality Publishing Collective.

Federici, Silvia. 1975. *Wages Against Housework.* London: Power of Women Collective.

Federici, Silvia. 2014. *Caliban and the Witch.* Brooklyn, N.Y.: Autonomedia.

Fellows, Will, ed. 1996. *Farm Boys: Lives of Gay Men from the Rural Midwest.* Madison: University of Wisconsin Press.

Ferguson, Roderick. 2003. *Aberrations in Black: Toward a Queer of Color Critique.* Minneapolis: University of Minnesota Press.

Floyd, Kevin. 2009. *The Reification of Desire: Towards a Queer Marxism.* Minneapolis: University of Minnesota Press.

Foucault, Michel. 1977. *Discipline and Punish: The Birth of the Prison.* Translated by Alan Sheridan. London: Allen Lane, Penguin.

Foucault, Michel. (1978) 1990. *The History of Sexuality, Volume I: An Introduction.* Translated by Robert Hurley. New York: Vintage.

Frank, Nathaniel. 2010. *Don't Ask, Don't Tell: Detailing the Damage.* Santa Barbara, Calif.: Palm Center. http://unfriendlyfire.org/research/files/report.pdf.

Frankenberg, Ruth. 1993. *White Women, Race Matters: The Social Construction of Whiteness.* Minneapolis: University of Minnesota Press.

Gates, Gary J. 2006. *Same-Sex Couples and the Gay, Lesbian, Bisexual Populations: New Estimates from the American Community Survey.* Los Angeles: Williams Institute.

Ghaziani, Amin. 2015. "Lesbian Geographies." *Contexts* 14 (1): 62–64.

Ghaziani, Amin, and Matt Brim. 2019. *Imagining Queer Methods.* New York: New York University Press.

Gluckman, Amy, and Betsy Reed. 1997. *Homo Economics: Capitalism, Community, and Lesbian and Gay Life.* New York: Routledge.

Gopinath, Gayatri. 2005. *Impossible Desires: Queer Diaspora and South Asian Public Cultures.* Durham, N.C.: Duke University Press.

Gordon, Avery. (1997) 2008. *Ghostly Matters: Haunting and the Sociological Imagination.* Minneapolis. University of Minnesota Press.

Gordon, Avery. 2004. *Keeping Good Time: Reflections on Knowledge, Power, and People.* Boulder, Colo.: Paradigm.

Gordon, Avery, and Christopher Newfield, eds. 1996. *Mapping Multiculturalism.* Minneapolis: University of Minnesota Press.

Gossett, Reina, Eric A. Stanley, and Johanna Burton, eds. 2017. *Trap Door: Trans Cultural Production and the Politics of Visibility.* Cambridge, Mass.: MIT Press.

Gray, Mary L. 2009. *Out in the Country: Youth, Media, and Queer Visibility in Rural America.* New York: New York University Press.

Gray, Mary L., Colin R. Johnson, and Brian Joseph Gilley, eds. 2016. *Queering the Countryside: New Frontiers in Rural Queer Studies.* New York: New York University Press.

Greer, Germaine. 1970. *The Female Eunuch.* London: MacGibbon & Kee.

Griffin, Maryam. 2020. "Transcending Enclosures by Bus: Public Transit Protests, Frame Mobility, and the Many Facets of Colonial Occupation." In "Occupations in Context: The Cultural Logics of Occupation, Settler Violence and Resistance," edited by Mona Bhan and Haley Duschinski, special issue, *Critique of Anthropology* 40 (3): 298–322.

Gupta, Hemangini. 2019. "Testing the Future: Gender and Technocapitalism in Start-Up India." *Feminist Review* 123: 74–88.

Halberstam, Jack. 1998. *Female Masculinity.* Durham, N.C.: Duke University Press.

Halberstam, Jack. 2005. *In a Queer Time and Place: Transgender Bodies, Subcultural Lives.* New York: New York University Press.

Hall, Kim. 2011. *Feminist Disability Studies.* Bloomington: Indiana University Press.

Halpin, Sean, and Michael W. Allen. 2004. "Changes in Psychosocial Well-Being During Stages of Gay Identity Development." *Journal of Homosexuality* 47 (2): 109–26.

Hanhardt, Christina B. 2013. *Safe Space: Gay Neighborhood History and the Politics of Violence.* Durham, N.C.: Duke University Press.

Haritaworn, Jin. 2010–11. "Queer Injuries: The Racial Politics of 'Homophobic Hate Crimes' in Germany." *Social Justice* 37 (1): 69–89.

Hartmann, Heidi. 1979. "The Unhappy Marriage of Marxism and Feminism: Towards a More Progressive Union." *Capital & Class* 3 (2): 1–33.

Hegde, Radha S., ed. 2011. *Circuits of Visibility: Gender and Transnational Media Cultures.* New York: New York University Press.

Hemmings, Clare. 2011. *Why Stories Matter: The Political Grammar of Feminist Theory.* Durham, N.C.: Duke University Press.

Hennessy, Rosemary. 2000. *Profit and Pleasure: Sexual Identities in Late Capitalism.* New York: Routledge.

Hennessy, Rosemary. 2013. *Fires on the Border: The Passionate Politics of Labor Organizing on the Mexican Frontera.* Minneapolis: University of Minnesota Press.

Herdt, Gilbert, ed. 1996. *Third Sex, Third Gender: Beyond Sexual Dimorphism in Culture and History.* New York: Zone.

Herek, Gregory M. 1988. "Heterosexuals' Attitudes towards Lesbians and Gay Men: Correlates and Gender Differences." *Journal of Sex Research* 25 (4): 457–77.

Herring, Scott. 2010. *Another Country: Queer Anti-urbanism.* New York: New York University Press.

Howard, John. 1999. *Men Like That: A Southern Queer History.* Chicago: University of Chicago Press.

Howard, John. 2006. "Of Closets and Other Rural Voids." *GLQ: A Journal of Gay and Lesbian Studies* 13 (1): 100–102.

Howard-Hassman, Rhoda. 2001. "The Gay Cousin: Learning to Accept Gay Rights." *Journal of Homosexuality* 42 (1): 127–49.

Hughes, Howard. 2003. "Marketing Gay Tourism in Manchester: New Market for Urban Tourism or Destruction of 'Gay Space'?" *Journal of Vacation Marketing* 9 (2): 152–63.

Hunter, Nan. 1991. "Marriage, Law, and Gender: A Feminist Inquiry." *Law and Sexuality* 1: 9–30.

Irving, Dan. 2008. "Normalized Transgressions: Legitimizing the Transsexual Body as Productive." *Radical History Review* 38 (100): 38–59.

Jackson, Peter. 2009. "Capitalism and Global Queering: National Markets, Parallels among Sexual Cultures, and Multiple Queer Modernities." *GLQ: A Journal of Lesbian and Gay Studies* 15 (3): 357–95.

Jagose, Annamarie. 2009. "Feminism's Queer Theory." *Feminism & Psychology* 19 (2): 157–74.

James, Selma. 1983. *Marx and Feminism.* London: Crossroads.

Jarman, Michelle. 2012. "Dismembering the Lynch Mob: Intersecting Narratives of Disability, Race and Sexual Menace." In *Sex and Disability,* edited by Robert McRuer and Anna Mollow. Durham, N.C.: Duke University Press.

Jimenez, Stephen. 2013. *The Book of Matt: Hidden Truths about the Murder of Matthew Shepard.* Hanover, N.H.: Steerforth.

Johnson, Colin R. 2013. *Just Queer Folks: Gender and Sexuality in Rural America.* Philadelphia: Temple University Press.

Johnson, E. Patrick. 2008. *Sweet Tea: Black Gay Men of the South.* Chapel Hill: University of North Carolina Press.

Johnson, E. Patrick. 2016. *No Tea, No Shade: New Writings in Black Queer Studies.* Durham, N.C.: Duke University Press.

Johnson, E. Patrick. 2018. *Black. Queer. Southern. Women: An Oral History.* Chapel Hill: University of North Carolina Press.

Johnson, E. Patrick, and Mae Henderson. 2005. *Black Queer Studies: A Critical Anthology.* Durham, N.C.: Duke University Press.

Johnston, Lynda, and Robyn Longhurst. 2010. *Space, Place, and Sex: Geographies of Sexualities.* Plymouth, U.K.: Rowman and Littlefield.

Johnston, Lynda, and Gill Valentine. 1995. "Wherever I Lay My Girlfriend, That's My Home: The Performance and Surveillance of Lesbian Identities in Domestic Environments." In *Mapping Desire: Geographies of Sexualities,* edited by David Bell and Gill Valentine. London: Routledge.

Joseph, Miranda. 2002a. *Against the Romance of Community.* Minneapolis: University of Minnesota Press.

Joseph, Miranda. 2002b. "Analogy and Complicity: Women's Studies, Lesbian/ Gay Studies and Capitalism." In *Women's Studies on Its Own: A Next Wave*

Reader in Institutional Change, edited by Robyn Weigman. Durham, N.C.: Duke University Press.

Jung, Karen Elizabeth. 2011. "Chronic Illness and Educational Equity: The Politics of Visibility." In *Feminist Disability Studies,* edited by Kim Hall. Bloomington: Indiana University Press.

Kafer, Alison. 2013. *Feminist, Queer, Crip.* Bloomington: Indiana University Press.

Kazyak, Emily. 2012. "Midwest of Lesbian: Gender, Rurality, mand Sexuality." *Gender and Society* 26 (6): 825–48.

Kazyak, Emily, and Mathew Stange. 2016. "Examining the Nuance in Public Opinion of Pro-LGB Policies in a 'Red State.'" *Sexuality Research and Social Policy* 13 (2): 142–57.

Keeling, Kara. 2019. *Queer Times, Black Futures.* New York: New York University Press.

Kelley, Robin D. G. 2002. "Keeping It (Sur)real: Dreams of the Marvelous." In *Freedom Dreams: The Black Radical Imagination.* Boston: Beacon.

Kelly, Jack. 2019. "More Than Half of U.S. Workers Are Unhappy in Their Jobs: Here's Why and What Needs to Be Done Now." *Forbes.* https://www.forbes .com/sites/jackkelly/2019/10/25/more-than-half-of-us-workers-are-unhappy -in-their-jobs-heres-why-and-what-needs-to-be-done-now/#899032f20247.

Kennedy, Elizabeth Lapovsky, and Madeline D. Davis. (1993) 2014. *Boots of Leather, Slippers of Gold: The History of a Lesbian Community.* New York: Routledge.

Kirby, Kathleen. 1993. "Thinking through the Boundary: The Politics of Location, Subjects, and Space." *Boundary* 2 20 (2): 173–89.

Kulick, Don. 1998. *Travesti: Sex, Gender, and Culture Among Brazilian Transgendered Prostitutes.* Chicago: University of Chicago Press.

Lance, Larry M. 1987. "The Effects of Interaction with Gay Persons on Attitudes Toward Homosexuality." *Human Relations* 40 (6): 329–36.

Lipsitz, George. 2007. "The Racialization of Space and the Spatialization of Race." *Landscape Journal* 26 (1): 10–23.

Lukács, George. 1971. *History and Class Consciousness: Studies in Marxist Dialectics.* Cambridge, Mass.: MIT University Press.

Luongo, Michael. 2002. "Rome's World Pride: Making the Eternal City an International Gay Tourism Destination." *GLQ: A Journal of Lesbian and Gay Studies* 8 (1–2): 167–81.

Manalansan, Martin F. 2003. *Global Divas: Filipino Gay Men in the Diaspora.* Durham, N.C.: Duke University Press.

Manalansan, Martin F. 2014. "The 'Stuff' of Archives: Mess, Migration, and Queer Lives." *Radical History Review* 2014 (120): 94–107.

Manalansan, Martin F., Chantal Nadeau, Richard T. Rodriguez, and Siobhan B. Somerville, eds. 2014. "Queering the Middle," special issue, *GLQ: A Journal of Lesbian and Gay Studies.*

Marinucci, Mimi. 2010. *Feminism Is Queer: The Intimate Connection between Queer and Feminist Theory.* Northwestern University: Zed Books.

Massad, Joseph A. 2008. *Desiring Arabs.* Chicago: University of Chicago Press.

McGarry, Molly, Fred Wasserman, and Mimi Bowling. 1998. *Becoming Visible: An Illustrated History of Lesbian and Gay Life in Twentieth-Century America.* New York: Penguin.

McKittrick, Katherine, and Clyde Woods. 2007. *Black Geographies and the Politics of Place.* Cambridge: South End Press.

McNaught, Brian. 2011. "Why Gays Should Come Out at Work." *CNN.* http://www.cnn.com/2011/OPINION/06/28/mcnaught.gays.workplace/index.html

McRuer, Robert. 2006. *Crip Theory: Cultural Signs of Queerness and Disability.* New York: New York University Press.

McRuer, Robert, and Anna Mollow. 2012. *Sex and Disability.* Durham, N.C.: Duke University Press.

Millett, Kate. 1971. *Sexual Politics.* New York: Columbia University Press.

Moore, Mignon. 2011. *Invisible Families: Gay Identities, Relationships, and Motherhood among Black Women.* Los Angeles: University of California Press.

Muñoz, José Esteban. 1999. *Disidentifications: Queers of Color and the Performance of Politics.* Minneapolis: University of Minnesota Press.

Muñoz, José Esteban. 2006. "Stages: Queers, Punks, and the Utopian Performative." In *The Sage Handbook of Performance Studies,* edited by Soyini Madison and Judith Hamera. Thousand Oaks, Calif.: Sage.

Muñoz, José Esteban. 2009. *Cruising Utopia: The Then and There of Queer Futurity.* New York: New York University Press.

Musser, Amber Jamilla. 2018. *Sensual Excess: Queer Femininity and Brown Jouissance.* New York: New York University Press.

Nair, Yasmin. 2010. "Who's Illegal Now? Immigration, Marriage, and the Violence of Inclusion." In *Against Equality: Queer Critiques of Gay Marriage,* edited by Ryan Conrad. Lewiston, Maine: Against Equality Publishing Collective.

Namaste, Vivian. 2000. *Invisible Lives: The Erasure of Transexual and Transgendered People.* Chicago: University of Chicago Press.

Nyong'o, Tavia. 2018. *Afro-Fabulations: The Queer Drama of Black Life.* New York: New York University Press.

Osborne, Karen Lee, and William Spurlin. 1996. *Reclaiming the Heartland: Lesbian and Gay Voices from the Midwest.* Minneapolis: University of Minnesota Press.

Ott, Brian, and Eric Aoki. 2002. "The Politics of Negotiating Public Tragedy: Media Framing of the Matthew Shepard Murder." *Rhetoric & Public Affairs* 5 (3): 483–505.

Patsavas, Alyson. 2014. "Recovering a Cripistemology of Pain: Leaky Bodies,

Connective Tissue and Feeling Discourse." *Journal of Literary and Cultural Disability Studies* 8 (2): 203–18.

Pellegrini, Ann. 2002. "Consuming Lifestyle: Commodity Capitalism and Transformations in Gay Identity." In *Queer Globalizations: Citizenship and the Afterlife of Colonialism,* edited by Arnaldo Cruz-Malave and Martin Manalansan. New York: New York University Press.

Petersen, Jennifer. 2011. *Murder, the Media, and the Politics of Public Feeling: Remembering Matthew Shepard and James Byrd Jr.* Bloomington: Indiana University Press.

Phelan, Peggy. 1993. *Unmarked: The Politics of Performance.* London: Routledge.

Podmore, Julie. 2001. "Lesbians in the Crowd: Gender, Sexuality and Visibility along Montréal's Boul. St-Laurent." *Gender, Place and Culture* 8 (4): 333–55.

Pollitt, Katha. 2015a. "There Are No Abortion Cakes." *The Nation.* https://www.thenation.com/article/archive/there-are-no-abortion-cakes/.

Pollitt, Katha. 2015b. "There's a Reason Gay Marriage Is Winning While Abortion Rights Are Losing." *The Nation.* https://www.thenation.com/article/archive/theres-reason-gay-marriage-winning-while-abortion-rights-are-losing/.

Puar, Jasbir. 2002a. "Circuits of Queer Mobility: Tourism, Travel, and Globalization." *GLQ: A Journal of Lesbian and Gay Studies* 8 (1–2): 101–37.

Puar, Jasbir. 2002b. "Transnational Feminist Critiques of Queer Tourism." *Antipode* 34 (5): 935–46.

Puar, Jasbir. 2007. *Terrorist Assemblages: Homonationalism in Queer Times.* Durham, N.C.: Duke University Press.

Puar, Jasbir. 2017. *The Right to Maim: Debility, Capacity, Disability.* Durham, N.C.: Duke University Press.

Reddy, Chandan. 2008. "Time for Rights? Loving, Gay Marriage, and the Limits of Legal Justice." *Fordham Law Review* 76 (6): 2849–72.

Reddy, Chandan. 2011. *Freedom with Violence. Race, Sexuality, and the US State.* Durham, N.C.: Duke University Press.

Roscoe, Will. 1991. *The Zuni Man-Woman.* Albuquerque: University of New Mexico Press.

Rosenberg, Gabriel. 2015. *The 4-H Harvest: Sexuality and the State in Rural America.* Philadelphia: University of Pennsylvania Press.

Rosenberg, Jordana, and Amy Villarejo. 2012. "Introduction: Queerness, Norms, Utopia." *GLQ: A Journal of Lesbian and Gay Studies* 18 (1): 1–18.

Rosenfeld, Michael J., and Byung-Soo Kim. 2005. "The Independence of Young Adults and the Rise of Interracial and Same-Sex Unions." *American Sociological Review* 70 (4): 542–62.

Rubin, Gayle. 1975. "The Traffic in Women: Notes on the Political Economy of Sex." In *Toward an Anthropology of Women,* edited by Rayna R. Reiter. New York: Monthly Review.

Rubin, Gayle. 1984. "Thinking Sex: Notes for a Radical Theory of the Politics of Sexuality." In *Pleasures and Danger: Exploring Female Sexuality,* edited by Carole S. Vance. London: Routledge.

Rupp, Leila. 1999. *A Desired Past: A Short History of Same-Sex Love in America.* Chicago: University of Chicago Press.

Rupp, Leila. 2009a. "Loving Women in the Modern World." In *Feminist Frontiers,* edited by Verta Taylor and Nancy Whittier. 8th ed. New York: McGraw-Hill Higher Education.

Rupp, Leila. 2009b. *Sapphistries: A Global History of Love between Women.* New York: New York University Press.

Rupp, Leila, and Verta Taylor. 2003. *Drag Queens at the 801 Cabaret.* Chicago: University of Chicago Press.

Russo Garrido, Anahi. 2020. *Tortilleras Negotiating Intimacy: Love, Friendship, and Sex in Queer Mexico City.* New Brunswick, N.J.: Rutgers University Press.

Rust, Paula. 1993. "Coming Out in the Age of Social Constructionism." *Gender & Society* 7 (1): 50–77.

Salton-Cox, Glyn. 2013. *Cobbett and the Comintern: Transnational Provincialism and Revolutionary Desire from the Popular Front to the New Left.* PhD diss, Yale University.

Samuels, Ellen. 2003. "My Body, My Closet: Invisible Disability and the Limits of Coming-Out Discourse." *GLQ: A Journal of Lesbian and Gay Studies* 9 (1–2): 233–55.

Samuels, Ellen. 2014. *Fantasies of Identification: Disability, Gender, Race.* New York: New York University Press.

Schattenkirk, Kevin. 2014. "Matthew Shepard, Music and Social Justice: Discourse on the Relationship Between Homophobic Violence and Anti-Gay Sentiment in Two Performative Contexts." *Eras* 16: 83–95.

Schneider, William, and Irwin A. Lewis. 1984. "The Straight Story on Homosexuality and Gay Rights." *Public Opinion* 7 (1): 16–20.

Schweighofer, Katie. 2016. "Rethinking the Closet: Queer Life in Rural Geographies." In *Queering the Countryside: New Frontiers in Rural Queer Studies,* edited by Mary L. Gray, Colin R. Johnson, and Brian Joseph Gilley, 223–43. New York: New York University Press.

Scott, Joan Wallach. 1991. "The Evidence of Experience." *Critical Inquiry* 17 (4): 773–97.

Sears, Alan. 2005. "Queer Anti-Capitalism: What's Left of Lesbian and Gay Liberation?" *Science & Society* 69 (1): 92–112.

Sedgwick, Eve Kosofsky. (1990) 2008. *Epistemology of the Closet.* Los Angeles: University of California Press.

Seidman, Steven. 2002. *Beyond the Closet: The Transformation of Gay and Lesbian Life.* New York: Routledge.

Shah, Nayan. 2011. *Stranger Intimacy: Contesting Race, Sexuality, and the Law in the North American West*. Berkeley: University of California Press.

Shah, Svati. 2014. "Queering Critiques of Neoliberalism in India: Urbanism and Inequality in the Era of Transnational "LGBTQ" Rights." *Antipode* 47 (3): 635–51.

Sikk, Helis, and Leisa Meyer, eds. 2019. *The Legacies of Matthew Shepard: Twenty Years Later*. New York: Routledge.

Skeggs, Beverley. 1999. "Matter out of Place: Visibility and Sexualities in Leisure Spaces." *Leisure Studies* 18 (3): 213–32.

Skidmore, Emily. 2019. *True Sex: The Lives of Trans Men at the Turn of the Twentieth Century*. New York: New York University Press.

Smith, Andrea. 2013. "Unsettling the Privilege of Self-Reflexivity." In *Geographies of Privilege*, edited by France Winddance Twine and Bradley Gardener. New York: Routledge.

Soderling, Stina. 2016. "Queer Rurality and the Materiality of Time." In *Queering the Countryside: New Frontiers in Rural Queer Studies*, edited by Mary L. Gray, Colin R. Johnson, and Brian Joseph Gilley, 333–48. New York: New York University Press.

Solis, Santiago. 2007. "Snow White and the Seven 'Dwarfs'—Queercripped." *Hypatia: A Journal of Feminist Philosophy* 22 (1): 114–31.

Somerville, Siobhan. 2000. *Queering the Color Line: Race and the Invention of Homosexuality in American Culture*. Durham, N.C.: Duke University Press.

Spade, Dean. 2015. *Normal Life: Administrative Violence, Critical Trans Politics, and the Limits of Law*. Durham, N.C.: Duke University Press.

Stanley, Eric, and Nat Smith, eds. 2015. *Captive Genders: Trans Embodiment and the Prison Industrial Complex*. 2015. Oakland, Calif.: AK Press.

Stein, Arlene. 1997. *Sex and Sensibility: Stories of a Lesbian Generation*. Berkeley: University of California Press.

Stein, Arlene. 2002. *The Stranger Next Door: The Story of a Small Community's Battle Over Sex, Faith, and Civil Rights*. Boston: Beacon.

Stone, Sandy. 1991. "The Empire Strikes Back: A Posttranssexual Manifesto." In *Body Guards: The Cultural Politics of Gender Ambiguity*, edited by Kristina Straub and Julia Epstein. New York: Routledge.

Stryker, Susan, and Stephen Whittle, eds. 2006. *The Transgender Studies Reader*. New York: Routledge.

Swarr, Amanda Lock. 2012. *Sex in Transition: Remaking Gender and Race in South Africa*. Albany: State University of New York Press.

Taylor, Verta, and Leila Rupp. 2014. "Are We Still Queer Even Though We're Married?" *Contexts* 13 (2): 84–87.

Thompson, Brock. 2010. *The Un-Natural State: Arkansas and the Queer South*. Fayetteville: University of Arkansas Press.

Thomsen, Carly. 2013. "From Refusing Stigmatization to Celebration: New Directions for Reproductive Justice Activism." *Feminist Studies* 39 (1): 149–58.

Thomsen, Carly. 2015a. "The Post-Raciality and Post-Spatiality of Calls for LGBTQ and Disability Visibility." In "New Conversations in Feminist Disability Studies," edited by Kim Q. Hall, special issue, *Hypatia: A Journal of Feminist Philosophy* 30 (1): 149–66.

Thomsen, Carly. 2015b. "The Politics of Narrative, Narrative as Politic: Rethinking Reproductive Justice Frameworks through the South Dakota Abortion Story." *Feminist Formations* 27 (2): 126.

Thomsen, Carly. 2016. "In Plain(s) Sight: Rural LGBTQ Women and the Politics of Visibility." In *Queering the Countryside: New Frontiers in Rural Queer Studies*, edited by Mary L. Gray, Colin R. Johnson, and Brian Joseph Gilley, 244–66. New York: New York University Press.

Thomsen, Carly. 2019. "Matthew Shepard, Hate Crimes Legislation, and Queer Rurality." In *The Legacies of Matthew Shepard: Twenty Years Later*, edited by Helis Sikk and Leisa Meyer, 57–78. London: Routledge.

Thomsen, Carly, and Grace Morrison. 2020. "Abortion as Gender Transgression: Reproductive Justice, Queer Theory, and Anti-Crisis Pregnancy Center Activism." *Signs: Journal of Women in Culture and Society* 45 (3): 703–30.

Tongson, Karen. 2011. *Relocations: Queer Suburban Imaginaries.* New York: New York University Press.

Tongson, Karen, and Scott Herring. 2019. "The Sexual Imaginarium: Reappraisal." *GLQ: A Journal of Lesbian and Gay Studies* 25 (1): 51–56.

Towle, Evan, and Lynn Morgan. 2002. "Romancing the Transgender Native: Rethinking the Use of the 'Third Gender' Concept." *GLQ: A Journal of Lesbian and Gay Studies* 8 (4): 469–97.

Tuan, Yi-Fu. 2011. *Space and Place: The Perspective of Experience.* Minneapolis: University of Minnesota Press.

Tucker, Edmon W., and Miriam Potocky-Tripodi. 2006. "Changing Homosexuals' Attitudes Towards Homosexuals: A Systematic Review of the Empirical." *Research on Social Work Practice* 16 (2): 176–90.

Tyburski, Susan J. 2015. "Exploring Popular Culture Narratives of Gender Violence." In *Violence in American Popular Culture*, edited by David Schechter. Santa Barbara, Calif.: Praeger.

Valentine, Gill. 1997. "Making Space: Lesbian Separatist Communities in the United States." In *Contested Countryside Cultures: Rurality and Sociocultural Marginalisation*, edited by Paul Cloke and Jo Little. London: Routledge.

Visser, Gustav. 2003. "Gay Men, Tourism and Urban Space: Reflections on Africa's 'Gay Capital.'" *Tourism Geographies* 5 (2): 168–89.

Vitulli, Elias. 2010. "A Defining Moment in Civil Rights History? The

Employment Non-Discrimination Act, Trans-Inclusion, and Homonormativity." *Sexuality Research and Social Policy* 7: 155–67.

Walters, Suzanna Danuta. 2001. *All the Rage: The Story of Gay Visibility in America*. Chicago: University of Chicago Press.

Ward, Jane. 2010. "Gender Labor: Transmen, Femmes, and Collective Work of Transgression." *Sexualities* 3 (2): 236–54.

Ward, Jane. 2016. "Dyke Methods: A Meditation on Queer Studies and the Gay Men Who Hate It." *Women's Studies Quarterly* 44 (3/4): 68–85.

Ward, Jane, and Amy Stone. 2011. "From 'Black People Are Not Homosexual' to 'Gay Is the New Black': Mapping White Uses of Blackness in Modern Gay Rights Campaigns in the United States." *Social Identities* 17 (5): 605–24.

Warner, Michael. 1993. *Fear of a Queer Planet: Queer Politics and Social Theory*. Minneapolis: University of Minnesota Press.

Warner, Michael. 1999. *The Trouble with Normal: Sex, Politics, and the Ethics of Queer Life*. New York: Free Press.

Weed, Elizabeth, and Naomi Schor. 1997. *Feminism Meets Queer Theory*. Bloomington: Indiana University Press.

Weeks, Kathi. 2011. *The Problem with Work: Feminism, Marxism, Antiwork Politics, and Postwork Imaginaries*. Durham, N.C.: Duke University Press.

Weil, Abraham. 2017a. "Psychoanalysis and Trans*versality." *TSQ: Transgender Studies Quarterly* 4 (3–4): 639–46.

Weil, Abraham. 2017b. "Trans*versal Animacies and the Mattering of Black Trans* Political Life." *Angelaki: Journal of the Theoretical Humanities* 22 (2): 191–202.

Weil, Abraham. Forthcoming. "Transmolecular Revolution." In *Schizoanalysis of Trans Studies*, edited by C. Cremin and I. Buchanan.

Wesling, Meg. 2012. "Queer Value." *GLQ: A Journal of Lesbian and Gay Studies* 18 (4): 107–25.

Weston, Kath. 1995. "Get Thee to a Big City: Sexual Imaginary and the Great Gay Migration." *GLQ: A Journal of Lesbian and Gay Studies* 2 (3): 253–77.

Wienke, Chris, and Gretchen J. Hill. 2013. "Does Place of Residence Matter? Rural–Urban Differences and the Wellbeing of Gay Men and Lesbians." *Journal of Homosexuality* 60 (9): 1256–79.

Woods, Clyde. 1998. *Development Arrested: Race, Power and the Blues in the Mississippi Delta*. New York City: Verso.

Index

Page numbers in italic refer to illustrations.

LGBTQ organizations, xlii, xlv, 49,
60, 62, 63, 77, 78, 102, 106, 118,
134, 173n22
LGBTQ people of color, xxxiii, 37,
38, 136; disabled, 68, 70; target-
ing, 22–23
LGBTQ rights, xx, xxviii, xxxi,
xxxvii, li, 12, 21, 64, 82, 111, 115,
117, 173n22; support for, 134
LGBTQ studies, xi, xxxiii, xlv, xlix,
li, 1, 32, 119, 137, 141, 147, 161–62,
171n3, 172n13, 178n8; city-centric
nature of, xiv
LGBTQ workers, 98–99, 109; authenticity and, 115–16; homonormativity and, 113; outness of,
113, 116
LGBTQ youth, xxxv, 140
LGBT Resource Center, 104, 110
LGBT Rural Summit, lii, 118, 120,
127–30, 132–35, 138, 139, 141,
168, 184n25
LGBT Technology Partnership and
Institute, 140
liberals, viii, x, 1, 13, 23, 134
liberation, x, xviii, xli, lv, 88
Limbaugh, Rush: lesbian farmers
and, 127–29; liberal responses to,
130–35
Longhurst, Robyn, 171n1
"Love(EXPLORE)" (Suburban and
Rural Gay Life), *123*
Lozito, HB, 139
Lukács, George, 90
L Word Mississippi (film), 183n9

Manalansan, Martin, xlviii
March on Washington, xxxi
marginalization, ix, x, xxxii, liv, 30,
66, 69, 70, 71, 82, 89, 99
Maril, Robin, 137
Mariposas (film), 95

marriage, 29; legal, xxxii, 50, 52.
See also same-sex marriage
Marsden, Jason, 9
Marx, Karl, 88
Marxism, 86, 90, 91, 92, 180n18,
181nn19–22, 181n24; queer, 93,
94–96, 112
Marxist feminists, 87, 89, 90, 91,
181n20
Marxists, 89–94; queer, xxix, 87, 89,
90, 93, 94
Mashable, 124–25, 126
Massad, Joseph, 41
Matthew Shepard and James Byrd,
Jr., Hate Crimes Prevention Act,
12, 132
Matthew Shepard Foundation, 3, 9,
11
McKinney, Aaron, 3, 5, 6, 11, 13, 20,
21; described, 7; methampheta-
mines and, 4
McNaught, Brian, 97
McRuer, Robert, xxx, 30
media, xlii, l, 6, 7, 13, 16; multi-
platform, 125; rurality and, 5
Media and Gay Rights activists, 14
Media Matters, 13, 14
Medicaid, 114
Men Like That (Howard), xxxiii
"Men Seeking Men" (Craigslist), xlv
methamphetamines, l, 3–4, 5, 9–10,
18, 20, 22, 23
metronormativity, x, xiii, xiv, xvi,
xxv, xxxi, xxxii, xxxvi, xliv, lv, 1,
13, 14, 15, 17, 21, 24, 30, 31, 64,
69, 111, 130, 138, 139, 141, 159,
160; assumptions of, 71; *Book
of Matt* and, 4–10; challenging,
xxxiv–xxxv, 147; concept of, 161;
discussions of, 65; enabling of,
xxxv; gay rights work and, 65;
hegemony of, xlix; as legacy, l;

logics of, xxxvii, 142; reliance on, 23; reproducing, 32–33; resisting, 153; sexual imaginarium and, xxxiv; ubiquity of, xxxvi, 134; visibility and, lii, 32, 119

Meyer, Leisa, 174n1

Midwest, xxvi–xxvii, xxviii, xlix, 72, 78, 126, 135; analysis of, 171n2; representations of, xliv; rural, 31, 119, 123

Midwestern, 37; term, xxiv, xxvii–xxviii

migrants, homophobic, 12–13

Mock, Janet, xxxix

Moore, Mignon, 41

Moreau, Julie, 129–30

Movement Advancement Project (MAP), 63

multiculturalism, 31, 68

Muñoz, José, 4, 33; disidentification and, li, 36, 37, 38, 39; majoritarian culture and, 40

narratives, 21, 32, 40, 111; cultural, xiii, xxxiii, 36; dominant, xiii, xvi, 121; metronormative, xvi, xxxvi, 30, 65; queer theory, xxiii, 92

national, term, xxiv, xxviii

National Center for Lesbian Rights (NCLR), vii, lii, 63, 118, 120, 128, 129, 131, 136, 184n25

National Center for Transgender Equality, 136

National Coming Out Day, vii–viii, 98

National Gay and Lesbian Task Force, 98, 109, 136

nationalism, 91, 111

National LGBTQ Task Force, 63

Native Americans, 30, 55, 76, 77, 102

neoliberalism, xv, 29, 97, 99, 114

Newsome, Jene, l, 30, 119, 124, 174n1,

175n19, 176n26; DADT and, 25–26, 27; estrangement for, 31; legislation against, 32; marriage of, 28; media coverage of, 24–27, 32; metronormativity and, 1; story of, xlii–xliii, 31; support for, 27, 32, 33

Newsweek, 86

New York City Pride Parade, 152, 153

New York Times, 5, 117

normalcy, 157; performance of, 153–64

normativity, xxxvii–xxxviii, xli–xlii, 39

Obama, Barack, 12, 117, 128, 141

"On 'Coming Out' and Gay Visibility" (Christmas), 35

One Iowa, 129

Other, 30, 31, 96

Out in the Silence (film), 52

Outloud, 139

"out, loud, and proud," xxxvi, 49, 51, 58, 59, 63, 64, 89, 109–10, 161

outness, 49, 113, 159, 163; power of, 114; prioritization of, 136; social value of, 85; visibility and, xxxvi, 36, 159; workplace, 84, 85, 86, 96, 97–100, 114, 116

out there, xlii–xlix, 50, 53–54

Palm Center, 26

Pan Visibility Day, viii

"Passing and Disability," 63

performance, 86; autoethnographic, 37–38; sexual, 96

Pew Research Center, data from, xvii, *xix*, xxii

Phelan, Peggy, xxx

Piker, Hasan, 133

place, xiii, xxvii, 37, 163, 171n1; backwards, 88; lines of, 71; nonurban,

Carly Thomsen is assistant professor of gender, sexuality, and feminist studies at Middlebury College.